THE MASQUE OF FEMININITY

Theory, Culture & Society

Theory, Culture & Society caters for the resurgence of interest in culture within contemporary social science and the humanities. Building on the heritage of classical social theory, the book series examines ways in which this tradition has been reshaped by a new generation of theorists. It will also publish theoretically informed analyses of everyday life, popular culture, and new intellectual movements.

Recent volumes include:
Symbolic Exchange and Death
Jean Baudrillard

Sociology in Question
Pierre Bourdieu

Economies of Signs and Space
Scott Lash and John Urry

Religion and Globalization
Peter Beyer

Baroque Reason
The Aesthetics of Modernity
Christine Buci-Glucksmann

The Consuming Body
Pasi Falk

Cultural Identity and Global Process
Jonathan Friedman

The Established and the Outsiders
Norbert Elias and John L. Scotson

The Cinematic Society
The Voyeur's Gaze
Norman K. Denzin

THE MASQUE OF FEMININITY

The Presentation of Woman in Everyday Life

Efrat Tseëlon

SAGE Publications
London • Thousand Oaks • New Delhi

© Efrat Tseëlon 1995

First published 1995

Published in association with *Theory, Culture & Society*,
School of Human Studies, University of Teesside

SAGE Publications Ltd
6 Bonhill Street
London EC2A 4PU

SAGE Publications Inc
2455 Teller Road
Thousand Oaks, California 91320

SAGE Publications India Pvt Ltd
32, M-Block Market
Greater Kailash – I
New Delhi 110 048

British Library Cataloguing in Publication data

A catalogue record for this book is available from the
British Library

ISBN 0 8039 8806 0
ISBN 0 8039 8807 9 (pbk)

Library of Congress catalog card number   95-069789

Typeset by Photoprint, Torquay, Devon, UK.
Printed in Great Britain at the University Press, Cambridge

To my parents, Aya and Ariè,
with my love and gratitude

CONTENTS

ACKNOWLEDGEMENTS

This book is the harvest of four years' work. It was sparked off by my doctoral thesis in psychology which looked at clothes as communication and it echoes my personal and intellectual development.

It is not by coincidence that I chose to complete my book in the same supportive and inspiring settings of Wolfson College and the Department of Experimental Psychology at Oxford where I got my PhD. Once again, I enjoyed a helpful hospitality in both places.

The final shape of the manuscript was born just days after the birth of my daughter, Milette. And it was the tremendous help from my parents and my husband, Søren Riis, that made this final delivery possible.

My work benefited from the precious research time and resources that were made available to me by the Faculty of Cultural and Education Studies at Leeds Metropolitan University.

In addition, I would like to thank the following for kind permission to use previously published articles: *Theory & Psychology, Theory, Culture & Society, Journal for the Theory of Social Behaviour, Semiotica, Symbolic Interaction, Studies in Symbolic Interaction* and Blackwell.

I would also like to thank Louise Murray and Rosemary Campbell from Sage for their support, and Susan Kaiser for some helpful comments. Finally, I would like to thank Valerie Steele, Halla Beloff, Mike Hepworth and Mike Featherstone for their encouragement.

INTRODUCTION

This book is a story. My story. A story which attempts to weave various threads of information and insight to explain a central enigma of my life and experiences. It attempts to describe the sources and explain the ways in which the woman presents herself in Western culture. It starts off from Goffman's observation in *Gender Advertisements* (1979) that if categories of gender are the cultural correlates of sex, then gender display is 'the conventionalised portrayals of these correlates'. But my intention is to do more than just present the ways in which Western woman is expected to appear. I also look at the ways these expectations shape her own self-perceptions. I examine contemporary perceptions but locate them within cultural traditions that produced a particular visual expectation. In so doing I bridge a gap which constantly frustrates me when I read accounts of gender display in the literature. Because the literature seems to fall into two basic traditions: one which documents but does not go far enough in a theoretical analysis, and the other which offers imaginative interpretations without grounding them in a solid empirical basis. What I have tried to do here is to combine the two approaches into a construction that is daring in its theoretical links while drawing on solid data as well as on anecdotal evidence. And while my interest is in contemporary woman 'like myself' I constantly move in leaps and bounds between historical periods and current theories in order to question the concepts, and to suggest an explanation.

Being a social psychologist my understanding is perhaps more deeply rooted in perspectives and methods of the social sciences. But I am not an orthodox social psychologist. I began as one, but the journey down the path of my PhD work took me from the empiricist landscape to a dialectical interpretative one. Alongside the paradigm shift in the social sciences my empirical work led me to question the methods and assumptions of the experimental paradigm (see Tseëlon, 1989; Tseëlon, 1991b). It has highlighted the dilemma involved in a delicate trade-off between rigid precision and colourful richness. The result was that I moved away from the control of a single paradigm, and the restrictions of a single discipline. I positioned myself in the space which I define as cultural psychology, because I range across many frameworks and domains. This position is rather risky as it appears sacrilegious to those who adhere to one framework passionately. It has the advantage, though, of allowing me to treat all theories and approaches as tools of the trade without committing myself to any one in particular. It provides a critical edge which is lacking in those who are true believers. Such a position involves choices both of material and of scope. I have not included all the theories or all contemporary thinkers who have participated in all the current debates I am alluding to. Nor have I surveyed all the debates – only those which suited my story and my understanding. The result is a construction and not a scientific truth. And it is judged in terms of how valid its building blocks are, and how persuasive their combination is. It is not judged in terms of being the only, or even the best account.

By not limiting myself to a single period, or a social group or a theoretical framework, I have opened myself to the criticism of trying to universalise; of trying to speak of differences, or of characteristics as if they were essential and immutable features of the female (and by implication of the male) psyche. On the other hand, rooting oneself in the socio-historico specifics means losing the scope and the possibility of discovering novel and unexpected connections that are visible only from a bird's eye view. Put slightly differently, this dilemma between contradictory modes of thought *logos* and *mythos* is as old as the Hellenic mind. The former refers to that which can be stated in rational terms, the latter – to that which follows the rules of the imagination.

I have tried to balance the dialectic of the concrete and the metaphysical by moving back and forth between the level of specific examples (or empirical data), through the paradigmatic level of theory, to the metaphoric level of myth and symbol.

In putting together the story I have used a method which I might call creative critical analysis. It is a dialogue between analytic knowledge and creative readings of social phenomena. The sources I have drawn on inspired my thinking, which in turn, led me to seek inspiration in more diverse directions. In my analysis I have combined elements from social theory, psychology, cultural history, literature, semiotics, religion, feminist theory and psychoanalysis. And I have mixed myth and legend together with empirical data from my own doctoral research work.

The result is a story about an impossible creature who is given a space and no space at all, who is offered a position while being denied that position, who embodies a thing and its opposite at one and the same time.

That creature is the woman. In defying any categorical designation she constitutes herself as a paradox, a perpetual deferrence, an image of reality with the unavailability of desire, an absent presence. Her mode of existence is subject to the law of the return of the repressed: it highlights what it denies in the act of denying. The central metaphor defining her essence is placed in the collective imagination between the fantasies of the phallic mother and the castrating mother; the bliss of paradise, and the expulsion from it. It is a paradox which denies the woman's place together with defining it. The roles that are available to her (social, psychological, visual) place her in another impossible position. If she embraces them she is supporting the ideology which defines her in the first place. If she rejects them outright she denies herself a certain amount of options, now marked, that would have otherwise been available to her.

Paradoxicality, however, is not unique to women. As Freud has argued we are all subject to the law which governs the operation of defence mechanisms. Their function is to protect us by hiding a certain reality from our field of vision. But the defence mechanism itself calls attention to that which it tries to disguise. And psychoanalysis has also taught us that desire is by definition unattainable – it is always a yearning for a paradise lost. Thus paradoxicality is part of the human condition. But the woman has become a cultural signifier for it. And collective consciousness as crystallised in group myths provides individual minds with the materials of their imagination.

My book traces the paradoxical existence of the woman with respect to the quintessentially feminine: personal appearance. In an effort to under- stand 'the presentation of the woman in everyday life' it explores some of the paradoxes which frame the feminine experience in contemporary West. It examines the role of personal appearance in defining her social position, but also in influencing the way she comes to think of herself. In that sense it departs from analyses which focus on identifying patterns alone. It adds a psychological dimension, and uses social theory to link cultural practices and personal meanings.

It is a common cliché that the woman cares about appearance, that fashion is a feminine affair, and that appearance is superficial – an antithesis to substance. Young women, goes the nursery rhyme called 'Natural History', are made of 'ribbons and laces/and sweet pretty faces'. What is missing from a plethora of semiotic and sociological analyses of fashion styles and trends, historical accounts or psychological experiments is the reasoning given by the wearers themselves. Cultural analyses regard clothing as a cultural artefact which signifies social or historical processes. Psychological analyses take the here and now approach and examine the influence of various clothing styles on perception (of self and other). Alternatively, clothing behaviour which is judged as deviating from norms is treated as a symptom of some disorder. My approach is different.

The departure point for my work is the notion that a cultural designation is instrumental in shaping a personal one. There is a dialectical dialogue between cultural categories and the people who embody them: the act of representation modifies the nature of the represented object. The work, therefore, starts off by departing somewhat from the tradition of studying people, or theorising them without taking their own perspective into account. It adds a layer of meaning of appearance as given by the wearer to that superimposed by the cultural analyst. Thus each chapter consists of a theoretical discussion, supplemented by an empirical illustration.

The empirical work that I use for rhetorical illustration consists of a number of studies, as well as analysis of 160 written interviews completed for me by readers of women's magazines. The readers responded to a call for volunteers which was placed in the November–December 1986 issues of three UK magazines. Each magazine was targeted to a slightly different audience: *Elle* – to the young upmarket fashion-conscious; *Options* – to the career woman; *Women's World* – to the housewife; as well as in an internal newsletter of a professional women association *Network*. The questionnaires comprised 35 (mostly) open-ended questions pertaining to the influence of audience, situation and self – on explaining clothing choice and meaning.

In analysing the interviews I have paid special attention to insights provided to me by the interviewees themselves who offered a step beyond the cliché, an attempt to make connections, of thoughts perhaps unarticulated before, sometimes in brackets, sometimes as an afterthought, or a candid reflection on the reason of why things might be the way they are.

But I also examined them beyond isolated cases to identify recurrent themes, to locate the kind of concerns that are more existential than strategic, to see if they form a consistent pattern. The pattern has two reference points: one is the questionnaire context (her own context, as well as the body of questionnaires as a whole). Some questions, for example, when considered at face value in isolation from the rest of the questionnaire seem to be telling a rather different story than when embedded in a whole range of other responses. A woman, for example, may say that she dresses to please herself alone, or that her own judgement of her appearance is the most important to her. She then may go on to provide details to specific questions which betray a whole range of concerns with other people's views. This, of course, is very much a contextual matter. With some people she may feel more or less comfortable; and on some occasions more or less vulnerable. It is not a matter of getting into a 'deeper truth'. Maybe it has to do with different ways of understanding or interpreting the question. But most likely it is a case of going beyond a unidimensional–conventional understanding into a complex one which contains inconsistencies and contradictions.

The other reference point is the wider cultural context. The cultural practices and conceptions that inform and ground specific behaviours, and mould her shape in their own image. This dual referencing has the advantage of going some way towards linking cultural practices with personal experiences.

The book is not exhaustive. It makes no claims about non-Western women, issues of ethnicity, class or sexual orientation. It also leaves out men. It can be argued that some of the phenomena I discuss are more 'general' than 'female'. Indeed, Bauman (1992), Featherstone et al. (1991), Giddens (1991), Harré (1991), and Shilling (1993) have recently argued that within a cultural framework of late Capitalism, in a consumer culture obsessed with appearance, the status of the body has been transformed from a fixed natural given, to a malleable cultural product. Regimes of dietary management, building and maintenance, as well as complete reshaping and sculpting of the body are associated with its conception as an instrument of pleasure, and self expression. The preservation of the body-beautiful, body-young, and body-healthy indicate on the one hand a desire to control nature by defying mortality, on the other hand the fashioning of personal identity.

While acknowledging these social trends I want to suggest that they have different meanings for men and women. And while my study focuses on the story of the woman, my intention is not to add my voice to an essentialist discourse which reifies gender differences. I would not argue that the processes I discuss are exclusively female. While some aspects of the story I tell may be inherently feminine, a lot are historically so. As Goffman put it, gender patterns reflect a historical habit: the frequency of playing a certain social role on the historical stage. And a concern over carrying off an appearance does not necessarily imply a deep and abiding identification with that appearance (1979, p. 51). Thus the feminine experience and perspective may be treated as a paradigm that, while excluding some women no doubt applies to some men, and given the direction of social trends, will apply to more.

Rather, I wish to highlight a partial picture. A picture that is simultaneously taken from the point of view of the woman, and focuses on the woman as its central object. Rather, I would like to direct my attention and offer explanation to the specificity of the female experience – the particular assumptions about her nature and character – which makes these processes uniquely relevant to her. I would want to argue, with Elias, that a certain interpersonal dynamic, and a particular set-up of structural relationships modified patterns of emotion management. These, in turn, have been projected onto and internalised by the woman. Further I would argue that by her definition as inextricably bound with the original sin the woman internalised a certain existential apologetic standpoint. As Mead (1934) and Sartre (1943/1966) taught us, we all have a derivative social existence in the sense that we depend on the Other's acknowledgement. But as a result of her definition as a spectacle, the woman internalised a *more heightened* awareness of her derivative nature than that which is common to all.

Finally, I would like to avoid an ideological position. Ideologies have a way of ironing out uneven surfaces in order to produce a smooth effect. And while guilty of using unavoidable generalisations, I would hope to take issue with some of them as well.

More specifically the book explores five paradoxes:

- Chapter 1: the modesty paradox – the woman is constructed as seduction – to be for ever punished for it.
- Chapter 2: the duplicity paradox – the woman is constructed as artifice, and marginalised for lacking essence and authenticity.
- Chapter 3: the visibility paradox – the woman is constructed as a spectacle while being culturally invisible.
- Chapter 4: the beauty paradox – the woman embodies ugliness while signifying beauty.

- Chapter 5: the death paradox – the woman signifies death as well as the defence against it.

Finally, the concluding chapter will examine the founding assumption of my thesis: that dress and appearance cues still possess a signifying function in spite of postmodern claims to the contrary.

1

FATAL SEDUCTIONS:
'AND GOD CREATED WOMAN'

The Mermaid, an embodiment of female threat is modestly covered in
Western reproductions and boldly exposed in a Mexican counterpart.

My purpose in this chapter is to examine the links between the traditional
conceptions of the woman, and the way they continue to frame women in
contemporary society. More specifically I am looking at how cultural
expectations of the woman have been translated into specific appearance
expectations, and how they influence the way the woman perceives her
own look. The paradox that runs through this analysis is one which defines
the essence of the woman on the side of the matter (body and appearance)
as opposed to spirit, and simultaneously denounces her for her inferior
essence. I would propose to trace present-day self-conceptions of women
with respect to appearance to a long tradition which positioned the woman

in a space of danger and desire, and unconscious fears. The theoretical landscape which I evoke to place explanations and data, in this as well as subsequent chapters, is one which examines the construction of present-day woman as a point on a historical continuum. Examination of my empirical research (Tseëlon, 1989), as well as further research in this area inspired me to focus my search on explanations painted with a broad brush, often at a mythical level, rather than on local and highly specific theories, and explanations on an individualistic level. This is not to say, for example, that I search for essentialist theories of gender. Rather I would argue that even archetypal phenomena which transcend time and space are only sustained within a given set of social conditions. And that the mythical level (which is like the collective unconscious) reflects, but also inspires the private unconscious. In Lacan's terms, I take on board both the idea that the subject's conscious experience is structured by a pre-existing symbolic order (language), and that the unconscious experience is also a cultural product 'the unconscious is the discourse of the Other' (1975/1991, p. 85). The social theories that I engage in are of the kind that is marked by vision and force, and combines individual and social levels of explanation.

But first I have to define the limits of my project. For it is presumptuous to subsume historical or contemporary attitudes to 'women' and 'femininity', under simple homogeneous categories. Nor do I attempt to present an exhaustive historical survey of those conceptions. Rather I would start by sketching the contours of the Western picture of the woman through illustrative landmarks of the first woman: the Hellenic Pandora, the Christian doctrine of Eve, and the Jewish legendary Lilith. Produced in different religions and centuries apart, and representing only one of the possible gallery of female constructions in each of their respective cultures, these versions of the myth of origin of the first woman nevertheless share some characteristics. Together they throw a light on a powerful force that shaped the collective imagination of the Judeo-Christian world. Next, I would outline the processes which identified the woman with her appearance while distancing the man from his. Finally, I would trace the link between female modesty in dress to male anxieties of the woman.

Female essence: the first woman

The first story I will examine, that of Pandora, sets the scene for linking together beauty and sin – both of which have come to encode 'the fair sex'. It was Hesiod, the most famous poet to have told the genealogy of the Greek gods (adding, in the process, his own misogynist slant; see Graves, 1955/1981, p. 148) who characterised Pandora as the beautiful evil. She was created by Hephaistus to punish humans for Prometheus's theft of fire. Pandora was endowed by the gods with all the possible gifts, and was married to Prometheus's brother. But she was also endowed with danger-ous qualities. Her beauty is a cunning device, her frivolity is a weakness of character, and her curiosity is a propensity to sin. While in her home, she was unable to resist a strong desire to open the lid to a forbidden vessel. By so doing she released all the troubles of humankind – ills and mortality – trapping hope inside as she closed the lid.

Moving on to the Biblical story of creation of the woman, centred in paradise, the connection between adornment and sin becomes a bit more complex. In the Garden of Eden Eve and Adam lacked nothing but were denied one fruit. Eve succumbed to the temptations of the serpent and ate from the only forbidden fruit, and even offered some to Adam. Her act brought an end to their paradisic existence and opened the gateway to hardships and mortality. Genesis offers two versions of the story of the creation of Eve. In the first, both man and woman were created equal, out of dust. In the second, Adam was created first, and his helpmate was created from his rib. According to the Jewish legend both of them were extremely beautiful (Ginzburg, 1909/1937). The Jewish rabbinic commentary on the Pentateuch, The Genesis Midrash (in Hebrew *Bereshith Rabbah*), elaborates various female customs and precepts that relate to Eve's original sin: that of bringing death into the world. Thus we learn that women cover their head while men go bareheaded because 'she is like one who has done wrong and is ashamed of people'. Women walk in front of a corpse in a funeral because 'they brought death into the world'. The precept of menstruation was given to them because they shed the blood of Adam (by introducing death), and the precept to sanctify the 'dough' – 'because she corrupted Adam, who was the dough (hallah) of the world'. And they were given the precept of lighting the Sabbath candles (*Bereshith Rabbah* 18: 8; Ginzburg, 1909/1937, p. 67). But however antifeminist these precepts appear to be, it is misleading to speak of a single Jewish attitude to women. According to the *Judiaca Encyclopedia* (1971) the variety of attitudes contained in rabbinic literature consists of a duality of condemnation and respect (after all, Eve, whose name in Hebrew means 'living' brought into the world not only death but also life). And precepts which, like the above, appear to express an attitude of punishment, are in fact an expression of a privilege.

The attitude of the Christian church to the same creation myth was, however, quite different. In their attitude to women the early church fathers in the first centuries of Christianity drew on the Apocrypha (intertestamental writing: composed after the completion of the latest book of the Hebrew Bible, and before the completion of the New Testament). This literature (for example, *Jubilees*, *Life of Adam and Eve*, *Testaments of the Twelve Patriarchs*) partly reflects Jewish ideas two centuries before and one century after Christ, and it presents a negative view of Eve and womankind. For example in *The Testament of Reuben* (from *Testaments of the Twelve Patriarchs*) it is said

Pay no heed to the beauty of women . . . for evil are women . . . and since they have no power or strength over man, they use wiles by outward attractions . . .

> women are overcome by the spirit of fornication more than men, and in their
> hearts they plot against men . . . for a woman cannot force a man openly, but
> only by a harlot's bearing she beguiles him. (4: 1, 5: 1–4)

In the apocalyptic Enoch literature (uncanonised apocalypse from the
fourth century, found in Qumeran caves) a Near Eastern rebellion myth
becomes part of the Judaic tradition. This theology replaces human
responsibility for evil with an angelic one. It attributes evil to the angels'
revolt (headed by Satan) against their roles, culminating in a descent to
earth and in lusting after the daughters of men. The revolt resulted in the
flood, and in human access to forbidden knowledge such as the art of
working of metal. This, in turn, delivered tools of warfare to men, but also
the secret of adornment with precious metals to women in order to lure
men. Both, in the view of these Judean authors, are the sources of human
misery (Forsyth, 1987). The Jewish apocalyptic form of the combat myth
influenced the New Testament. The following transformation of the
combat myth in the hands of one of the church fathers, Tertullianus (1869),
shifts the blame from the angels back to the woman. This reanactment of
Eve's story is a telling example of the essence of the paradox of woman and
appearance. First, the sin of the angels is described:

> Those angels . . . who rushed from heaven on the daughters of men . . . this
> ignominy also attaches to woman. For when . . . they had disclosed certain well-
> concealed material substances, and several not well-revealed scientific arts – if it
> is true that they had laid bare the operations of metallurgy . . . they conferred
> properly . . . upon women that instrumental mean of womanly ostentation, the
> radiance of jewels wherewith necklaces are variegated, and the circlets of gold
> wherewith the arms are compressed, and the medicaments of orchil with which
> wools are coloured, and that black powder itself wherewith the eyelids and
> eyelashes are made prominent. What is the quality of these things may be
> declared . . . from the quality and condition of their teachers; in that sinners
> could never have either shown or supplied anything conducive to integrity,
> unlawful lovers anything conducive to chastity, renegade spirits anything
> conducive to the fear of God.

Then, the women are made to be the cause both of their own, and of the
angels' sins:

> Women who possessed angels [as husbands] could desire nothing more; they
> had, forsooth, made a grand match! Assuredly they who, of course, did
> sometimes think whence they had fallen, and after the heated impulses of their
> lusts, looked up toward heaven, thus requited that very excellence of women,
> natural beauty, as [having proved] a cause of evil, in order that their good
> fortune might profit them nothing . . . Sure they were that all ostentation, and
> ambition, and love of pleasing by carnal means, was displeasing to God.
> (pp. 306–7)

The combat myth particularly influenced the teachings of Paul. Here, too,
the woman continues to represent the instrument of evil. Satan becomes
the adversary of human salvation and the opponent of Christ, and the
woman is demonised through her alleged liaison with Satan, embodied by
the serpent.

It was Augustine, the most forceful personality among the church fathers (around the fifth century), who bequeathed to the Middle Ages the combat myth. His doctrine of the original sin is premised on the precept that evil is passed on through bodily pleasure which is turning away from God. According to him we are born with inherited guilt, and bondage to sin and to the devil. Only grace can liberate us. The Fall from grace and the expulsion from paradise charge Eve with the introduction of desire, and of death into the created order. Through Eve the original sin becomes sexualised and demonised. Her temptation to eat the forbidden fruit becomes seduction, and the seducer – the serpent – a demonic infusion between evil and sexuality. In the Middle Ages the story of Eve's beauty and curiosity was conflated with that of Pandora adding the element of evil beauty as an instrument in carrying out evil designs (Phillips, 1984). In the late Middle Ages the devil was to attain his greatest power over Christian imagination during the witch-hunts of the fifteenth to the seventeenth centuries. I will return to that later.

The sexual interpretations of the Fall became validated through the doctrine of chaste Mary. The doctrine of the second Eve, the obedient and sexually pure, reified and atoned for the sinful Eve. To rid herself of sin and overcome her inferior nature the woman must not possess even the capacity to sin. To this end Christianity offered her one road to salvation: to embody the impossible space of Mary which combines virginity and motherhood untainted by the desires of the flesh. In the writings of the church fathers virginity was extolled as a touchstone of female purity. By the ninth century devout Christian women had created an alternative for the woman from her destiny as wife and mother. Women could devote themselves to spiritual concerns, and renounce their femininity by becoming 'brides of Christ' (Anderson and Zinsser, 1988). This embedded the woman in a complex paradox. Because not only is the moral ideal of virginity an antithesis to sexuality. It is also an antithesis to procreation. The solution embodied by Mary of immaculate conception is a phantasy solution.

Whether as an instrument of evil, or as incarnating evil, in Hellenic, Judaic and Christian accounts the woman is presumed to have been born overdetermined. Both Pandora and Eve were 'designed to sin' – Pandora because she was created as a punishment, and Eve because she was created from a faulty material. Born imperfect she cannot be virtuous because virtue, as Aquinas put it, is an inborn inclination. In *The Summa Theologica* (1932) he writes:

> the woman should not have been made in the first production of things . . . the female is a misbegotten male . . . nothing misbegotten or defective should have been made at that first production. (p. 268)

> God foresaw that the woman would be an occasion of him to sin. (p. 269)

> the production of woman comes from defect in the active force or from some material indisposition. (p. 270)

The inquisitor in Bohemia and Moravia, and the Dean of the faculty of Theology at the University of Cologne who produced in 1486 the authoritative explanation, diagnosis, and punishment of witches, *Malleus Maleficarum* (*The Witch Hammer*) similarly note:

> the law punishes those who have done evil as if they had acted for the sake of doing evil. Therefore if the devil works by means of a witch he is merely employing an instrument; and since an instrument depends upon the will of the person who employs it and does not act its own free will, therefore the guilt of the action ought not to be laid to the charge of the witch, and in consequence she should not be punished. (Kramer and Sprenger, 1486/1951, p. 12)

They nevertheless proceed to condemn the witches for colluding with the devil to bring about evil (p. 18).

But if Pandora and Eve are evil by design, Lilith is evil by choice. According to the Jewish rabbinic commentary (Midrash) (Alphabet of Ben Sira 23a–32b; 33a–33b, see Ginzburg, 1909/1937), Lilith is Adam's first wife featured in the first creation story where Adam and Eve were created equal, from earth. She demanded equality in sexual intercourse, and when he refused her, she turned to Satan. Modelled on a Babylonian spirit she appears as a female demon with long hair and wings. In medieval Jewish mysticism (Cabbalistic midrash of *The Zohar*) Lilith has two roles: to seduce men sleeping on their own, and strangle newborn babies. She is the bearer of seduction and of death. When she sets out to pursue a man she puts on sumptuous clothes and ornamentation. When she has trapped him she comes dressed ablaze – in the fire of destruction to claim his soul (see Cohen-Alloro, 1987, p. 21). In other words, she is another version of the major sins blamed on Eve and Pandora: beauty and adornment together with a treacherous character.

Between them, the archetypal features of the woman encoded in the legends of Pandora, Eve and Lilith inform Western moral attitudes towards the woman's character and personal appearance. Together they frame the woman as cunning and gullible, untrustworthy and evil. She is portrayed as disguising behind false decoration, using her beauty and finery as a vehicle to dazzle men to their destruction. Primordial fascination with the mystery of the woman is fused with unconscious fears.

Female appearance and morality

To counter those fears, and to offer the woman a path to salvation, female sexuality had to be controlled. Thus, a discourse of modesty and chastity in dress came to encode female sexuality. As a symbol of seduction and sin, the woman was redeemed in chastity and pardoned in modesty. She came to be a site of cultural messages and displaced fantasies. The history of Christian Europe bears witness to the fact that even though finery in general was considered a vice, it became conflated with the very conception of the essence of the woman. From early Christianity to medieval

Christianity the importance of female apparel formed part of the theological discourse.

For example, for the early church fathers modesty in dress is a moral duty born by Eve's burden of guilt 'in memory of the introduction of sin into the world through the woman'. Adornment is singled out particularly for condemnation 'you destroyed so easily God's image, man. On account of your desert – that is death – even the son of God had to die. And do you think about adorning yourself over and above your tunics of skins?' (Tertullianus, 1869, p. 305). Similarly, for the medieval Thomas Aquinas finery is a sin pardonable if committed heedlessly out of frivolity or vanity for the sake of ostentation. But if done to provoke lust – it is a mortal sin which entails a spiritual death (1932, pp. 309–10).

Central to the notion of chastity is the requirement of virginity. Virginity is an angelic state that has existed in paradise before the Fall. It is a mediator between the human and the divine (Brown, 1986). But in Christian theology virginity is not merely abstinence of sexual behaviour. It is chastity of body and mind in every form: desire, thought, speech and look. And it extends beyond the subject's own mind. In the requirement *to appear pure* as well as *to be pure*, modesty is located not only in the woman, but also in the way she is perceived by others. Her responsibility extends beyond herself to the eyes that are looking at her as a sexual object. Herewith lies a paradox. First, never to be desired means never to be seen. It means a complete victory over, and denial of the flesh. This conception betrays a death wish. Taken to its logical conclusion – that is, the only true virgin is a dead one (Bloch, 1992). Further, by condemning all forms of display as being precursors to sin, the church has been instrumental in instilling into the female collective consciousness a permanent awareness of the way she appears, and the impact of her appearance on others.

Indicative are judgements such as we find in the writing of Tertullianus *On the veiling of virgins* (1870): 'seeing and being seen belong to the selfsame lust'(p. 157); and 'Every public exposure of an honourable virgin is [to her] a suffering of rape' (p. 158). Similarly Cyprian's opinion is that 'a virgin ought not only to be so, but also to be perceived and believed to be so' (1868, p. 337). Virgins who visit public baths frequently 'prostitute to eyes that are curious to lust bodies that are dedicated to chastity and modesty' (p. 346). If they are gazed upon immodestly they are themselves polluted 'together with the clothing of garments, the honour and modesty of the body is laid aside; virginity is exposed' (p. 347).

These attitudes of the church fathers writing in the second and third centuries, influenced and inspired ecclesiastical medieval misogyny. In a moralistic treatise against sinful fashions (translated from French by Edward Cooke, 1678) we find a bolder and more vivid expression of the idea of the sinful gaze

a double crime for a woman to be fashion'd after the mode of this world, and so to bring her innocence into dispute through her immodest nakedness; because she her self not only sins against shame, but causes others also to sin against purity, and at the same time she renders her self suspected. (p. 6)

to glorify God by the flesh the woman has to offer a body pure and chaste, and ought not to expose it to the view and the desires of all men . . . but to cover it with modesty . . . she ought to avoid the evil there is in tempting them by her nakedness. (p. 137)

In a sense one can trace here the origins of 'the mirror psyche' of the woman – the public gaze which is inscribed even into her private self (see Chapter 3).

The roots of the renunciation of the body lie in the transformation from paradisic unashamed nakedness into shamed nakedness after the Fall, which required some form of covering (Smith, 1978; Perniola, 1989). According to the Jewish legend, before the Fall Adam and Eve were clothed with garments of light ('Or' in Hebrew), like those of the angels. After the Fall, the celestial clothing which enveloped them disappeared to leave them wearing garments of skin ('Or' in Hebrew as well). The garments of skin are degraded as they are only for the body, not for the soul (Ginzburg, 1909/1937, p. 75, notes 69 and 93; *The Zohar*, 1931, I, 36b). And since the Fall is blamed on the woman, the links between sin, body, woman and clothes are easily forged.

The tradition that was laid down with regard to the first woman carried over to female adornment more generally. Here the moral language was specifically about sexual morality, because clothes, through their proximity to the body encode the game of modesty and sexual explicitness, denial and celebration of pleasure. Clothes veil the body. Do they provide a kind of disguise to the body's nakedness, or enhance the body's nudity that is fantasised behind? A lot of the allure in clothes lies in the interplay between the covered and the partially clothed. The half naked woman, the suspended promise, is always more erotic than the naked. Is that a quality of the dress, the wearer, or the eyes that are looking? I will return to this later.

In Western civilisation clothes served the dual function of indicating status and gender. Starting from the eleventh century the development of trade heralded economic and social transformations. In Europe's expanding markets cloth production was emerging as a primary trade commodity, and cloth products as a mark of social distinction. Many mercantile cities started regulating through sumptuary laws the fabrics and styles that were allowed in the dress of the various social strata. Fashion has functioned as a technology of social control, legitimising social distinctions. But in the case of women, fashion was regulated along lines of gender and sexuality rather than lines of social distinction. This it has achieved by becoming a signifier of moral virtue. The major distinction in female dress was between the noblewoman and the prostitute (Owen Hughes, 1992). Moral transgression consisted in violation of gender sartorial codes, in showing vanity of display, and in deceiving through make up and false hair. While from a Christian perspective all finery is a signifier of Eve's sin, and display in dress is a sign of vanity and pride, some sartorial forms were perceived as more wicked than others.

There were two kinds of vices. The first, which was common to men and women, that of transgressing gender lines, constituted a threat to the natural order. Already Clement of Alexandria writing in the second century warns that 'to such an extent . . . has luxury advanced, that not only are the female sex deranged about this frivolous pursuit, but men also are infected with the disease' (1867, p. 284). The appearance of the sexes belongs to the created order 'for God wished women to be smooth, and rejoice in their locks alone growing spontaneously . . . but has adorned men . . . with a beard' (p. 286). Therefore 'let the head of men be shaven . . . let the chin have the hair. But let not twisted locks hang far down from the head, gliding into womanish ringlets' (p. 317). And it is not just the body, but also its covering 'let the woman wear a plain and becoming dress, but softer than what is suitable for a man . . . And let the garments be suited to age, person, figure, nature, pursuits' (p. 315).

Being criticised for a sartorial transgression was not a female preroga- tive. But there was a gender difference. A criticism of male fashion is inherently different from the criticism of female fashion. It always implies a warning against effeminisation. This is because the woman has been made to embody the essence of fashion, the qualities of fashion have become one with her flesh.

Thus men's adoption of female fashion (such as long trains, and close fitting clothes) was considered in the twelfth century as evidence of moral decline by the monastic chroniclers (Owen Hughes, 1992). At the end of the sixteenth century men cultivated growing hair or wearing powdered periwigs curled and perfumed. In the seventeenth century male dress was embroidered and trimmed with lace and spangles. Even the semi-formal look (vest and breeches and coat) evidenced effeminate element (the breeches were like petticoats, the coats flared out like a woman's dress). All these types of sartorial behaviour drew out criticism varying from ridicule to moralistic warnings. These criticisms, however, were a warning but they were not an all out condemnation. In contrast, sartorial deviations in women were of a different order. If effeminate clothes in men produced ridicule, female appropriation of male attire produced near hysterical reactions. Like the uncanny (the familiar that has become estranged through repression, see Chapter 5), time and again the old motifs kept recurring. The spectre of the woman created desires to contain her uncontrolled sexuality, to underlie her inferior nature, and to expose her weakness of character (Ribeiro, 1986).Women's sartorial deviations were seen as confirming their essential flaw. When in the fifteenth century, guided by divine voices, Joan of Arc led the French to victorious battles against the English, she was taken prisoner. Her refusal to wear female clothing throughout her imprisonment served to underlie her indepen- dence and defiance and she was perceived as the agent of the devil, not of God (Barrett, 1931, p. 55). In the sixteenth and seventeenth centuries female use of false hair and make-up, or versions of male attire – like masculine doublets and men's hats – produced alarmed criticisms of artificiality and falseness, akin to alignment with the devil. And in the nineteenth century the divided skirt was declared unwomanly and unhealthy in the prestigious medical journal, the *Lancet* (1883, p. 921).

The woman, it seems, could never get it right. Whatever she wore became synonymous with some negative characteristic. Whether she wore feminine or masculine clothes, natural or artificial she was condemned. Anything that was excessive, rich in material (like trains, hooped skirts, high headgears) or extravagant (like sumptuous luxurious materials and colours) was denounced for its vanity. Tight-lacing and corsetting were denounced as a health hazard. The dramatically wide dresses that became fashionable in the eighteenth century were criticised for their complexity, indulgence and artificiality, and crinolines (in the nineteenth century) on grounds of practicality and modesty (excessive, taking too much space, can blow up in the wind). At the same time headgears were towering to enormous heights, sometimes more than three feet, generating similar criticism. It was a common belief that women who spent too much on their clothes might be inclined to a life of idle frivolity. But if the artificial and the excessive or the masculine look were morally condemned, so was the flowing, soft natural and feminine dressing gown which was beginning to replace the structured gown in the seventeenth century, and at the end of the nineteenth century for informal occasions. It was quickly equated with looseness of morals, and soft clothes with soft minds (Ribeiro, 1986).

The second kind of vice blamed on fashion was, however, singular to women: immodesty for the sake of temptation. Styles which exposed too much of the body were condemned for their enticement. Such fashions were considered as appropriate for a prostitute, but not for a virtuous woman. Fashions which created false impression (such as dyeing of hair, painting of face, or adorning with jewellery) were tainted with a devilish seduction since 'Whatever is born is the work of God. Whatever, then, is plastered on [that], is the devil's work. To superinduce on a divine work Satan's ingenuities, how criminal it is' (Tertullianus, 1869, p. 321).

From 1100 to 1600 male fashions were as much eroticised as women's (as, for example, the cod-piece that covers the genitals worn in Tudor times over tight leggings; Banner, 1992). But it was the woman alone who was accused of using the seductive role. In the seventeenth century, for example, the loose-bodied gowns and the low neckline were the main targets for the attack on the immodest dress. Both were regarded as negative metaphors of character. Starting in the eighteenth century criticism of female fashion took on a different note. The moral discourse was giving way to other kinds of rhetoric while maintaining its judgemental edge. Just as manners moved from the Renaissance tradition of aristocratic 'courtesy', to the bourgeois tradition of nineteenth-century etiquette (Curtin, 1985), sartorial offence moved from being defined as a moral transgression to being defined as a social transgression. While the former is indicative of a character flaw, the latter indicates lack of gentility, education and civilised behaviour.

In the nineteenth century a discourse of health was beginning to replace the discourse of social graces. For example, when dress reformers introduced the Bloomer costume (voluminous trousers gathered in at the ankle), they provoked a tidal wave of critical comment. The *Lancet* declared that 'The divided skirt is clearly not likely to advance the interests or improve the health of the sex . . . it is unnatural, and must be productive of unwomanly ways which are to be deprecated' (1883, p. 921).

The medical discourse was to be succeeded in the twentieth century by a psychopathological discourse. The diagnostic and statistical manual of mental disorders (DSM III) lists such syndromes as male transvestism, and the psychiatric literature has recently defined a female 'dressing disorder'. The description of this disorder exemplifies how social criticism, and even social prejudice, can disguise as an account of individual pathology. This disorder which appears in female adolescents is expressed in 'spending inordinate amounts of time, money, and energy on clothing' and in 'an inflexible insistence on being dressed identically with peers, or in what is believed to be the contemporary mode, no matter how uncomfortable, expensive, or aesthetically distasteful the fashion'. The disorder is chronic and cureless, and is exacerbated by 'living in a consumer-oriented society' (Frankenburg and Yurgelun-Todd, 1984, p. 147).

Moral criticism of female apparel indicates that the sartorial continues to signal moral qualities. It is perhaps best exemplified in a discourse which undresses and sexualises women in contexts where this is particularly irrelevant, typically, as a sort of desperate measure to disqualify the woman's move towards increased equality, and by implication, power. On 11 November 1992 the ruling body of the Anglican church secured a narrow majority in a historical vote to ordain women into the priesthood. In the long debate that preceded and followed the decision a picture unfolded which appeared to be centred on relations of power, now enshrined in a long tradition. The subtext, though, harked back to some ancient themes and attitudes. These were found in many responses as well as in media reporting. The decision to usher in women was treated by opponents as a decision to usher in evil, and by supporters as a necessary evil. Eve/Pandora was threatening to upset the old order again. In an editorial entitled 'Eve ordained' (12 November 1992), *The Times* cautioned that the ordination 'will jeopardise the progress of ecumenism and the hard-won understanding achieved between Rome and Canterbury'. In an age where discrimination and sexism have become unacceptable codes for civilised talk old prejudices needed more subtle outlets. The *Daily Express* described the victory as 'a clarion call to the liberals who wanted to change the craggy, male dominated face of the Church for *something softer and more fragrant*' (emphasis added). While The *Guardian* sketch intimated that perhaps what influenced the waverers was the image of 'blatant fitness' projected by the candidates to the priesthood: 'They were mostly women wearing matronly hairdos, reading glasses and quietly coloured clothes'. The seductive sexualised aspect of the female threat was painted, for example, between the lines of journalistic rhetoric. The *Sun* headed its rather slim first page coverage (ironically overshadowed by a voyeuristic chapter in the Royal saga about the Prince of Wales and his female friend: 'What the Royal cop saw – they kissed and then slid down sofa'): 'Church say yes to their vicars in knickers'. One is reminded of the antifeminist tone referring to a suffragette demonstration at the turn of the century as a 'procession of petticoats', or deploring the possibility of a 'petticoat-elect cabinet' (Latham, 1911, p. 28, quoted in Rolley, 1990).

From essence to appearance: the civilising process

Why were women's modesty and chastity guarded with such passion? What was at stake? And how justified are we in making a particular case for women's clothes? Flügel (1930/1971, pp. 17–24), for example, defines modesty as a site of struggle between unconscious tendencies such as desire and its inhibitory opposite – disgust, or between hiding the naked body and calling attention to it. Modesty, he noted, was greater among 'civilised' cultures than among 'primitive' ones. He located the reason in the increase in modesty which took place with the rise of Christianity (following the collapse of the Graeco-Roman world). Because of the body–soul dualism upheld by Christianity, a tendency to cover the body was a means to repress attention devoted to the body, and divert it to the soul. This caused a displacement of the interest in the naked body on to clothes. Consequently, the church disapproval was extended to clothes and decorativeness.

In his analysis of the European courts from feudal to premodern times, Elias (1939/1978; 1939/1982) opens another possibility. He traces the development of civility along the history of the Christian West. Up to the eighth and ninth centuries, Europe was subject to successive waves of migrating tribes (Hellenic, Italian, Celtic, German, Arab, Slavonic, Hungarian and Turk) which populated its empty spaces. Once the external threat was diminished (between the ninth and the fourteenth centuries) population started to grow, and with it land shortage pressure. This society where land ownership was the important currency, was marked by struggles between nobility, church and princes for their share of the land. Feudal society witnessed the transition from centralisation to decentralisation (from the control of the conquering central ruler to the warrior class), and back to centralisation (when smaller knights were drawn towards closer integration into bigger courts, consolidating 'absolute' power in the hands of a single prince). The instability, violence and low drive-control which characterised the feudal age gave way to the stability, refinement and moderation of the 'age of absolutism' (1939/1982, pp. 3–37). Elias observed that in European courts from the sixteenth century onwards, alongside the centralisation of political power around the prince (and later the nation state), a 'civilised' code of behaviour developed. This code consisted of a shift in the kind of control of instinctual urges, restraint of emotions, and concealment of the body and sexuality. This concealment created new zones of modesty (shame, guilt and embarrassment) and transfer of emotions from action to spectating. In societies which were becoming more centralised and specialised, the growing interdependencies between people changed the rules of the social game. Thus state diplomacy replaced open conflicts, contests replaced real battles, and the pleasure of looking was substituted for the pleasure of participating (Elias, 1939/1978).

Elias's argument articulates two principles. First, *although the impetus for the oscillation between centrifugal and centripetal tendencies is economic* (a change from a local self-sufficient barter economy, to a global, specialised, monetary economy), *the driving force for the change is interpersonal*. In the course of a civilising process physical fears of attack are gradually replaced by social fears of shame and embarrassment. This is mediated by the level of interrelationships between people. The knight had 'a short chain of interdependence'. He lived on his sword in an isolated estate. But in an increasingly complex and internally pacified society, the way people were bonded to each other was different. In the court one had to be attuned to a greater number of people, or lose courtly status.

Such a formulation takes us away from the historical specificities of one period or another, since, as Elias reminds us, social processes do not have a 'zero point'. Rather they are rooted in a dynamic 'web of human relationships'. In other words, the process is capable of forward as well as backward movements. This way we can account for lapses in 'civilised behaviour' even in a postmodern context if the stability of the social institutions or the quality of interdependencies deteriorates. To translate it into relevant contemporary reality: the 'interdependencies discourse' has a contemporary ring in issues related to a loss of sense of community, deterioration of the public space etc.

The second principle posits *a parallel development of the social and the individual*: 'One needs to investigate the transformation of both the personality structure and the entire social structure' (1939/1982, p. 287). Such an investigation reveals that alongside the transition from a warrior to a courtier society, a change occurred in the psychological make-up of the individual; a sort of a social construction of emotions. The knight did not feel compelled to impose restraint on himself. His affects roamed free – from uncontrolled joy of the moment to wild outbursts of violence (1939/1978). In psychodynamic terms he had little developed superego. In contrast, for the courtier drive-control was the key to prestige (1939/1982, pp. 264–78): 'In a sense, the danger zone now passes through the self of every individual' (ibid., p. 298).

Elias's theory seems to provide a theoretical framework for explaining the specificity of female modesty, but the 'civilising process' is about men, not women. As Ribeiro (1986) shows, for women, modesty and shame regarding body and dress existed since the Greeks and Romans, early Christianity and Judaism. With women's behaviour being regulated by men, modesty and obedience have always been the requirements of a good woman. Born into the sin of Eve, women have been chastised and restrained either by the teachings of the church or the jealous power of their men. It was men, not women, who acted on their sexual urges in medieval times. But it was the woman who was actually always vulnerable to an attack of a violent or sexual nature, from a stranger, a master or a husband. The attitude of men towards women was one of contempt and distrust. They were regarded as inferior beings whose task is to gratify the man's physical pleasure (Elias, 1939/1982, pp. 73–82). Women were treated more harshly in courts for adultery, and punished severely by father or husband for unchaste behaviour. And when they had been raped or bore illegitimate children it was they and not the men who were stigmatised (Anderson and Zinsser, 1988). Elias notes that 'The pressures on the libidinal life of women are throughout Western history (with the exception of the great absolutist courts) considerably heavier than on men of equal birth' (1939/1982, p. 82).

So how does men's increasing affect control relate to women's modesty? In order to provide an explanation I would like to look at the intersection between Elias and Freud. Perhaps the best paradigm to explain the collective patriarchal displacement of male sexuality onto women's body is psychodynamic. Psychoanalytically speaking, Eve was made responsible for the castration from the symbiotic unity with the all powerful (phallic) mother, represented by the lost paradise. Similarly, Pandora was charged with the guilt of the voyeuristic look. In myth and lore the look is enticing and menacing – like Medusa, the Greek sea-demon whose glaring eyes turned those who gazed at her into stone (Freud, 1940; see also Flügel, 1924). In his effort to deflect the woman's menacing look – the man converts her desire to look into its opposite; a desire to be looked at. The man's desire to look, however, is projected onto the woman. She becomes a spectacle. This is how man's fear of the threat represented by female sexuality is displaced onto the woman, and becomes the woman's modesty.

In order to illustrate the transformation from instinctual desires into refined affects, and from actual action to ritualised action, I would like to draw on the example of the transition from chivalry love to courtly love in the thirteenth century. Chivalry love is carnal and is based on a daring action, courtly love is spiritual and is based on abstinence. The desire underlying chivalry love is realised. The desire underlying courtly love is idealised, restrained in a set of rituals. Thus, sublimated, it transforms into honour. In Provence, the cradle of courtly love, troubadours praised discretion and delighted in the anguish of anticipation of satisfaction. The locus of pleasure shifted from immediate satisfaction of desire to delayed gratification (Duby, 1992). The politics of the courtly love game is an affirmation of a power structure in which a socially inferior knight (knight without land) is in the service of the high ranking lady, but both are subordinated to the lord.

This process, according to Freud, is analogous to the individual sexual development. Not unlike Elias who sees a connection between political processes and development of emotions Freud notes that: 'the process of human civilization and the developmental or educative process of individual human beings . . . are very similar in nature, if not the very same process applied to different kinds of object' (1930, p. 333).

In both, the essence of the process is the integration of the individual into a group, at a cost. The personal and the cultural processes share similar aims and employ similar means. On the individual level when sexual wishes cannot be fulfilled they are diverted. The aim of this diversion is to protect against the suffering that comes from the inability to satisfy those instinctual impulses. This protection is secured by subjecting those impulses to reality constraints. One of the means by which it is achieved consists of transforming the instinct into an impulse with an 'inhibited aim'. Thus the impulse (libidinal energy) is displaced away from sexual aims to 'finer and higher' cultural sublimations (for example, artistic, scientific or moral paths). Other means include killing off the impulse, abstaining (suppressing) from it, or deriving satisfaction from an illusion (phantasy). The cost paid for subjecting the 'pleasure principle' to the 'reality principle' is a reduced sense of happiness through a heightened sense of guilt.

Similarly, on the cultural level, as Elias pointed out, the task of integrating individual feudal knights into a court, or a state, requires 'sublimation' of brute and open (instinctual) conflicts into state diplomacy and ritualisation. And courtly love is a signifier for this process. It was intended as a showcase for values of virility, and the skills of a cultivated and refined person. In courtly love women were portrayed as objects of love. Love, not the woman herself, caused the hero to act. It gave him an excuse for self-restraint, and provided a test of honour and virtue. This tradition manifested itself in two ceremonies: gazing on the naked lady, and the test of love – the Assag (Nelli, 1989). It elevated female beauty into an incarnation of godliness. Idealised and idolised this beauty was a spiritual, not a carnal, pleasure. And the psychoanalyst Lemoine-Luccioni reminds us that 'contemplating woman's beauty and not consummating the sexual act are one and the same thing' (1987, p. 129). This is because the love of the form (which is female beauty) denies the Other as a subject, while confirming its status as an object of (the male) desire by distancing it.

The politics of desire encoded in the troubadour's lyric is the twin patriarchal fantasy of the two-faced lady. One face of this lady is a virginal perfect woman who embodies divine virtues, a supporting helpmate, and a desexualised object of adoration. The other face is the erotic but demonic heartless seductress whose earthly sensuality makes her a sexual (but unattainable) object of desire (Burns, 1985). The first image personifies the lover's dream, the other his nightmare. This ambivalence towards the woman, the fact that she is not loved for herself but as a medium for acquiring virtue, together with the narcissistic accounts of the anguish enjoyed by the lover, complete the analogy between individual neuroticism and the 'neurotic values institutionalised in courtly love' (Askew, 1965).

On the face of it the chivalrous code is empowering the woman since 'whenever men are forced to renounce physical violence, the social importance of women increases' (Elias, 1939/1982, p. 81). But in fact it is a game 'as carefully regulated as a bullfight. The lady could no more escape her fate than the bull in the ring' (Duby, 1992, p. 262). The woman's freedom was apparent. Her body belonged to her husband. She was expected to succumb to her persistent lover honourably and discreetly. Yet it is not exactly empowering for the man either. The troubadour's love is actually a test of power of will, an activity of self-restraint. Through the psychic mechanism of 'replacement by opposites' (Freud, 1915a) it actually betrays not adoration of the woman, but fear of the female's irresistible sexual power. On a cultural level it represents, to use Freud's concept, 'a compulsion to repeat' (Freud, 1920) the childhood trauma of submitting to the temptation of Eve. Except that this time the troubadour shows resilience where Adam yielded.

But it was not only fear which fuelled the mechanism of courtly love, there was also desire. The more self-restraint and dictates of propriety the courtly code imposed, the greater was the need of the repressed desire to idealise, fantasise and transfer the power of action to the power of gaze. When he could no longer force himself on her he undressed her in his mind. An inevitable corollary of affect control and self-restraint – the shame of the naked body – emerged in the sixteenth century in the court society. It coincided with the development of the private space. And together with the development of the private space, and of (male) modesty, the woman continued to be defined as 'public', through being an object of the gaze (see Chapter 3).

From appearance to essence: decline of the male peacock

Female modesty, I have argued so far, represented a displacement onto her body and clothes of two images: desire and fear. More specifically, it was male guilt (repressed desire) and fear which, projected onto the female body, created modesty. This argument can be further supported through a combined 'civilising process' and psychodynamic explanations of another sartorial process: the reduction in male decorativeness. In *The Psychology of Clothes* Flügel (1930/1971) calls the demise of the playful narcissistic element of male dress 'The great masculine renunciation'. Up until the nineteenth century male fashions were sumptuous and decorative, no less, and even more than women's (Banner, 1992). Around the nineteenth century male fashions began to show more sobriety, and became progressively more sombre and drab. In contrast, women's dress continued for a long time to be flamboyant and fancy, and for ever more imaginative, playful, and aesthetic. What we tend to associate with the feminine decorativeness is only a Victorian phenomenon.

Fashion theorists have been puzzled by the question of why 'men gave up their right to all the brighter . . . more elaborate and more varied forms of ornamentation . . . men abandoned his claim to be beautiful' (Flügel, 1930/1971, p. 111). Traditional explanations usually put it down to social and political developments (for example, Laver, 1937; Bell, 1947/1992; König, 1973; Davis, 1992). The French Revolution, goes the explanation, created a trend for abolition of rank distinctions. The decline of European aristocracy created a desire of the rising bourgeoisies to reflect these social attitudes in what they wore. Seeking to distinguish themselves further from aristocracy the bourgeoisie adopted a different propriety code which rejects the corrupt aristocratic claims to elegance, leisure and romantic adventure that became so encoded into pre-nineteenth century dress. Further, the Industrial Revolution intensified the private/public split (a distinction between the domestic sphere of reproduction and the work sphere of production) and stimulated urbanisation. Male attire evolved to encode the centrality of work and career for male identity, and became more simple, unchangeable and sombre. And it seemed to evade urbanisation's opportunities too. The city heralded an era of anonymity where appearances could be manipulated. And in the post industrial revolution period, with increased commercialism, the premium on appearances became even greater (Wilson, 1985). Yet male garb continued to encode expressive constriction. Female garb, on the other hand, encoded expressive excess. Lacking any substantial 'socio-economic currency', women served as tokens of conspicuous consumption and displayed the family status through their appearance (Veblen, 1899/1912).

Another explanation for such gender distinctions in dress can be advanced from the perspective of the singularity of the relationship between the woman and fashion. This singularity is captured by a seventeenth century fashion analyst in France of Louis XIII – M. de Grenaille. Comparing the attitudes of men and women towards fashion he characterises men's relation to fashion as passion and esteem, but brands women's interest in fashion as obsession and idolisation (quoted in Owen Hughes, 1992, p. 136). But why? The association between women and fashion goes back to the Biblical Israelites and to imperial Rome. A style of criticism and mockery of women because of their attachment to clothes practised by moralists and prophets inspired the early Christian church fathers, and the later medieval ones. The woman became one with fashion, and the qualities of fashion clung to her character. Like fashion itself she was believed to be ephemeral, changeable, illusory and extravagant. Yet it was not only misogyny that was expressed in these attitudes. The association of man with mind and women with flesh created a feminisation of the flesh. The flesh embodies material corruption as well as decay and mortality – which is why it was threatening. But however hard it is resisted, the threat cannot be denied. This is the fear of the woman in every body (Bloch, 1992) and of the mortality of everybody (see Chapter 5).

Flügel's explanation draws on psychoanalytic concepts. He notes that desires connected with denied satisfaction are either inhibited or displaced. The desire in question is for self display. It is common to all people and many animals (Lowen, 1968). Men compensated for the loss of their exhibitionistic desires for self display by transforming them to active voyeurism (pleasure in looking). Alternatively, men projected their repressed desire onto beautifully dressed women.

Thus in the 'civilising process' when active satisfaction became limited and men's desire became regulated, women stopped being a signifier of their own desire alone, and took on the signification of men's repressed desire as well. The woman's position is somewhat like the portrait of Dorian Gray. In Oscar Wilde's classic, the hero remains eternally youthful while his portrait bears the marks of ageing, desire and corruption. The woman is the mirror image of the man: the more men became repressed, the more women's visual quality increased. Men's increasing modesty in the civilising process corresponded to an increase in the woman's display. Since fashion was created and controlled by men – when men moderated their desires, drives and affect – they compensated themselves by deriving pleasure in gaze and fantasy – focused on women's bodies and clothes. In the psychoanalytic logic of fetishism, the female dress became the substitute for fulfilling this desire.

Fear of the woman

On a mythical level the woman represented a seductive threat (although in reality it was the woman who was actually always vulnerable to violent or sexual assault). Within the framework of a psychoanalytic metaphysics, the woman functions like a symptom: she represents a threat while being constructed as a defence against that threat.

One particularly violent form of resisting the mythical female power was the witch-hunt which spread over Europe in the sixteenth and seventeenth centuries accusing women of liaising with the devil, and claiming the lives of about 100,000 women. According to Russell (1972), the European witchcraft was a form of social discontent and religious dissent against the (male) establishment between the fourteenth and the seventeenth centuries. The witch was a rebel against Christ because she believed in a cosmology which extends beyond the limits tolerated by the church, to include the Devil and demonic forces. Once gendered as feminine in the fifteenth century (in the *Malleus Maleficarum*), the image persisted. It was a clear case where fear of the outsiders – who set themselves apart from the Christian world order – was superimposed over the irrational 'fear of women [which] lies deep in the mythic consciousness of men' (Russell, 1972, p. 283). More than outcasts of Christian society, the witches were singled out for a particularly strong hatred because they were not physically identifiable, hence more threatening (ibid., p. 269). Paradoxical as it may sound, I would suggest that both witch-hunt and courtly love are two sides of the same coin. It is this duality of denial/affirmation that underlies such ambivalent treatment of women as allied with demonic forces (during the witch-hunt) on the one hand, and idolised as the incarnation of the love and beauty of God (by Provençal troubadours) on the other. Metaphorically these two phenomena illustrate the dialectics of nudity and clothing and their relationship to metaphysical essence (Perniola, 1989). The witch-hunt illustrates the *debasement* of women as representing demonic vice, in spirit and in body. Courtly love illustrates the *exaltation* of women as representing Godly virtue, in spirit and in body. In some way, both allude to the story of the Fall from grace of Adam and Eve. Although courtly love has been paraded as an antithesis to treating the woman as a sinful daughter of Eve, on one level it embodies the same principle as persecuting women for alleged sexual union with the devil. In both cases what is being affirmed is the mystical powers the woman exercises on men's imagination and sexuality. The witch-hunt represents a brute outburst of the fear of that power, courtly love a more refined way of resisting that power. The lover derives virtue out of self-control which indicates a deeper feeling. But he also shows that he, unlike Adam, can resist the temptations of Eve. And Bloch noted that:

> Antifeminism and courtliness stand in a dialectical rapport which, like the dialectical relations of the images 'Devil's gateway' and 'Bride of Christ' among the early church fathers [places the woman] in the overdetermined and polarized position of being neither one nor the other but both at once. (1992, p. 164)

A cross-cultural and historical survey (for example, Flugel, 1930/1971, Ch. 4; König, 1973; Ribeiro, 1986) reveals modesty to be a relative concept. To the Chinese and the Victorians exposure of the feet would seem immodest, while Muslim women will show bare feet but veil their faces. For a late Middle Ages sensibility and for orthodox Jews a chaste woman is not to expose her hair (but cover it with the aid of a jewelled net in the former case, or a wig in the latter). Bare breasts were an accepted form of ceremonial sumptuousity since the fifteenth century but are regarded as over the top in the twentieth century (Bell, 1947/1992, pp. 46–7). Flügel (1930/1971) advanced the theory of 'shifting erogenous zones' arguing that Woman is a desirable sexual object which cannot be consumed all at once. Therefore men choose different parts of female anatomy at different times and eroticise them through fashion. What is common to those divergent practices is that no single part of the human body is considered inherently more or less chaste than others, and that from the thirteenth century standards of modesty are practised by men on women. In *Fashion and the Unconscious* Bergler (1953) defines modesty as a feeling of acute self-consciousness due to appearing different. He sees it as the result, not the cause, of dressing in a particular way. According to his account, in patriarchal societies men had the power over women's conduct, and they enforced modesty on the woman in order to ward off man's unconscious fears of the castrating mother. Feminine clothing is, thus, a fetishistic strategy of defence: an 'improved skin, minus the frightening genitals'. Bergler argues that unconsciously every man is afraid of the woman, and proceeds to discuss a number of passive baby fears which originate in its relationship to the mother and generalise to women as a whole. These are fears of being starved, devoured, poisoned, choked, chopped to pieces and drained. All these fears culminate in a phallic castration fear. And they lead the man into developing an unconscious powerful portrait of himself. Bergler calls this portrait 'He-Man'. He-Man is virile, active, determined:

> He is sound but daring, faithful but conquering – in short, a hero . . . where other mortals would despair, he remains undaunted . . . his vocabulary does not include the word 'fear' . . . physically, He-Man is composed of a miraculous material, firm but resilient, hard as steel and at the same time elastic. (1953, p. 42)

The hero of the cult TV series *The Prisoner* (written and played by Patrick McGoohan; see Carrazé and Oswald, 1990) was one such manifestation. In the series a 'superman type' hero resigns from the secret services and is subsequently abducted. He finds himself on an island run by invisible tyrants with a closed-circuit surveillance system, where everyone is a number, and from which there is no escape. His captors try to break him and get out of him the reason for his resignation. But he, No. 6, faced with the most bizarre and character testing experiences, remains unswerving, resourceful, brilliant and suspicious (of men and women). It is a good example (more so than, for example, James Bond who does have a soft spot for women) because it represents the fantasy in its full ambivalent nature. Yet this power is but a charade because whenever he has an illusion of having figured out one hurdle, he finds himself still tied up to the same umbilical cord. And when he tries to escape, a huge balloon-like monster is summoned which presses against his face like an amniotic sac and threatens to choke him. The intensely metaphoric nature of this series renders it a good candidate for symbolic reading. In one episode, for example, he spends the whole time fighting the cunning tricks of 'a woman named death' who designs all the schemes possible to kill him. And in the last episode the identity of the ultimate tyrant, No. 1, is finally revealed to be the hero's own alter ego.

Like No. 6, the helpless baby transforms himself to the active man. This is accomplished through an 'unconscious repetition compulsion' – a general unconscious tendency to repeat actively what has been passively experienced (Freud, 1920). Thus the fantasy of activity compensates for inner passivity. The attraction of female clothing is the revival of an infantile fantasy of being attracted to women, combined with the experience of the 'uncanny forbidden'. Female clothing allows the man to control his fear by an attitude of aggressive peeping and undressing in thought. Psychologically, man's attitude towards women is influenced by the narcissistic wound caused by the fact that as a baby he was dependent on them. By way of evidence for his thesis Bergler points at the fact that women's clothes have a moth-to-flame attraction for men. Particularly, men are turned on by the game of half-exposure/half concealment. The partly clad is more alluring than the nude. Anthropological evidence also supports the observation that the scanty covering is a powerful sexual stimulus. Undergarments which by their nature embody the dialectic of concealing and revealing became significantly more erotic and less practical in the course of the civilising process (Willett and Cunnington, 1951/1981). What is the allure of the partly naked? The case of the exposure of breasts can illuminate the process.

In the Middle Ages the breasts were covered and the abdomen emphasised. It is perhaps not surprising that the décolleté made its first appearance during the Renaissance, as the civilising process was getting under way. It fits in with the thesis that exposure of the body can only take place where individual self-controls are high (Elias, 1939/1978). The plunging neckline and the ostentatiously exposed breasts became a feature of high sumptuousity in the fifteenth century. Worn on indoor evening occasions, it was contrasted with the completely covered daytime look where exposure was less selective. A similar rationale characterises the appearance of the bikini and the topless bathing costume in the 1960s. Seen within the general context of informalisation of dress in the twentieth century it indicates a degree of (male) self-control that allows women to expose their body without being accused of immodesty. Goffman (1963b) made a similar point when he noted that body exposure is a way of expressing security and trust. A woman who reveals more of her body in ceremonial occasions declares her trust that she can expose herself without being exploited.

But in order to understand the meaning of display and disguise of the female body we need to compare the way it was perceived by both men and women. When the low-cut cleavage made its first appearance it unleashed the wildest moral criticism for its allurement. In line with the prevailing theological climate, it was also seen as a sign of alliance with the devil. In a treatise entitled *Just and Seasonable Reprehension of Naked Breasts and Shoulders* (Cooke, 1678), the author condemns various fashions. Among other things he reasons that:

> our women, whose arms, breasts, and shoulders are naked and bare, are the true Amazons of the Devil. (p. 27)

> by their nakedness they do not only become the seat, but the Thorne of Satan . . . he does not only repose himself upon their breasts and shoulders exposed to the view of men; but he reigns and has an absolute dominion there. (p. 28)

Because

> God has an aversion to all kinds of nakedness about the body, and . . . the Devil is most pleased and delighted with it . . . God hates nakedness, it is the cause of

sin; and the Devil loves it, because it is a proof of our misery . . . God hates nakedness because he cherishes us . . . the Devil loves it, because he hates us and makes that instrument to our destruction. (p. 49)

Women, however, exhibited a more 'natural' attitude to the revealing cleavage. For they did not regard it as a direct provocation, but an aesthetically tamed eroticism. Flügel (1930/1971, pp. 106–10) and König (1973, pp. 134–5; 193–7) point out that in women the principle of concealment and revealing of the body often gets mistaken for immodesty. Within a psychodynamic framework, they locate the reasons for such a response in the differences between male and female sexuality (a reasoning which has since gained currency among psychoanalytically oriented feminists; cf. Irigaray, 1977/1985). These differences are manifested both in showing the body, and in looking at it. Because female sexuality is diffused in the whole body, women are simultaneously more modest and more exhibitionistic, and their sublimation of exhibition from body to clothes is less complete. In contrast, male sexuality is more localised in the genitals, his exhibitionism is wholly invested in his clothing, and it is easier to symbolise a single sexual zone (the phallus) in garments than to symbolise the whole body.

In traditional societies even today the attitudes towards exposure of the breasts are more similar to those of medieval Europe where female sexuality was most threatening, than those of a contemporary nudist camp where total nakedness demystifies sexual feeling (Flügel, 1930/1971). Thus, for example, in Singapore where anti-exposure norms are strong across all age groups, daringly cut dresses do not sell. Chua (1992), who did an observational study of customers in an exclusive designer shop, notes a response of a woman in her mid-40s who was offered a bra-less evening dress: 'I am a mother of four children, not me!'

The equality of women, says Bergler, is alien to man's unconscious: 'Basically, he is afraid of women, and consequently deprecates them in a silly-supercilious way' (1953, p. 44). Men's fear of the bleeding (castrated) female genitals is evidenced both from clinical experience, and anthropological data about treatment of menstruating women and puberty girls. More recently, the disapproval of adverts for sanitary napkins on British television proves a similar point: 'There is irony, when one realizes how illogical is the cultural yardstick which forces man, the weaker sex, to act the stronger sex' (1953, p. 47).

Within the space outlined by Bergler, Elias and Flügel, female chastity and modesty appear to be a displacement of men's fear and their own uncontrolled desire by inversion. Within this framework the history of moral criticism of dress takes on a particular meaning. Criticisms from religious or medical authorities are but another expression of the 'masochistic pleasure' involved in an interplay between fear of the woman, and fear of the uncontrolled desire of her.

Modesty in dress

The link between female modesty and dress, derived from the intimate connection between clothes and body, need not be interpreted psycho-dynamically. Social psychology offers other explanations. If clothes identify the person, they call attention to the body as well as mark it as part of a particular social category. Goffman talks about two levels of messages: those that mark the individual as similar to other members of some broad category (for example, occupational or ideological category), and those messages which identify how the individual is different from all others (1963a). This interplay between the desire to convey an individual message and a social message can be interpreted in various ways. Social psychological theories explain it as a conflict between conformity and uniqueness tendencies. It involves striking a fine balance between being sufficiently similar to others to claim group membership, and sufficiently different not to lose one's own identity (Markus and Kunda, 1986, p. 860). This balancing game is then traced to two fundamental motivations underlying social behaviour: to attract (to be loved) and to conform (to be approved of) (Buck, 1988). When it comes to clothes, whether or not one wants to conform or to make an individual statement has a sexual dimension. If identification is the text, sexuality is the subtext. This is evident from the observation that every transgression from the requirement of female modesty threatens to put her in the category of the prostitute. Historically, a prostitute was conceived of as the ultimate woman, who is both in touch and in charge of her sexuality. Such a woman was simultaneously desirable and dangerous. She embodied male fears of female sexuality. The prostitute was not originally from a lower class. Until the last century she was from the educated classes, and her desires were genuinely to have an independent life: sexual, intellectual and social. Prostitution was, for most of history, the only way a woman could earn her living independent of a male guardian. But in so doing the woman was undermining the basis of her reputation. In fact her independent sexuality puts her more in common with present-day feminist than with a 'sexy' woman (Roberts, 1992). The fears of the sexually independent woman have been transferred to the contemporary single independent woman (Showalter, 1991) and the 'Other woman' (single independent woman having an affair with married men; Richardson, 1985). More on that in Chapter 4.

The religious legacy equates display with prostitution, while psycho-analytically informed theories suggest how the 'civilising' of instinctual urges transformed male exhibitionism into pleasure in gazing at female display. As a result, display (existing for the Other's eyes) seems to be almost a design feature of the woman. At the same time modesty finds expression in the fear of display that comes across as a prostitute. In my survey of British women the questionnaires reveal an almost paradoxical mixture of a desire for display and a fear of display, both indicating internalisation of cultural expectations. The motif of the prostitute/

independent sexual woman and the fears it engenders expressed themselves in the kind of concerns signified by the desire to stand out or blend in.

One question inquired 'Do you prefer to turn heads or blend in?' On the face of it the issue is about confidence and self-esteem, and a conflict between social and individual messages. On another level it encodes the ambivalence of modesty and display. A typical answer ran 'I like to be well dressed and noticed for being well dressed. However, I do not like to draw attention to myself through my appearance'. Yet neither strategy seemed to be an optimal position: there are advantages and drawbacks in both standing out and blending in. Blending in is reassuring ('it would show I wasn't outrageous in my dress'), but it runs the risk of being unattractive ('too rigid conformity, boring and unimaginative'). Standing out, on the other hand, is rewarding ('if I made an effort I do stand out, this is not unpleasant'), but also threatening. It can invite attention ('when I take trouble I draw attention to myself so probably I only want to draw it when I'm capable of dealing with it!'). It might lead to erroneous attributions of intention ('I would only dress adventurously where I might feel superior or slightly superior or don't like the persons or don't want to be part of the occasion'). It might also lead to mistaken attribution of character ('I don't want to appear eccentric but like to think I have individuality').

That reservations from standing out are related to social (dis)approval is evident from the guilt expressed while enjoying it. For example:

> 'I like to turn heads sometimes . . . but not all the time. There would be something wrong with one's ego if it were necessary all the time.'

> 'It's probably vanity but I want to turn heads by looking good but slightly different. If someone asks me why I look like I do I say that its everybody else who's strange by being boring with their appearance. I want to be creative. I'm against everyone being the same. Conforming. Oh, I've probably got too much of an ego. I love the comments.'

At the same time just as much moral reservation was expressed at the idea of blending in by following fashion. And while women admitted that they would not want to look 'dated' they strongly rejected the idea of looking like 'fashion victims'. Common answers acknowledged that 'I note the trends and bend them to suit my looks and life style' but qualified that with 'I wouldn't follow slavishly if it didn't suit me'. Yet they make concessions to fashion even when they would rather not follow it closely: 'If I'm honest, there are certain colours and styles that I still like but no longer want to wear because they might be last year's'.

A French fashion journalist once observed that while the French follow fashion to look good, Englishwomen follow fashion to look interesting (*Elle Magazine*, 1986, p. 54). Yet what seems to be at stake is not a matter of taste, or creativity, but the difference between a (French) culture of pleasure, and a (British) culture of puritanism. This was evidenced by the observation that across age and marital status, occupational status and level of confidence, the overriding concern of the women in my sample was with *not giving the wrong sexual signals*. Asked about undesirable messages they *do not want* to convey through their clothes the most common response was some sort of a sexually available message. Looking cheap or tarty, inviting or available, free and easy, needy or provocative is wrong. So is making men 'getting ideas of me' or 'leading anyone on'. This expectation, however, is also tainted with a web of contrary expectations. Because while being overtly sexual is wrong so is a total desexualised message. In the words of one woman, the message to avoid is 'I'm a right old tart and available to all', but also 'I think sex is an unfortunate evolutionary mistake and I'm available to nobody'. The permissible territory again borders on impossibility: signalling desire while denying it – being suggestive, but understated enough so as not to be blatantly seductive:

'I would not like to be seen as a sex object (although I do still want to look attractive).'

'I would not want to be saying I'm available. I hate tarty clothes – really tight ones. A hint is so much more sexy.'

'I would not want to look tarty, or consciously seductive – unconsciously is another matter, of course.'

'I like to look reasonably sexy. Not tarty but slightly fanciable.'

'I like to stand out . . . I don't dress to turn male heads – not at least consciously.'

The concern with sexual overtones echoes the absent presence of 'the prostitute in every woman'. It highlights the desire/fear conflict with regard to standing out or blending in. This ambivalence came across very clearly from many respondents. It conceals a denial of sexuality, a fear of getting the wrong kind of attention for the wrong reason: that which depends on packaging rather than content: 'If you stand out for some reason, I find a certain type of man is attracted to you . . . very superficial appraisal usually means they are more interested in your looks than your brain and personality'.

The fear is of uncontrolled male sexuality. Being sexy risks inviting undesirable male attention, and is therefore preferable in situations where the woman feels less vulnerable: 'It's nice to feel attractive, so long as I'm in a controlled environment i.e. party'. Another way of feeling protected is through male company, which is why many women admit to being more adventurous in their clothes when with a male companion. For example, one teenager explained: 'I am more daring with my boyfriend . . . [because] . . . I feel extremely vulnerable and insecure if I'm aware older boys are eyeing me up in case I get into a difficult situation which I can't handle'. This concern is not limited to teenagers though. It is reflected in the practice that allowed the married woman in the nineteenth century to be more erotic and sumptuous than the unmarried one, and sanctioned body exposure in eveningwear, among one's social equals more than in daywear where exposure is less selective (Steele, 1985).

Other undesirable messages the women were careful to avoid were 'boring', 'outrageous', and 'unfeminine'. Each in their own way conveys on one level a concern with propriety. On another level they all reflect the anxiety of getting the right balance between appearing coy and enticing. And indeed the concern with social appropriateness is a Victorian version of the same age-old concerns of chastity versus sexuality. Originally associated with the nobility, refinement and decorum were appropriated by the rising middle classes who sought to establish a genteel image by being 'more aristocratic than the aristocrats'. The aristocrats 'can do, say, wear and look like anything they want without undue feelings of shame which is largely a bourgeois feeling' (Fussell, 1984, p. 45). In Elias's terms, the middle classes are most highly interdependent, hence their greater affect control and its counterpart shame.

Thus trapped again between impossible alternatives where cultivating her appearance is evidence of her unsubstantive essence, but failing to do so is bad form, the woman is treading the fine line carefully. And while almost every woman found fault with some part of her appearance and admitted to making various degrees of effort of personal enhancement – the majority drew the line at cosmetic surgery, and other excessive forms of time consuming beauty procedures. But this already takes us to Chapter 4.

2

MASKING THE SELF:
THE LADY IS A FAKE

The multi-faced woman captured by this participant in the carnival in
Venice where fantasy peronae are clothed and enclosed.

The paradox which underlies this chapter has its roots in a long tradition
which defines female identity as non-identity. My claim is that this tradition
covers very different theoretical explanations. It ranges from mythological

and theological descriptions which define the essence of the woman as dissimulation, to psychoanalytic accounts and contemporary social theory which define the 'essence' of femininity as an inessential social construction. The objections to my claim might point out that lumping together a misogynist essentialist picture with a feminist, deconstructionist one under the same 'tradition' masks the fundamental difference between them. The difference is that while the former imprisons its object of discussion (that is, Woman) in rigid categories, the latter liberates it through an ideological critique of the categories.

These objections, far from disputing my claim, in fact underline it, because they serve as an illustration of the paradox that cuts across this chapter. The paradox is that in some sense both ideological and counter-ideological attitudes trap the woman in the same impossible space where her essence is defined as non-essence. The main difference between these two positions is moral. In the theological discourse femininity is fake. It is duplicitous. In the psychoanalytic discourse femininity is masquerade. It is socially constructed. Implicit in both approaches is the issue of authenticity, or the relationship between appearance and essence. In other words the question which frames the debate is whether the 'appearance of femininity' (decorativeness, fashions, beauty procedures) is indicative of inauthenticity of character, or is external to the self. One voice, however, is constantly missing from this kind of discussion: the actor's own. Given that women are placed in these feminine roles, do they experience them as alien or as part of the self?

In what follows I want to pick up these various themes. Revisiting and building on some notions elaborated in Chapters 1 and 4, I will start by illustrating the ancient theological and the current constructionist position. Then I will present women's own account based on my research. I will show how the continuity that can be traced between old misogynies and new psychological and sociological theories regarding the Eve-woman is disrupted when it comes to women's own experience.

Artifice as a sign of deception and evil

In mythological and theological representations the woman features as synonymous with artifice, inauthenticity, and duplicity. She appears as made up, claiming false identity, trying to appear for ever younger and prettier than nature made her. Artificiality is not threatening in itself. It is a means to an end. The end is to seduce the man, to lure him to his destruction. Embodied in the legendary sea-demons such as Medusa (whose beauty and bewitching gaze are deadly to men), or the Sirens (the half fish/half woman beauties whose enchanting singing allures sailors to their death) is the primordial fear of the archetypal woman who is for ever menacing. Seduction and threat are built into her design features. The mythical figures of Pandora and Lilith represent the threat to paradisical existence. In the creation stories Pandora and Lilith concealed a treacherous self behind a façade of beauty, and Eve's essence is bound up with decoration. In the Jewish legends God has made a number of attempts to create Eve out of various materials, but Adam rejected them all. When God finally created her out of a part of Adam, and presented her to him adorned with jewellery and plaited hair, Adam accepted her. Consequently, the woman must use a perfume because she was created from a bone, and a bone putrefies. Because Adam was created from earth the man does not require a perfume (*Bereshith Rabbah*, 17: 8; Ginzburg, 1909/1937). The creation of Eve from Adam's rib emphasises her derivative nature. Another implication of the Eve story is the woman's inessential nature. Both her creation and her being are predicated on dissimulation. She is made to stand for manipulation of beauty, adornment and feminine charms to lure people. She is artifice pretending to be what she is not. Christian interpretations consider her decorativeness as endemic to her sex, and as profoundly sacrilegious. The authors of the medieval authoritative explanation of the phenomenon of the witches *Malleus Maleficarum*, the inquisitors Heinrich Kramer and James Sprenger blame the woman's natural tendency upon her formation: 'there was a defect in the formation of the first woman, since she was born from a bent rib . . . through this defect she is an imperfect animal, she always deceives' (1489, p. 44).

Improving on nature through the 'wicked arts' of false and dyed hair, make-up and coloured clothes constitute, according to the church fathers, offences against God, self and men. By decorating herself the woman betrays mistrust in the work of the Creator of all things and defiles His creation. In the words of Clement of Alexandria, 'they dishonour the Creator of men, as if the beauty given by Him were nothing worth' (1867, p. 278). 'Those things, then, are not the best by nature which are not from God, the Author of nature. Thus they are understood to be from the devil, from the corruptor of nature' (Tertullianus, 1869, p. 312).

The sin against the soul is in cultivating values of falsehood instead of seeking truth. Falsehood ultimately resides in the body, not in spiritual matters: 'For applying things unsuitable to the body, as if they were suitable, begets a practice of lying and a habit of falsehood' (Clement of Alexandria, 1867, p. 269), and 'elaborate braidings, and infinite modes of dressing the hair, and costly specimen of mirrors in which they arrange their costume . . . are characteristic of women who have lost all sense of shame . . . they turn their faces into masks' (ibid., p. 280). Another sin implied by adornment is against people, that is men. By adorning herself for display the woman distracts the minds of men, and tempts them to sin. The notion that women use their beauty and finery, false hair and cosmetics to trap men is one of the constant themes in thirteenth century poetry (like *Roman de la Rose*).

In all these acts the woman's demonic quality is lurking behind. If she defies God and distracts men through feminine charms she is in alliance with the devil: 'when she becomes fond of finery, she falls away from God' (Clement of Alexandria, 1867, p. 260), and 'what is superfluous, Scripture declares to be of the devil' (ibid., p. 256).

> For they who rub their skin with medicaments, stain their cheeks with rough, make their eyes prominent with antimony, sin against Him. . . . they censure, the Artificer of all things! . . . when they amend, when they add to [His work] taking these their additions, of course, from the adversary artificer . . . that is the devil. (Tertullianus, 1869, p. 320)

This conception of the woman is by no means confined to religious circles, ancient times or medieval misogyny. Schopenhauer, for example, expresses a similar mistrust of the woman when he says:

> nature has equipped . . . woman with the power of dissimulation as her means of attack and defence . . . to make use of it at every opportunity is as natural to her as it is for an animal to employ its means of defence whenever it is attacked . . . A completely truthful woman who does not practice dissimulation is perhaps an impossibility. (1970, p. 83)

A recent addition to the metaphysical meaning of women's appearance is its dismissal as unimportant. This view owes its existence to the turn gender fashion has taken at the end of the eighteenth century. This period marks a real differentiation in men's and women's clothes in terms of general style. It marks the departure of male clothing from decorativeness, colour and flair. Female clothing, on the other hand, continued to be flamboyant, imaginative and playful. These changes coincided with, and came to signify, significant social changes. While the French Revolution did away with aristocratic type leisure attire, the Industrial Revolution created a division between public/work and private/home. From the point of view of the woman, the victory of the bourgeoisie marked a regression. For bourgeois values emphasised her domestic role and redefined her in the territory of the home. The public sphere, symbolised by the suit, was man's world. The private sphere was the woman's kingdom. And by implication, the public world was invested with importance, while the domestic was trivialised as 'women's world'. Nietzsche, for example, in *Beyond Good and Evil*, expresses both conceptions of the woman: triviality and falsehood when he refers to the woman's 'genius for finery' as evidence of an 'instinct for secondary role' (1885/1987, p. 84), and when he reads her self adornment as signifying a rejection of truth: 'what is truth to a woman! From the very first nothing has been more alien, repugnant, inimical to woman than truth – her great art is the lie, her supreme concern is appearance and beauty' (1885/1987, p. 145).

The much acclaimed film *Dangerous Liaisons* (based on a play by Christopher Hampton, adapted from the novel *Les Liaisons dangeruses* by Choderlos de Laclos) tells the story of an eighteenth century upper class Parisian seducer, while portraying the paradigmatic picture of the archetypal inessential woman. The protagonist is no common seducer. Expert in the subtleties of the charmer's craft he is not satisfied with easy victories (of young innocent girls), but prefers the challenge of virtuous women. His motives and pursuits are like an open book to another society lady, an ex-lover who has perfected the manner of living dangerously usually reserved for men. She leads an independent sexual and social life, and plays the games of love strategically and artfully. The message which is unambiguously packaged in the film is that it takes a shrewd and calculating woman to persevere in this game. Familiar with the seducer's weakness and vanity she manipulates him into participating in one of her little revenge schemes. The plot eventually leads to a ruin of the players. The seducer, realising that he destroyed the only woman he actually cared for, allows himself to be defeated in a duel and dies. Setting a contemporary film back in time is a simple but powerful device of conveying a mythological truth in the guise of history. The film is overlaid with all the motifs of the Eve genre. The heroine is a woman trying to survive in a man's world by beating them in their own game. Both she and her partner for the scheme are depicted as exploitative and heartless. But there is a difference. While his vice is portrayed as redeemable because he does have a soft spot of genuine emotions for his last victim, the woman is painted as evil incarnate in pitch black with no shades of human colour. She is unyielding and unemotional – until she realises that her schemes boomeranged against her. The opening and closing scenes of the film – showing her put on her mask of make-up and attire, and wiping off her masked paint after the defeat – frame her as the quintessential woman whose glorious appearance is nothing but an artifice used as a tool in her evil designs.

Masquerade as a sign of an inessential construction

Psychoanalysis extended the argument of inessential femininity to theorise it as masquerade. This conception was first discussed by Riviere, more recently by Lacan, and in theories of female spectatorship in the cinema (e.g. Doane, 1982). The idea (premised on the Freudian notion that the libido is male; Freud, 1905) is that the essence of femininity is a dissimulation of the female unconscious masculinity. It is a 'charade of power'. It is because of her anxiety of the man's retribution for challenging his power that she disguises herself as an object of desire (the castrated 'feminine' woman) (Heath, 1989). One finds here echoes of the church fathers' insistent demand on feminine chastity through transcending the body. This requirement implies that the woman can only equal man if she transcends her essential nature: if she renounces that which is quintessentially feminine: the flesh (Bloch, 1992, pp. 106–7). And if the 'real woman' is a man, a feminine woman is a masquerade. Riviere introduced the masquerade in 1929 in her analysis of the behaviour of some professional women who flash their femininity to signal that they are not really so threatening, and to reassure that their power is just a charade. Femininity is thus a disarming disguise: it is donned, like masquerade, to disguise the female's desire of the phallus (of power). Afraid to challenge the male who possesses the phallus directly, the woman deflects attention from her desire for power through its opposite: constructing a very feminine, non-threatening image of herself. For Riviere the display of femininity hides an unconscious masculinity. The masquerading woman becomes the father through her masculine success, having exhibited herself in possession of the phallus. Having thus 'castrated' her man, she seeks protection from his expected revenge, offering herself now as the castrated woman through a mask of womanliness, or as the MacCannells (1987) put it 'Beauty is only male insecurity displaced'. According to this argument, femininity is a representation of the woman: not an essential, but a constructed identity. In Lacan's formulation femininity is like a fetish: pretending to hide what is in fact not there – a castrated lack-in-being. In *The Signification of the Phallus* (1966/1977) Lacan writes:

> Paradoxical as this formulation may seem, I am saying that it is in order to be the phallus, that is to say, the signifier of the desire of the Other, that a woman will reject an essential part of femininity, namely, all her attributes in the masquerade. It is for that which she is not that she wishes to be desired as well as loved. (p. 290)

Whether from Riviere's or from Lacan's position, masquerade reveals the claim for authentic femininity to be like the structure of 'bad faith': in both cases I constitute myself as 'a thing' in order not to be 'that thing'. The effort 'to be authentic' implies a twofold paradox. According to Sartre the very attempt to be 'authentic' (that is, feminine) suggests that originally 'one is being what one is not'. In other words: the woman is not originally authentically feminine but can become one with effort. Second, 'being authentic' implies an act of objectifying oneself, of seeing oneself through the eyes of the Other. And a being which is for-others cannot be authentically for-itself (Sartre, 1943/1966, p. 100).

Historically, the concept of masquerade has some relevance to the woman, if by no means unique. It emerged alongside the concept of privacy as a result of the civilising process (Elias, 1939/1978). The notion of privacy, which was quite absent from Medieval life, created a change in patterns of interaction among strangers. Coupled with the belief that people's thoughts and character can be read from their faces (Sennett, 1976), people developed practices of turning their faces into inscrutable masks and avoided staring at strangers. Thus masks became a device for creating a private sphere even in public. Not surprisingly this coincided with the emergence of the public masquerade which combined the desire for public interaction with keeping private boundaries intact. Masquerade operated not only on a formal level, but also on an everyday one. In a medieval society where people knew each other, the stranger was a threatening entity. But in premodern times, with the development of urban centres which were 'communities of strangers' people exercised forms of 'civil inattention' (such as not staring at others) in order to allow others their space. It became common for women, for example, to wear a black mask when in public so as to protect their privacy and reputation from uninvited eyes (Heyl, 1994).

From a feminist perspective, the concept of masquerade is double edged. On the one hand it implies the instability of the feminine position. Like fetishism, it defines subjectivity through distance, a denial of, and a defence against a threatening reality. The threatening reality is the 'castration' of the woman in the case of fetishism, and the power of the woman in the case of masquerade. On the face of it, as Doane (1988–9) argues, the concept of masquerade facilitates an understanding of the woman's status as spectacle rather than a spectator. But, she goes on to suggest, it has an empowering feature as well. The patriarchal notion of femininity is one of closeness and immediacy, hence lacking the distance (between the object and the sign) which is a prerequisite for the use of language. The consequence is that femininity (and women) are positioned outside language (and power). For the woman to embrace the 'authentic femininity' is to affirm her own disempowerment. The masquerade, through its distance from any 'authentic' or stable position appears to challenge this patriarchal notion. But in fact, it remains dependent upon masculinity as a frame of reference for its very definition. Further, the notion of femininity as disguise does not necessarily imply bad faith. In some ways it manifests the structure of a defence mechanism, or a symptom (which is a failed defence). In both cases the defence simultaneously disguises and calls attention to what it tries to hide, in the process of hiding it.

Even the notion of gender as a construction (see, for example, West and Zimmerman, 1987) is only liberating to a limited extent. In the face of persistent social realities and documented sexual differences in the wider natural realm, it might appear like an escape into phantasy. Feminist criticism of socio-biology may be justified, but it backfires against feminism's own claim: that the denial of our embodied identity is itself a patriarchal tradition.

Once again the justification for looking at the specificity of the female experience comes from the gender meaning assigned to appearance. When it comes to the woman appearance and essence are intertwined. When vanity, artificiality, and extravagance in fashion are condemned, they are not seen as external behaviours, but are given metaphysical meanings. They are seen as indicators of female (in)essence. But if the woman is considered as artifice and fake, is it the case that she hides her real essence, or is she only a series of masks with no essence? In order to examine this question I propose to look at interview material with women. These interviews reveal how women perceive the role of appearance in their life, and how sartorial identities are related to their sense of self. More specifically, it addresses the question of whether sartorial self-presentation is sincere or manipulative. I examine this question in the light of two social theories that deal with the issue of self-presentation: impression management and dramaturgical psychology (see also Tseëlon, 1992a; 1992d). The central question these theories address is how to account for the multiplicity of appearances. And they do it from different starting points. Impression management is using the language of sincerity/manipulation. Dramaturgy uses the language of dramatisation and performance.

Self-presentation *à la* Goffman

In his classic book *The Presentation of Self in Everyday Life* (1959) Goffman provides an account of social life which is modelled on the theatre. He details how people qua actors plan and execute different performances in front of various audiences, and how participants (actors and audience) cooperate in negotiating and maintaining a definition of the situation. The self for Goffman is not an independent fixed entity which resides in the individual. Rather, it is a social process: 'In dramaturgical analysis the meaning of the human organism is established by its activity and the activity of others with respect to it . . . selves are outcomes not antecedents of human interaction' (Brissett and Edgley, 1975, p. 3).

In his book Goffman articulated a principle which enjoys the dual merit of being both a culturally specific phenomenon and 'a universal human possibility'. The 'façade self' represents a particular variant of bourgeois social character. The construction of 'fronts' and the threat of being caught in embarrassing situations is, however, a 'human constant' (Kuzmics, 1991). Two concepts are central to understanding Goffman's position on the issue of sincerity of presentational behaviour: *region behaviour* and *audience segregation*. Region behaviour refers to the discrepancy between one's behaviour when with different kinds of audience (for example, strangers, own 'team members'):

> when one's activity occurs in the presence of other persons, some aspects of the activity are expressively accentuated and other aspects, which might discredit the fostered impression, are suppressed . . . there may be another region – a 'backregion' or 'backstage' – where the suppressed facts make an appearance. (1959, p. 114)

> Audience segregation refers to a device for ensuring that those before whom one plays one of his parts won't be the same individuals before whom he plays a different part in another setting. (1959, p. 57)

This device summarises Goffman's conception of *private* and *public*. It is a dynamic concept which refers not to a *place*, but to the *experience* of being visible or invisible (Foddy and Finighan, 1980). Thus, although Goffman uses the metaphor 'stage' and 'backstage', or 'private' and 'public', a careful reading of his account, suggests that he uses them as different kinds of stage, not as a true private and a false public. Goffman's actor has no interior and exterior. Rather she or he has a repertoire of 'faces' each activated in front of a different audience, for the purpose of creating and maintaining a given definition of the situation. Thus, according to Goffman 'region behaviour', 'audience segregation', as well as techniques of emphasis and dramatism are designed to conceal irrelevant information, not some real truth. Acting, for him, is an existential metaphor. From a symbolic interactionist perspective, Goffman's distinction between 'private' and 'public' (or backstage and stage) is not a structural one. It is not the difference between sincere and managed behaviour, but between unself-conscious and self-conscious behaviour. In other words it is the distinction between a subjective experience of being visible or invisible (Tseëlon, 1991a).

In Goffman's view the essence of self presentation is that it is just as important to represent oneself as possessing a certain quality as to actually possess a quality one is claiming (1959, p. 81). As Harré (1979) pointed out, despite the differences between theatrical and 'real' behaviours both share a common feature. In order to claim a certain identity it is not enough to *be* it, because: 'to be a given kind of person is not merely to possess the required attributes, but also to sustain the standard of conduct and appearance that one's social grouping attaches thereto' (Goffman, 1959, p. 81).

Goffman himself did not take issue with the question 'when is performance more sincere?' because he regarded even sincere performance as still constructed. He stressed that while all dishonest behaviours are 'staged', not all 'staged' behaviour is dishonest: 'While people usually are what they appear to be, such appearances could still have been managed' (1959, p. 77). Goffman, however, was more concerned with the mechanics of creating an appearance and less with the relationship between appearance and reality:

> there are many individuals who sincerely believe that the definition of the situation they habitually project is the real reality. In this report I do not mean to question their proportion in the population, but rather the structural relation of their sincerity to the performances they offer. (1959, p. 77)

Self-presentation *à la* impression management

An alternative interpretation of self-presentation was developed by *impression management* social psychologists. Impression management traces its roots to Goffman's dramaturgical metaphor. But in contrast to Goffman, it appropriated this metaphor to portray a very different type of actor. 'Impression management' (see for example, Arkin, 1980; Schlenker, 1980, 1985; Tedeschi, 1981; Baumeister, 1982, 1986; Buss and Briggs, 1984; Snyder, 1987) took Goffman's stage metaphor literally. And just as dramatic actors have indeed an off-stage persona and a stage persona, the social actor *à la* impression management has 'private realities' and 'public appearances'. Their interpretation regard behaviours which appear spontaneous as sincere, and behaviours that are managed as deceptive. The model of a person underlying the impression management perspective is that of a manipulator who tries to control the impression people will form of them through situationally appropriate behaviours. Such behaviours are designed by the actor to establish particular desired images in the eyes of various audiences (see for example, Schlenker, 1980; Tedeschi, 1981; Baumeister, 1986; Snyder, 1987).

At issue here are two approaches to presentation of self: representation or mispresentation. The difference between these two approaches to presentation of self is in the meaning attributed to the social game. The Goffmanesque approach views people's presentational behaviour as a process of negotiation. According to this view people offer definitions of themselves in various interaction contexts which the audience either accepts or challenges. This 'game' is the point of the interaction, *an end in itself*. It is a game of *representation*. In contrast, the position advanced by 'impression management' researchers views presentational behaviour as strategic acts of creating images. Unlike Goffman's approach, this 'game' is not an end in itself but *a means to an end* of gaining benefits. It is a game of *mispresentation*. This assumption actually runs counter to Goffman's own treatment of staged behaviour. He observed that 'these dichotomous conceptions [sincere versus false] providing strength to the show they put on, but a poor analysis of it' (Goffman, 1959, p. 77).

Jones and Pittman summarised the differences between the two approaches as the difference between actors' *expressions*, and between actors' attempt to create *impressions*:

> Goffman crystallized one viewpoint on impression management. Goffman's emphasis, however, was on the subtle ways in which *actors project or convey a definition* of the interaction situation *as they see it*. Attempts on the part of the actor to *shape others' impressions* of his personality received only secondary emphasis. (1986, p. 231; emphasis added)

Impression management theorists use the term 'self-presentation' almost always as an equivalent of 'mispresentation' (contrasted with self-expression, private reality, etc.). Not all 'impression management' theorists defined 'self-presentation' as a misrepresentational concept. Some did try to distil a truly representational concept out of the self-presentational package. Schlenker's concept of *self-projection* (1980), Baumeister's concept of *self-construction* (1982), and Cheek and Hogan's concept of *self-interpretation* (1983) are such attempts. However, a manipulative model of the individual is implicit in much of impression management discourse and practices (cf. Baumeister, 1986).

The basic assumption of impression management research is that private views are different from public ones, and that the private self is sincere, while the public persona is designed to form a false impression. The model of the individual underlying this approach is that of a manipulator who makes cost-oriented calculations of how and when to gain credit falsely without risking disrepute. This is evident, for example, in the rationale for the paradigm typically employed in impression management research. The research paradigm consists of experimental manipulations intended to create a discrepancy between so-called private and public reporting conditions (for example, Tedeschi and Rosenfeld, 1981). The inherent assumption is that the private condition is true while the public condition is false. The paradigm usually involves two identical situations which differ only in that some circumstances are public in one situation but private in the other. These situations are then compared. A discrepancy between the two, then, is taken to indicate the operation of self-presentation. The private condition is interpreted as the 'true' self; the public condition as the 'presented' self (Baumeister, 1982, p. 4).

A paradigmatic case is the technique developed to investigate self-presentational behaviours by Jones and Sigall (1971) called 'the bogus pipeline'. This is essentially a mock lie-detector which is aimed at catching the subjects 'off guard' in order to get at the 'real truth' of their behaviour. Arkin et al. described the bogus pipeline technique as a strategy 'for reducing distortion and dissimulation in verbal responses . . . convincing the subjects that the experimenter is capable of detecting whether they are telling the truth, thus leading subjects to be more frank in revealing socially undesirable information' (1980, p. 28). Thus, the two theories use the terms 'private' and 'public', in different ways. While Goffman uses them as indicators of self-consciousness, impression management theorists use them as indicators of sincerity (private) versus duplicity (public) (for a discussion see Tseëlon, 1991a).

From Goffman's perspective the distinction between the 'real' (private) and the 'staged' (public) is a matter of *style* rather than *substance*. His account of the rhetorics of self-presentation is given in *amoral* terms (Edgley and Turner, 1975, p. 8),while impression management (and some of Goffman's critics) interprets self-presentation in *immoral* terms.

The analysis I want to present is based on an open-ended questionnaire study introduced in the introductory chapter. The study comprised 160 questionnaires. But the analysis was carried out on a sample of 40 questionnaires selected in such a way as to match the general population, as close as possible, in terms of sociodemographic status (for details of questionnaire and sample see Tseëlon, 1989).

If impression management theory provides an accurate account of women's behaviour we would expect the following corollaries to be true:

1. Presentational efforts in front of familiar audience indicate insincerity.
2. Attempts to present an improved image in front of less familiar others is evidence of duplicity.
3. Paying conscious attention to one's appearance indicates an intention to conceal, or to present a false image.

If, however, the dramaturgical account captures female sartorial behaviour better, none of these propositions need be true. In terms of the conception of the woman that this chapter is addressing, impression management's view of the actor is similar to the theological view of the woman as fake and manipulative. The dramaturgical theory's picture, on the other hand, is equivalent to the constructionist positions, which regard any essence as, in a sense, an appearance. The analysis was organised along the lines of each proposition, and was designed to identify which of the contrasting accounts of human self-presentation (dramaturgical or manipulative) can be supported by the data.

Familiar audience

If, as the first proposition implies, conscious control of one's appearance implies insincerity, then there should be no point in manipulating our appearance in front of familiar others who know us anyway. Evidence from the questionnaires, however, indicates that presentational efforts are not limited to unfamiliar audience whom we want to impress. Rather, they are found even when the audience is self or familiar others.

The fact that we care about our appearance even when with familiar others whom we are not trying to impress was revealed in a number of ways. For example, one question inquired 'How important do you consider your appearance to be when you are: on your own, with people you don't know well, with your immediate family?' Respondents were asked to indicate the importance of appearance by colouring-in wedges in three pie-charts (one for each type of audience), consisting of 10 sections each. For the purposes of analysis, each wedge was treated as representing a score of 10, with the minimum being 0 and the maximum being 100. The general pattern of the results was that the importance of appearance was highest among strangers, next among family members, least when alone ($F = 112.91$; ($df = 2$); $p < .01$) (see Table 2.1).

These data indicate that the less one is familiar with the audience, the more one regards appearance as important in the interaction. So far, this finding is compatible with an 'impression management' interpretation. However, a closer examination of the reasons given for choosing a particular percentage point reveals a substantial variety in the initial level of importance attributed to appearance, the discrepancy between the lowest and the highest levels for each respondent, as well as the subjective meaning of a given rating. For example, the following opposite explanations were given for an appearance level point of 50 *when with family*. For one woman it represented a high level: 'My family is critical of the way I look. Husband and son particularly'. For another woman it represented a low level: 'They know me and don't mind how I dress'. In another example, two respondents offered similar explanations for different

Table 2.1 *Mean scores of the importance of appearance (N = 144)*

	Mean	Standard Deviation
When alone	35.52	25.64
When with strangers	76.74	21.28
When with friends/family	44.79	26.04

Sources: Tseëlon, 1989; 1992d.

appearance levels. One woman, rating the importance of appearance as 30 said: 'My family accepts me – I have no need to wear "gucci" shoes or a Vogue classic – they'd know I'd had saved up for them'. Another woman, rating importance of appearance as 70, also explained: 'I am more at ease and don't have to impress them'.

The 'self as audience' featured in various ways, ranging from the way one feels about oneself even when nobody is looking, through drawing a parallel between inner feeling and appearance ('When you look good you feel good'; 'If I look horrible, I am likely to feel that way too'), to stating that one's own judgement about one's appearance is most important. As for familiar people (family, friends) in the capacity of audience, different women reported having different expectations regarding them. Some were freer with friends, because they felt comfortable enough to display atypical appearances in their company. For example, responses to the question: 'When are you more conventional about the way you dress, and when more daring?' included:

> 'I am more daring at parties especially with friends – or when with "arty" people who inspire me to try and be different.'

> 'I am more conventional in unfamiliar situations where I don't really know how to dress . . . more daring when there is no restraint or pressure on what I wear – at home, with close friends, on my own.'

On the other hand, some felt more constrained with friends and family and freer when deindividualised, anonymous. For example:

> 'I am more daring on holiday as I feel free and can get away with more – also because I'm away from the people I know.'

> 'I am most daring with my clothes when with large groups of people that I do not know and most conventional with family and boyfriends.'

> 'More adventurous or individual when I'm on my own or with female friends. My husband has more conventional tastes. . . .'

Perhaps it is not really the type of audience that influences the way one feels about one's self and appearance, but the kind of *atmosphere* induced by that audience: whether supportive or disapproving, whether creating a feeling of visibility or invisibility, as the following answers imply:

> 'Depends mainly on whom I'm with – some people act as a dampener and then I tend to dress in a more conventional way.'

> 'With people who encourage me to be myself – would probably dress more outrageously as I would feel safe in their company like that.'

Indeed, it appears here that neither family nor friends provide an unconditional backstage. Family provides a different sort of environment for different persons. For some women, the family provides a judging audience: for example, 'How important do you consider your appearance to be when you are with your immediate family?':

> 'If I don't look OK they tell me I look run down.'

'Because they nag so if they don't think I look reasonable.'

'I wouldn't want my relatives to think I couldn't cope with a career and chores . . . I would want them to think me smart and attractive in spite of my age, limited funds and little spare time.'

For others appearance was a way of expressing an attitude towards their family:

'I don't see them often so I like to show off relatively new clothes – perhaps to show I'm doing OK – to seek approval.'

'Residual desire for even their approval of the way I dress.'

'I feel I owe it to people I love most.'

'One must not impose too dreary a sight to one's family.'

It is also clear that the freedom to dress as one pleases in the company of people one knows well is better thought of as a stage where one feels invisible and unself-conscious of the expectations, but not as an expectation-free stage:

'Unfamiliar people do not know how you normally dress etc. therefore if you are neither stunning nor drab with them you will just be one of the crowd. However, people who really know how you normally appear will be surprised perhaps if you turned out "not quite up to your usual standard".'

'I take greatest care especially when meeting people I haven't seen for a long time or meet very seldom. I suppose I want them to think, "My God, she's worn well!".'

'I believe your friends always expect to see you in a certain way (or perhaps I always want them to see me that way).'

An 'improved' self

The second proposition stated that duplicity is indicated through one's attempts to present an improved image in front of less familiar others. Evidence from the questionnaires indicated that the presented self is not necessarily an improved self.

The assumption of 'impression management' that people are trying to present an 'ideal self' for strategic purposes implies that they appear as something they are not. The closest equivalent of the 'ideal self' in clothing terms was found in dressing up behaviour which is sometimes like play-acting. In response to the question: 'What is your idea of dressing up?' some women explained that dressing up is an opportunity to present a more attractive and rare but realistic self, while others described a phantasy idea. In fact, this was the only question where women made reference to some sort of 'make believe' self which comes anywhere near the impression management vision:

'. . . there's always the feeling that something or someone special may come along . . .'.

'Verging on theatrical . . . can create the illusion of being another person.'

'Either over doing what I am or pretending to be what I am not.'

'To edge towards a fantasy, an image that is part of me, but not an everyday self. Queen for a day.'

'Adds another dimension to the way I look.'

The actual 'dressing up' clothes that were assumed to produce the above effects varied according to taste and personal norm, but represented something special which was a contrast to the ordinary:

'Beautiful fabrics – silk, velvet and lace, made up by a couturier for me only (that is a dream!).'

'Wearing something opposite to my "normal" style.'

'Wearing a dress (I usually wear separates).'

'Anything more than a person's norm.'

'Lots of jewellery. Big and bold.'

Responses to the question: 'How do you look your best?' ranged from descriptions of outfits (of all sorts, not necessarily glamorous) to descriptions of state of mind. For example:

'When I feel happy and confident and clean and fresh and relaxed, usually in casual clothes, but it doesn't really matter if I am feeling the rest.'

'When I am happy, when I have a sun tan, when I am in colours that I feel reflect my personality, and when I am comfortable.'

'After lots of thought about how to make myself look my best and lots of time attempting to put the thoughts into action.'

'When my skin is good, my hair goes as I want it to and the clothes I have selected work well together.'

Thus the responses to the question about looking one's best did not match the responses to the question about dressing up, because while dressing up carried some phantasy elements, looking one's best was entirely realistic and represented a choice out of the repertoire of one's existing selves.

Hence, the desire to present a 'larger than life' phantasy image to impress an audience was not a general feature of dressing but a specific behaviour expressed either at a social occasion purposefully designed as such, or on certain, special instances as indicated by responses to the question: 'Do you like dressing up?'

'It takes me out of my rut, makes me feel good, gets the urge to dress outrageously out of my system for a while.'

'. . . like projecting more of a fantasy idea of my personality.'

'The "vamp" in every woman likes to come out, albeit unconsciously.'

A more indirect way of learning how sincere people feel about their presentation inquired about the limits of self-improvement. It appears that here the respondents drew the line between representing *one part* of oneself and creating a *false part*. Cosmetic surgery and other 'oppressive' regimes as well as milder forms of 'obsessive' preoccupation with 'self-improvement' met with clear resistance. For example:

'I wouldn't want to pretend to be something I wasn't.'

'A slight gild to the lily is fun, but I don't like going over the top with . . . anything that would create a false impression.'

'I try to show different aspects of myself with clothes, but without trying to be someone else. . . .'

'Too many women spend too much time trying to change from being themselves.'

Even the way the women used the phrase 'to make an impression' implied a desire to project to unfamiliar people, *more of a summary image than a false image*, as the following extracts from a variety of questions demonstrate:

'I like the outer me to reflect the inner me.'

'I wish to give a message of my personality.'

'I would dress . . . to show my personality.'

'My clothes are telling people who I am . . . the only information people have to my identity.'

'to project a stereotyped image . . . which gives them a picture of me.'

Self-consciousness

The third proposition stated that conscious attention to one's appearance indicates an intention to conceal or to present a false image. However, the data suggest that conscious attention to appearance is a way of dealing with evaluation apprehension by generating the self-confidence needed to face stressful situations. Hence it can be a sign of insecurity not insincerity as the following examples suggest:

'I take more care over my appearance in the group I feel least secure with.'

'I do care about my appearance with people I don't know because I feel awkward and insecure at first and if I'm looking a bit scruffy, that only makes things worse!'

'I would take more care and worry about what I wore when I am unsure of myself.'

'I find if I feel I look a mess, I have no confidence in myself.'

Responses to the question 'When are you conscious of what you wear?' showed that the anxiety resulting from threats to self-validation occurs not only where there exists a potential failure to convey the self-image, but also in the very transition from anonymity to visibility:

'When bumping into people unexpectedly or when a superior at work has me to their office for a discussion.'

'When it could be supposed I'm the best-dressed person in the room (i.e., wearing something particularly striking).'

'When I take trouble I draw attention to myself so probably I only want to draw it when I'm capable of dealing with it.'

Confidence interacted with clothes in more than one way. For some, it was the wearing of certain clothes which actually boosted confidence, as indicated by responses to the question 'Do you ever feel that the clothes give you confidence?':

'If I am going to be in an unknown and/or hostile situation, I want to project a neutral image.'

'Expensive clothes give me confidence at business meetings.'

'I feel confident in a tailored black or grey suit but vulnerable in something frothy or flimsy.'

'A special dress improves my self-esteem.'

'Usually when I'm wearing something new.'

For other women the appearance that would make them confident was tied up to the state of mind generated by the clothes, not to a specific set of clothes:

'When I am wearing things that I really like, and feel good, and feel that the clothes say good things about me that I might not otherwise express.'

'When I know they suit me, are a particularly good fit, when I've been complimented on them before.'

'If I feel they complement my appearance.'

All the above fits in with a social anxiety model of impression management theory (Schlenker and Leary, 1982). According to this model, effort can be related to anxiety that occurs when individuals wish to convey a certain image and doubt their ability to do so convincingly.

I would now like to focus on a range of responses across the entire set of questionnaires to a few characteristic questions. The questions capture, in a nutshell, the essence of the 'self-presentational' approach, and the 'true' versus 'false' identity. They read:

1. Different women dress in different ways. Do you have a certain look which you could call 'the real me'?
2. Do you feel a different person in different clothes?
3. Do you ever feel that the clothes you are wearing are not you, that you are acting out a role?

A typical 'self-presentational' response to these questions would be: I have a 'real me' look *but* I feel a different person in different clothes, and I sometimes act out a role. A typical sincere response would be: I have a 'real me' look, I feel the same person in different clothes, and I never act out a role. Out of 160 respondents, about a fifth (22.5 per cent) answered all three questions in a 'self-presentational' way, and 1.8 per cent answered in a sincere way. The rest of the respondents exhibited various combinations that from the perspective of self-presentation would appear inconsistent. However, a closer look at the detailed responses reveals that the variety of ways each statement was interpreted suggests anything but a unified conception, and renders a superficial clustering irrelevant.

The *first* question, regarding the 'real me' look, was interpreted as inquiring not just about a typical essential look but also about 'the clothes you wear most often', 'the clothes that make you feel good/look best/look unique' and 'your idealized look'. The range of answers was also quite varied. While some were detailed and concrete, others were non-specific. For example: 'any outfit that makes me feel really confident feels like it's the "real me" '. And some made the categories used in the question themselves seem inappropriate:

> 'that really depends on what I'm doing. The real me at presentation is different from the one at the weekend.'

> 'I find that hard to answer because I'm not really certain who I really am! That may sound strange but when you are influenced so much and at the same time trying to find an individual identity, it's hard to say what I am really like "deep down". '

The *second* question, regarding feeling a different person in different clothes was interpreted to mean: 'do you *feel differently* in different clothes?'; 'do you feel *a different person* in different clothes?' and 'do you ever wear clothes in which you don't feel "yourself"?' Some of these interpretations when examined closely are more complex, and make subtle distinctions which are absent from the self-monitoring scale such as those between *appearing* differently and *feeling* differently, or between 'a different person' and 'a different aspect of the self'. For example:

> 'I try to dress in tune with the roles I play. Each role requires a slightly different type of clothes so I look somewhat different in each role, but don't really feel different as a person.'

> 'Yes definitely. Well, not exactly a "different person" but I feel a different side of me is dominant in, say, smart evening clothes as opposed to my everyday jeans + jacket or my weekend slouch clothes.'

The *third* question which inquired about feeling alienated from the clothes to the extent of feeling 'role distance' was interpreted to mean either 'do you find yourself in situations where you have to wear what you don't like' or 'do you possess clothes that you don't feel happy in'. In either case acting out a role was interpreted as a negative, not a neutral role playing. And responses such as: 'that I am acting out a role, yes, but not one that has been imposed on me, or that I am unwilling to undertake', and 'no, but I recognise the several selves I range between', were the exception rather than the rule. For the most part the answers given to this question by all, referred to various occasions where the respondents felt they were wearing something because it was expected of them, and felt uncomfortable about it.

Finally, another way of looking at these questions is by considering the entire set for each respondent. The rationales given for each question create very different systems of meaning that cannot be captured by simplistic true/false dichotomies. The following are a few examples.

The first example is of a woman who constructs a coherent meaning. Her real me is 'tracksuit & trousers', but other clothes enhance different moods: 'clothes promote a certain mood. I feel brisk and efficient in my business suits, relaxed in jeans and a sweater, ready for fun in a disco outfit.' Yet she can distance herself enough from the role of clothes in her presentation and see it as a social game: 'I amuse myself playing the role of an executive on the London shuttle – pinstriped suit, leather briefcase etc.'

The second example is of a woman who constructs an ambivalent meaning. She defines her 'real me' as 'trendy but not up to the minute fashionable + bright colours'. She explains how she feels differently in different clothes: 'Sometimes I'm a Laura Ashley girl in the garden. Others I'm the trendy Benneton Career woman. Sometimes I'm in tracksuit & slobbing it.' But when asked whether she ever feels like she's acting out a role she suddenly reflects: 'yes – but it's difficult to explain that as I'm not sure what the real "me" clotheswise is', in complete contradiction to her first answer.

Another respondent uses different definitions of self for each question. In the first answer she describes her 'real me' through clothes as 'elegant but not to a mindnumbing degree.' Asked whether she feels a different person in different clothes she distinguishes between *characteristics* and *personality*: 'I think clothes give me different characteristics but not a different personality'. And in response to the question about role acting she redefines her real self as one which is happy in what she wears: 'I go through my wardrobe every six months and give away clothes that I have not worn for a long time. I don't think I could buy something in which I didn't *feel happy*.'

The last respondent provides a rather complex discourse. She defines her real self as 'the genuine look of the 50s – tight black trousers, ballet pumps, very simple little dresses or suits etc.' In response to the second question about feeling different in different clothes she gives an ambivalent account of the influence of her clothes on how she feels. On the one hand she agrees 'I think so, but a few years ago I used to wear lots of very different things. Now I stick much more to one style anyway. I would feel different dressed very conventionally.' On the other hand she qualifies 'but I dress to suit mood or occasion, not the other way round, so the outfit wouldn't dictate how I felt.' In the third question she reveals two conceptions of dressing differently than she likes, only one of which she construes as acting out a role: 'only if I'm putting on unfamiliar things, say, to please my family . . . when I'm really dressed up it's *like* acting, but only a different side of me, not someone else.'

Thus the evidence from the questionnaires points towards 'a complex mode of consciousness' which allows us simultaneously to be 'lost in and aware of the action' (Harré, 1979). The fallacy advanced by 'impression management' theory which leads to the confounding of conscious attention with insincerity was defined by Goffman as the differential symbolic value given to:

> the perceptible difference between an act performed unthinkingly under the invisible guide of familiarity and habit, and the same act, or an imitation of it, performed with conscious attention to detail and self-conscious attention to effect. (1951, p. 300)

For Goffman, this is a difference in *style*, not in *sincerity*. And Harré noted that:

> except for the Machiavellian and socio-pathological individuals, people are primarily the parts they play, and the attitude of detachment that would allow them to see their actions as performances of parts is a frame of mind which has to be consciously adopted and may induce a stultifying self-consciousness inhibiting convincing performance. (1979, p. 224)

Thus Harré identified the two elements which may account for the confusion between consciousness and sincerity: *an attitude of detachment and stultifying self-consciousness.* First, he regards detachment as admitting the possibility of expressive control – control of the style of performance. This notion of control as enhancing one's style, rather than obstructing one's sincerity is equivalent to the Stanislavsky method of acting where the actor learns to subordinate inspirational creativity to conscious control until it becomes like a conditioned reflex. Second, a stultifying self-consciousness taints even the most sincere presentation with a shade of a not-sufficiently-rehearsed lie. But as Kuzmics points out in his analysis of one of Joseph Heller's literary characters: 'Green is sometimes a conscious, sometimes an unaware actor. But when he becomes the clumsy toady we can be sure that this is no longer acting, then he is for real' (Kuzmics, 1991, p. 21). Indeed, a reflexive consciousness, the ability to be at once a participant and an observer in one's life is from a symbolic interactionist perspective not a deceptive mode but the mode of existence *par excellence*. It is what Edgley and Turner define as: 'the act of standing outside ourselves looking at our own creations, knowing that they are real, but knowing also that we have made them' (1975, p. 6).

The results of the study take us away from the discourse of true/false (sincerity/insincerity) into a dialectical discourse, long articulated by William James of the self as both unitary and multiple: 'this generic unity coexists with generic differences just as real as the unity. And if from the one point of view they are one self, from others they are as truly not one but many selves' (James, 1890, p. 335). The results indicate that a series of personas need not be incompatible with sincerity. By implication the conclusions indicate that being 'the decorative sex', and having many 'sartorial faces' is not the same as being false, manipulative or deceptive. Nor, indeed, does it imply that the women are as deeply invested in any one of them. Because, as Goffman himself remarks in *Gender Advertisements* 'a concern over carrying an appearance off does not necessarily imply a deep and abiding identification with that appearance' in the same manner that an actor prepares seriously 'for a part he will never play again' (1979, p. 51).

Note

This chapter draws on the articles: E. Tseëlon (1992d), 'Self presentation through appearance: a manipulative vs. a dramaturgical approach', *Symbolic Interaction*, 15, 501–14; E. Tseëlon (1992a) 'Is the presented self sincere? Goffman, impression management, and the postmodern self', *Theory, Culture & Society*, 9, 115–28; and E. Tseëlon (1992b), 'What is beautiful is bad: physical attractiveness as stigma', *Journal for the Theory of Social Behaviour*, 22, 295–309.

3

THE GENDER OF THE SPECTACLE

The paradox that this chapter addresses is inherent in a female existence which is simultaneously socially invisible while being physically and psychologically visible, an object of the gaze. I would like to start by providing empirical illustration to the centrality of the gaze. The empirical illustrations draw mostly on a series of studies I conducted as part of my doctoral work (Tseëlon, 1989). Based on these studies, I will try to show how the mechanisms which structure the appearance of the woman become part of her psychological make-up. And just as the history of clothes does not indicate a particular style as being intrinsically more feminine or masculine than the other – my focus here is not on a particular style and its meaning, but on the relationship between cultural meanings and personal meanings. I am concerned not with a typology of the particular styles, but with the way cultural concerns get translated into personal concerns. The specific details vary according to period and according to country but the concerns are more robust. I will then examine the evidence in terms of a feminist psychoanalytic notion of the male gaze. Finally, I will trace the notion of the gaze to the private–public dichotomy, and discuss some problems arising from a simplistic application of the concept of the gaze to relationships of power.

The visible self

A strong sense that came out of the questionnaires and interviews I conducted was the crucial importance attached to the visible self. It goes beyond the importance of clothes, or making the right impression in certain contexts, or conforming to expectations. Feeling visible, exposed, observed or on show appeared to be internalised into the self-conception. It cuts across situations and the kind of people involved.

Fashion chronicles, sociological and semiotic analyses which have looked at dressing behaviour concentrated on *style*. Early psychological studies highlighted the distinction between formal and casualwear. This distinction, although valid, tells very little about what it means to wear a formalwear, or a casual one, when one would choose the one and not the other, or what the choice reveals about the wearer.

Besides being indicators of social trends and styles clothes are also encoded messages of attitudes towards others. While the formality of the occasion and one's individuality are indicated by a particular style, attitudes towards others evoke a more refined system of discrimination; one which may not be obvious to the observing eye. Women seem to be making subtle distinctions between dressing with *effort, care*, or *consciousness* of what they wear. *Effort* refers to the actual time spent in putting together an appearance (dressing, as well as beauty procedures). *Care* refers to the amount of worry and thought and planning and preparation. *Consciousness* refers to a particular kind of awareness: of being an object of the gaze of the Other. The Other need not be physically present. It can be evoked in preparation for an encounter, or it can be used metaphorically, as an imaginary Other, like the Sartreian notion of 'being for the Other'. It is a moment of realisation that I owe my existence to a reflection in the mirror that the Other is holding out to me. Women care about their appearance when there are important things at stake, when being judged, or when feeling unsure and anxious. They make effort with their appearance in the company of people they want to impress, in important situations (that require, for example, dressing up), or when there is a formal expectation (for example, work). But they are made conscious of their appearance when something goes wrong (if they are overdressed, underdressed, or inappropriately dressed), or when somebody comments on their appearance (compliment or criticism).

Three main elements seem to be influencing how and why the woman chooses what to wear. The situation, the people present and the state of mind she is in. And while situations structure the experience along the formal/casual dimension, it is the audience which mediates between the wearer and her clothes. People do not divide into formal/informal kinds. They fall into finer categories: they are familiar or unfamiliar, supportive or disapproving, high powered or unimportant, trendier or less well dressed than oneself. And with reference to the self they are constituted as either significant or insignificant. Significant audience is one whose opinion and judgement matter; insignificant audience is one whose opinion and judgement do not matter. While some situations are intrinsically more comfortable than others (for example, familiar as opposed to strange situations), it is the audience which creates a sense of a secure/comfortable environment or an insecure/uncomfortable one.

In a secure environment one feels approved, accepted, loved, inconspicuous – in short, confident and psychologically *invisible*. In an insecure environment one is on display, on show, being examined, and measured. One is invaded by scrutinising looks, attention or comments; overshadowed by other people's better presentation, or judgement. It is a feeling of being threatened and psychologically *visible*.

Some situations involve a mixture of significant and insignificant audiences (like being with friends in a restaurant) – in which case a mixed set of responses is invoked. Thus, for example when going to a restaurant which is a visible context with regards to the other people present, but in the company of people with whom one feels invisible the woman would feel simultaneously threatened and confident. The result will involve elements of *style* depending on the formality of the occasion, but also elements of *care* and *effort* which reflect both confidence and reassurance seeking.

The centrality of the visibility factor was demonstrated in a study where I asked a group of women from a wide range of backgrounds to group a list of situations according to their clothing concerns. The women were not limited as to the kind of criteria they were using – nor to a number of criteria. The similarity scores were then analysed using a multivariate approach. The multidimensional scaling method allows the researcher to recover the underlying structure of relationship between a set of objects, and to represent this structure onto a dimensional map. The advantage of using this method over traditional quantitative methods is that it combines the advantages of quantitative and qualitative methods. While being precise and independent of whoever carries out the analysis, it also offers freedom of response and does not reify context-free categories which the researcher imposes on the respondents (and on the data). Using this method, the following solution was obtained (see Figure 3.1). The multidimensional map provides dimensions, but not explanations to their interconnections. How does one interpret the proximity of A and B and their distance from C, for example? The clue was provided by the explanations given by the respondents themselves. From the reasons for grouping certain situations in a particular way, it emerged that the grouping principle that united the various criteria employed by different women was how visible or anonymous they felt. Thus the further up the map one goes, the more 'visible' the situation, and the further down, the more 'invisible'.

The visibility factor implies that while some clothing messages are overdetermined, a whole range of interpersonal messages which are encoded in one's appearance are not obvious, and cannot be detected without knowledge of the wearer's 'hierarchy of effort and affect' scale. It is difficult to tell just by looking whether the wearer feels in a secure or insecure environment – whether they feel visible or invisible. It is tempting but unreliable to link the two in a systematic fashion. For example, we can say that putting effort into one's appearance is a mark of respect (for the occasion, for the people). But one's level of effort is a relative construct. It depends on what the baseline level is. One woman's effort is another woman's weekend slob. There are no automatic connections between a particular state of mind and a particular appearance. For some women the difference is expressed in style. More conventional clothes (or formal) for the insecure situations and more individual (or informal) for the secure situations is one such common association. For others the difference is not in dress, but they would spend more (or less) time worrying about and choosing what to wear. Finally, a woman might signal two completely different emotions with a similar type of attire. While the motivation is different (for example, a reflection of her good feeling or covering up a bad

Figure 3.1   *A multidimensional map of social situations according to their clothing concerns. The top left corner (e.g. going to the races, funeral and fetching kids from school) indicates a space of high visibility. The bottom right corner (e.g. going to the local takeaway, answering the door to a service person or an unexpected caller) indicates a space of low visibility. (Source:* Tseëlon, 1989)

feeling) the result may be the same (for example, wearing brightly coloured and 'happy' clothes). Similarly, the same state of mind might be given very different looks.

In another study I invited a group of women previously unacquainted to an informal get together. They were requested to dress in a way which represented who they are in the best way. Upon arrival they were asked to decode each other's personal statements according to the way they dressed. They were also asked to indicate their own clothing messages. Both sets of statements (about self and about others) were elicited in a spontaneous as well as in a structured way, through rating scales. The scales referred to those dimensions that have been identified as the key ones in previous interviews and studies. They consisted of *effort, style,*

Figure 3.2   Figure 3.3

When intentions were compared with interpretations even the
stereotyped casual and smart codes 'failed' the test of accurate
communication (Tseëlon, 1989).

anxiety, visibility, fashionability, sexiness and *affluence.* Typically the scales
would be in the format of a question (how much she is aware that other
people are looking at her) with a series of options ranging from least (she
hardly feels) to most (she feels very much).

For each respondent the results were compared between what she said
about herself and what other women said about her. The comparison
between intentions and interpretations evidenced an overall poor fit (for
details see Tseëlon, 1989). Some of the discrepancies illustrate the limits of
inferring from clothing styles to inner messages. For example, the woman
in Figure 3.2 who came dressed in casual clothes for the road, and changed
just before the party to smart stylish gear was presumed to have put
together her outfit with a lot of effort, and to express more concern about
her appearance than she admitted to. While the woman in Figure 3.3 who
was wearing a studenty style outfit with some flair was attributed more
confidence than she claimed.

The clothed self

For women, so the questionnaires clearly suggest, the boundaries between self and dress are not clearly drawn. One woman describes the way she *looks* her best as 'more to do with how I feel, a mental attitude'. That material possessions are symbolic expressions of identity is well documented (Belk, 1988; Dittmar, 1992). But what appears to be a peculiarly female mode of experience is a lack of distinct boundaries between self and others, and by implication, self and possessions. There is experimental evidence to suggest gender differences when people are asked to choose favourite objects. Csikszentmihalyi and Rochberg-Halton (1981) conducted a study of the identity value of household objects. They found that while men tended to prefer objects which were symbolic of self and activities, women favoured objects of contemplation referring to memories and the immediate family. They explained the differences in terms of an organising principle of expressive versus instrumental orientations.

Very much along similar lines, Dittmar (1989) looked at the self meanings of favourite objects, and found statistically significant differences between the genders. In her sample, the characteristic male mode of relating to objects was object utility and self symbols (expressing individuality, personal goals or skills). Women's preferred mode, however, was emotional (indicating mood, security, confidence), and relational (symbolising relations with a person or a group). A similar trend with regards to a choice of favourite clothing was observed by Kaiser and Freeman (1989). In a qualitative study which compared men's and women's conceptions of their favourite clothing, men appeared to regard favourite clothing as a trophy or a memento (of a favourable event – for example, sports – or achievement). For women, on the other hand, favourite clothing was bound up with how they felt about themselves, and how they related to others.

There is a danger, however, of overdetermining the gender categories. For example, a recent quantitative study on the meaning of favourite clothing (Cox, 1993) found no support for the dimensional gender distinction. Instead, both men and women appeared to display some self-expressive orientations and some emotional/interpersonal ones. The only items which reached statistical significance indicated, for men, the importance of participation/belonging to a certain group (sporting or social), as well as a memory of childhood or past. For women the significant items emphasised expressing the self and feeling good about themselves, and more confident.

When it comes to clothes what appears to distinguish the women even in the last study is perhaps best captured in the tripartite typology of representations developed by C.S. Peirce. In this matrix the male approach to clothing could be cast as *causal-metonymic* – it is *a sign of* an event which is related to the self. The female approach, on the other hand, is a *similarity* one – the clothing *does represent* her self. If she met another woman at a party dressed like her, one respondent said she would not like it 'because I can't separate myself from my clothes' and another said 'I think one must "feel" her clothes like part of herself'. It is this sort of insight which runs through my questionnaires as well. (The third type in Peirce's system – *conventional* representation – would not concern us here although it can be said that both causal–metonymic and similarity are, to some extent, conventional.)

Umberto Eco provides a perceptive, if flippant angle on the notion of identity between self and clothes when he relates an experience of 'just' fitting into a pair of jeans having lost some weight:

> The jeans didn't pinch, but they made their presence felt. Elastic though they were, I sensed a kind of sheath around the lower half of my body. Even if I had wished, I couldn't turn or wiggle my belly *inside* my pants; if anything, I had to turn it or wiggle it *together with* my pants; Which subdivides so to speak one's body into two independent zones, one free of clothing, above the belt, and the other organically identified with the clothing, from immediately below the belt to the anklebones. I discovered that my movements, my way of walking, turning, sitting, hurrying, were *different*. Not more difficult, or less difficult, but certainly different.
>
> As a result, I lived in the knowledge that I had jeans on, whereas normally we live forgetting that we're wearing undershorts or trousers. I lived for my jeans, and as a result I assumed the exterior behaviour of one who wears jeans. In any case, I assumed a *demeanor* . . . I discussed it at length, especially with consultants of the opposite sex, from whom I learned.. that for women experiences of this kind are familiar because all their garments are conceived to impose a demeanor . . . Not only did the garment impose a demeanor on me; by focusing my attention on demeanor, it obliged me to *live towards the exterior world* . . . with my new jeans my life was entirely exterior: I thought about the relationship between me and my pants, and the relationship between my pants and me and the society we lived in. I had achieved . . . *epidermic self-awareness*.
>
> [The] woman has been enslaved by fashion not only because, in obliging her to be attractive, . . . to be pretty and stimulating, it made her a sex object; she has been enslaved chiefly because [her] . . . clothing . . . forced her psychologically to live for the exterior. (1986, pp. 192–4; emphasis added)

The 'epidermic self-awareness' that Eco is talking about appears to be a common experience among the women interviewed. Many supplied examples of how different styles of clothes become enmeshed in the way they experience themselves. A typical example is expressed by one of the women: 'I tend to sit very ladylike in tights, dresses and higher heeled shoes. I feel obliged to be dainty. I feel older and more sensible in dresses and skirts, and younger and more care-free in trousers.'

Given the bad name that dress enjoys as reflecting a rather superficial aspect of one's being, the questionnaires tell a surprising story of the intricate relationship that exists between one's appearance and one's sense of well being. They tell the story of the precariousness and the contextual nature of 'the sense of self-worth'. The precariousness of the image explains why the relationship between dressing and confidence is of crucial importance. In fact the effect is quite dramatic as it appears that regardless of age, experience and marital status – almost across the board (but more so for the younger woman) dress has a profound effect on the woman's sense of self-worth and well being. Clothes both confer a sense of self-worth and help creating it.

The fragile self

Wearing the right things, things that fit and look well and enhance the woman's best features seem to be a confidence booster. Similarly, an untoward appearance can diminish her sense of self-worth. And it does not take much to make someone feel insecure about her appearance. Being out of step with the others, being a target of attention or critical comments, being with someone who is trendier and better turned out, as well as a negative subjective mood of how clothes fit, whether make-up has 'gone right', hair looks clean and tidy, and how well body matches up to cultural ideals – all seem to be sure methods to ruin her faith in her right to claim the respect of the well presented person.

An often repeated phrase that 'if you look good you feel good' when examined within the context of other answers affirm clothes' formative role in reflecting vulnerability or boosting confidence. Looking good or bad is closely bound with feeling likewise. The identity between clothes and feelings works both ways. Looking good is a precondition, but not a guarantee of feeling good: 'I feel better about myself if I think I look good'; 'it is easier to feel attractive & sexy & good inside if you look it outside'. However looking bad is almost a guarantee for feeling bad. And there are many things that make women feel bad about their appearance. With very few exceptions most women list a variety of reasons that make them feel unhappy with the way they look. These include temporary states such as unwashed hair, badly fitting or creased clothes, but also fundamental dissatisfaction with their anatomy: height, weight, legs or facial features, are often defined as a problem, or flaw. When she feels bad, it becomes a question of effort not to signal the identity between self and clothes, so that 'when I'm feeling down I often wear clothes that I class as favourites, that I know I feel good in to hide what I'm really feeling' or 'when I'm depressed I might dress extra special which reflects that I'm perhaps happy'; 'if I feel facially grotty I feel less inclined to "celebrate" myself through my clothes. More inclined to merge inconspicuously'.

On the whole, almost every woman who answered the questionnaire admitted to derive confidence from clothes in some capacity. Clothes are used as armour against an uncomfortable situation, when feeling vulnerable, uncertain, when being in a new or strange environment, with unfamiliar or critical, powerful or trendy people – where one might feel put down and inferior, or pale by comparison. Being vulnerable is equated, unconsciously, with being naked, conspicuous, a visible target. And the natural instinct is to cover up, to put on a shield. For some women this shield is a smart dressy look, a suit or any formalwear. For others it is anything that makes them look their best, enhance their best features. So a certain type of dressing is remedial or booster of low confidence. But this sense of confidence is actually very precarious and is easily undermined 'if someone else's outfit seems "just right" and makes mine feel wrong' or 'if someone else (whose judgement I respect) undermines my confidence in an outfit' or even 'if I have not received at least one compliment during a party, function or whatever'.

Thus confidence in clothing is more like a veneer that allows one 'to forget about myself & concentrate on communication with the people I am with' while in fact, in the words of another respondent 'once I am all dressed, made-up, with accessories etc. and feel right and comfortable, I forget about my clothes. Although I suppose a little bit of me is always conscious of how I look'.

But the greater fragility of this kind of confidence is revealed when examining another question which looks at the possibility of meeting another woman dressed as oneself. The theme of the 'double' is a common folklore motif which represents death. Response to a hypothetical scenario of meeting one's 'double' revealed a similar reasoning. In many cases it was a cause for unhappiness, frustration and embarrassment. The responses fell into three categories: either women felt they would be upset because it would undermine their originality, individuality and uniqueness. Or they reasoned that if they looked better they would still come out on top. Alternatively, by the psychoanalytic logic of inversion they turned the threat into a compliment. Thus they saw it as a reinforcement of their good taste and said they would be flattered. Humour seemed to be a common strategy to deal with such a misfortune. Either way, all three solutions locate the self as the core of the situation and confirm the validating role that clothes play. One woman told that it once happened to her and she minded more than she thought she would. It was not a case of looking worse; quite the contrary. In fact the other woman looked cheap and tarty. Just like the picture of Dorian Gray she felt implicated by the tarty image as if it somehow reflected her too, or suggested another side to her, one that she did not want to imply.

What illustrates the self-validating role individual clothing has for some women is the fact that one of the possibilities mentioned as a favourable outcome of meeting a 'double' was outshining her. Outshining the other is in contrast with canons of good taste of sartorial civility. Often people wear more neutral clothes so as not to embarrass their companions. One respondent illustrated this contrast by admitting that she would have liked to look better than her 'double'. But admitting to a socially unacceptable way did not prevent her from endorsing the polite code in another context. In response to a question if she would ever modify her dress to suit others she responded 'I would never want to show anyone up, so may dress down if I thought it could make them more comfortable'. Such a contradiction need not be evidence of duplicity. Rather it may indicate a different way of conceptualising these two issues. The latter in the context of politeness, the former in the context of defining one's individuality. The contrast is reflected in ambivalence: a desire to outshine on the one hand, the desire to fit in on the other.

Another indicator of the constitutive role clothes play in constructing the self image is the role of appearance when alone. Dressing well is bound up with self-esteem and feeling good *even* on one's own. Respondents were asked to compare the role of appearance when alone with a situation of being with strangers or with family. Most rated appearance when alone as lower in importance. While some women seem to be concerned with appearance overall more than others it was the kind of explanation given for making effort with one's appearance when alone which deserves a closer scrutiny. Women talked about a measure of self-esteem, well being, lifting herself out of a gloomy mood, self-respect, fun, and a concern with an imaginary audience (self or Other). Thus, even when alone, many women think of themselves through the eyes they imagine as looking at them.

That body image and self-concept are closely related is well documented. In women, where the phenomena are more pronounced the association is usually made within some pathological discourse: a distortion of body image, abnormality in the perception of the body, eating disorders, and even a predominantly female dressing disorder defined as 'an inflexible insistence on being dressed identically with peers, or in what is believed to be the contemporary mode, no matter how uncomfortable, expensive, or aesthetically distasteful the fashion' (Frankenburg and Yurgelun-Todd, 1984, p. 147). Pathologising may be a useful way of defining and treating extreme, maladjustive forms of behaviour. But it misses the point. It reduces a *sign* of a general existential predicament into a *symptom* of a category, and it contaminates the issue by defining it as 'a problem'. This can be most clearly illustrated in the absurdity of the risk factors (predisposing and perpetuating) associated with this disorder. Those include: living in a consumer-oriented society, puberty, entering high school, perceived potential of a new significant relationship, lack of self-confidence, and a need to conform!

Being visible can be threatening and disempowering. It reveals a firm sense of self-worth to have a fragile base. Under a scrutinising gaze, or under the fear of one, the self-assured image seems to crumble. Good appearance is a shield which is easily pierced. Which is the reason why so many of us are willing to go to great lengths to reinforce this delicate construction.

The self-defining role of appearance of objects and procedures is also evident in the feeling of 'incompleteness' experienced in their absence. In their theory of symbolic self-completion, Wicklund and Gollwitzer (1982) suggest that low self-esteem is compensated by extending the self through objects. What characterises a self-completing object is a peculiar dynamics of dependency on that object. It echoes the relationship between people and their artificial limbs.

Interviewed in the BBC programme *Equinox* on 'bionic technology' (September 1994), a disabled person explained that when he has got his 'intelligent artificial leg' on it feels like a part of himself. But when he sees it in isolation he finds it disturbing and hard to relate to. Women often describe the experience of not wearing make-up or being ill dressed as feeling naked, or personally diminished. It is telling that the insights obtained in my studies correspond to those obtained by Stanley Hall in 1905 (and summarised by Flaccus, 1906). In a questionnaire-based study which looked at the 'psychology of clothes' among schoolgirls, being well dressed contributed to feeling equal to meeting the demands of social surveillance, a sense of confidence, self-worth and self-respect. While being ill dressed contributed to loss of confidence and self-esteem, and to fear of being thought less of, or laughed at:

> As one of the answers puts it: 'Clothing should be well cared for; it is part of us'. To what extent this integration has taken place is clearly brought out in the answers to [the] . . . question which deals with the exposure of parts of the body. For instance, going without gloves is said to give a feeling of being not fully dressed. (1906, p. 69)

Prevalent conceptions reproduce themselves in channels other than the 'real' or the 'symbolic'. They also feature in the 'imaginary'. The following example is from a children's book by a leading Israeli children's book writer. It encapsulates a psychic predicament and a social solution. It is a story of a little girl who dreads going to school because she is being teased about her 'sailing boats' ears. Her mother is busy looking after her baby brother leaving the girl to her own devices. Her solution is in phantasy. Trying on exotic hats (to hide her ears) takes her to exotic kingdoms where she is much admired. However, she promptly leaves each one before her secret is discovered. Finally when the clock strikes the time to go to school, she looks at the mirror and discovers her ears adorned with a pair of earrings. And with her new 'self-extension' she is proud to face the world, and to display her ears (Zarchi, 1993).

Some examples

I will now provide illustrations of several characteristic profiles. They tell candid stories of women who for one reason or another are more self-conscious of the relationship between self and dress. It is only when things go wrong that one discovers the working and the mechanics of the social processes one is part of, or subject to. Thus it is their reflexive discomfort which sheds insightful light on the process that otherwise appears obvious and ritualised – almost natural.

S is a musician. She plays in an orchestra, is in her 30s and soon to be divorced. She is very dissatisfied with her looks, and her unhappy preoccupation with her looks keeps coming up in response to many questions. For example, she admits to dressing 'subconsciously to attract attention, maybe especially from men as I feel generally that I am not particularly attractive and so I compensate by being friendly and wearing cheerful sets of colours . . . I would love to be a woman who turns heads but I am pretty short and have a not very pretty face so would not have the confidence to wear Joan Collins sort of clothes.' As a result, she covers her face behind make-up 'and if I don't people always comment and say I look tired or ill!' Generally she puts quite a lot of effort into her appearance when meeting new people because she wants to make a good impression, but feels self-conscious about her clothes at most times, especially when dressed up, or when dressed inappropriately. Her desire to get accepted through her clothes led her to conform to her husband's middle-class tastes – with the result of having a set of conventional classic clothes (pearl set, Burberry) in toned down colours. Since the motivation for wearing these clothes did not produce the desired effect and her marriage collapsed none the less (according to his wish), she has embarked on defining her own self by getting a set of new sporty outfits (for example, flying suit and baggy trousers in bright colours).

A is in her early 40s, a divorced mother, working full time. She lives on her own, therefore does not care too much about her appearance when alone 'in my weekend scruff'. This is her way of indicating that she does not have a special person in her life who justifies her putting effort in her appearance: 'if I lived with someone I would probably take more care of my appearance at home'. Yet she is not defensive about living on her own. She feels at ease in every situation, and therefore does not consciously define her appearance as tied up with emotions or insecurity. Other than her 'sloppy' weekend look she always tries to look presentable. She is not willing to expend tremendous efforts into looking nice, does not care much about fashion, and considers her own judgement regarding her appearance most important. 'I dress to please myself' she says, but she also admits to wanting to make a good impression in front of strangers because of a desire 'to create a good impression', to mind her appearance with strangers (8 out of a scale of 10) so as to 'make people like me'. She would also be quite upset if she realised that she is not dressed in a way she should be, or really likes, and it is too late to change. Being overweight makes her want to blend in, to be always conscious of what she is wearing, to envy women in lovely clothes not available in her size – but not to want clothes to hide her: 'I used to wear certain styles & colours to hide behind. Nowadays I'm trying to be my own mistress. To hell with convention, if I want to wear bright colours I shall.' She defines herself as rarely lacking in confidence, but would want to avoid clothes that would project a 'sex object' image. The answer to the question about preference for being adventurous or conventional seems to provide a handle on a complex and seemingly contradictory set of considerations. It boils down to her desire to be treated as a person – not as an embodied person, and to the self-validation conferred to her by her boyfriend: 'When I am with my boyfriend I am more adventurous with my clothes. Sexy even. He thinks I'm perfect. Doesn't notice my size at all. At work I am very conventional. I prefer to be accepted & treated as an equal not as a sex object.'

But what happens if the woman's self-worth is not validated by a sexual partner? Then her appearance is marked by a fundamental lack which cannot be compensated by other sources, however central to her core definition.

B is a self-employed professional in her late 40s, and a divorced mother. Accustomed to play the role of the smart business-like woman 'not to be exposed in a professional situation' she nevertheless feels it to be only an instrumental role (facilitating business contacts which might bring her new clients). Her professional persona is of great importance to her as she makes a point of stressing that what she would like to avoid is to be taken for a secretary. Her glamorous role is contrasted with what she regards as her drab appearance. The contrast is so marked that she is sometimes not recognised by people she knows who had previously seen her only in one of her smart images. She would have liked to have spent more on her appearance but has got neither the time nor the means to afford such luxury. Defining self-confidence as a mood rather than a permanent attribute she holds that when she looks good, or engages in a conversation with people, she forgets about her appearance. Even a woman looking identically does not seem to bother her all that much (perhaps because she does not regard it as a realistic possibility). But she does mind mistakes. She feels conscious of her clothes and unhappy about her appearance when inappropriately dressed, when in fashionable and very rich company, or when not living up to her idealised self: slim (which she is often not), wearing contact lenses (which she uses less as she cannot read with them), and being and looking happy (which is dependent on a male reassurance which she lacks). She dresses according to her moods: when she is low she opts for the 'safe' look, and when she dresses up for a fun occasion it has 'an accelerating spiral effect' on her as she always enjoys situations more if she feels she is looking good.

In a candid interview she lets out that her overriding concerns at present are being overweight and lacking a man in her life, and admits to being 'sex-starved and lonely and want a male partner'. She admits to regarding the 'implicit judgement of a man who is attracted to her' as the most important consideration regarding her appearance. She rates nightwear and underwear lowest in importance in her wardrobe because she has no lover hence sleeps alone. And she admits to being more daring in her appearance when with a lover, and taking quite a lot of trouble when dining out because she might just run into someone she knows who might introduce her to the life partner she is so desperate to find. 'It all hinges on the possibility of encountering a man who finds me attractive' she says.

The most significant observation about this interview is its situated nature. The respondent's own reflexive and self-aware insights ('because of my complex, tortured & unsuccessful life situation in every sphere *at present*') help to see that just as Goffman observed with regard to stigma, feeling good about oneself due to appearance is a temporary state. It requires some necessary conditions to exist such as looking good (according to prevailing canons of taste), and being reassured by acceptance from a significant male figure, as well as people who matter.

The cry for embodied social theory is problematic with regard to the woman. She suffers a schism between embodied existence which is sexy but not respectable, and a disembodied one (like the church saints) which is self-denial. Very telling is the comment (reminiscent of the Enlightenment maxim for mid-European Jews to be a Jew inside one's home, and a person outside it) made by one 30-year-old respondent: 'I like attention but overt sexual interest puts me on my guard. I go out of my way to be a person first, and a woman second in those situations.'

The gaze

The visible self, the clothed self, and the fragile self all point at the central role 'the gaze of the Other' plays in the construction of the female visual self. It is commonly accepted that direct gaze is a form of invasion. Therefore, the inclination to exploit the immediate vulnerability of others is suppressed, and strangers in public exercise 'civil inattention' (Goffman, 1977, p. 327). The principle of operation, as Goffman defines it is 'When bodies are naked, glances are clothed' (1971, p. 71). This principle is dramatically illustrated, for example, in the ideology of a nudist camp which disapproves of calling attention to one's body, and of direct staring (Weinberg, 1968).

But how can we explain the constitutive role of the gaze in the woman's self-conception, and what are the implications of an extreme position along this line? This question has been most usefully addressed within the terms of a feminist psychoanalytic perspective which theorises the male gaze as a 'technology of gender'. According to this view it is a way of objectifying the woman that fixes and frames relations of power and looking. The feminist psychoanalytic perspective has gained currency through its appropriation by feminist film theory. It was sparked by Laura Mulvey's (1975) article which advanced the notion that the cinematic gaze is male on account of the feminine image it constructs, and the mode of pleasure it offers the female viewer (see Figure 3.4). In the capacity of an image the woman is placed as an object of male desire (to be idolised and either conquered or destroyed). In the capacity of audience she has to assume a male spectator's position because idolising the woman is a form of fetishism, and the viewing of a film, like peeping through a keyhole is an act associated with a voyeuristic pleasure. Both fetishism and voyeurism are sexual male perversions representing solutions to unconscious conflicts (Freud, 1927). Fetishism is one solution to castration anxiety, voyeurism is one solution to

Male gaze	Female gaze
	The construction of the image of Woman
1. unidimensional	complex
2. posing for male audience: aware of audience	self absorbed; not self-conscious; oblivious to audience
3. glamorised, idealised, timeless	variable: both beautiful and plain, changing and aging, contextualised
4. accessible	unavailable
5. primarily an object of desire	a range of roles
6. defined by, through, for men	independent existence beyond and outside male discourse
7. pleasure in being a sexual object	pleasure in sexuality and autoeroticism
	Modes of pleasure
1. objectifying, fetishising	narcissistic identification
2. voyeuristic pleasure at a distance	pleasure in closeness

Figure 3.4   *Gendered Spectatorial Positioning (Tseëlon and Kaiser, 1992).*

exhibitionistic tendencies. Fetishism is triggered by the sight of the penis-less woman. The normal sexual object is replaced by a symbolic 'penis substitute': a part of the body or an item of clothing that belongs to the desired person. Voyeurism is a conversion of exhibitionistic tendencies from passive pleasure (displaying one's body) to active pleasure in looking. Mulvey later revisited her original analysis and concluded that the woman has another spectatorial position available to her: that of a man in woman's clothes. This masquerading idea to denote the position of the feminine is a longstanding one in psychoanalysis (see Chapter 2). It is based on the idea that femininity is a disguise assumed by the woman in order to disarm the male fear of her power (Riviere, 1929; Doane, 1982).

The debate in feminist film theory uses a psychoanalytic position as an analytical tool for deconstructing the patriarchal gaze. However, the debate is premised on a gendered gaze. Such a monolithic and homogenising model of spectatorship – which says that women can adopt either a male or a transvestite position – ignores complex forms of identification, multiple identifications, the plurality, contradiction or resistance that exists among feminine spectators, an active female gaze and feminist erotica (female pleasure in looking outside of male structures) (Kuhn, 1982, p. 65; Betterton, 1987, p. 7; Myers, 1988).

The argument equating gaze with masculine position and power is problematic. In the distinction between the man 'who is doing the gaze' and the woman who is the object of the gaze there is an assumption that one position, that of the onlooker, is inherently more powerful than the other. However, a careful examination of the use of 'invisible' and 'visible' shows them to encompass a dialectical rather than a unilateral meaning. Invisible as ignored and trivialised is powerless, but invisible as the source of gaze (that is, the one who is looking without being looked at) is powerful. Similarly, visible as objectified is powerless, but visible as prominent and dominant is powerful. It is also clear by the way these concepts are used that they are interpreted differently when applied to women and to men. Invisible when applied to women is always used to connote powerlessness even if their invisibility is like 'the principle of the veil' of Muslim women whose function is 'to permit the woman to see without being seen' (Tual, 1986, p. 58). At the same time invisible, when applied to men connotes power, as in the following observation that 'the powerful have greater access to the various devices and resources that facilitate the achievement of privacy'. Thus 'access to privacy achieving devices . . . can . . . symbolically define the powerful' while 'the very achievement of privacy can provide the psychological basis for greater power' (Foddy and Finighan, 1980, pp. 10–11).

The feminist discourse on the objectifying gaze is premised on Foucault's analysis of the disciplinary gaze. In *Discipline and Punish* (1975) Foucault examined the technology of surveillance developed from the eighteenth century. This technology was modelled on Bentham's Panopticon. The Panopticon is an architectural figure made up of a tower at the centre, surrounded by a ring of cells. The tower is equipped with windows facing the courtyard. The cells have two windows: one on the outside allows light in, the other, facing the courtyard laying them open to the scrutinising gaze of the supervisor in the tower. The Panopticon principle introduced a new element into power relations. It reversed the principle of the dungeon. Traditionally, power was seen, shown and displayed. This was symbolised by the political ceremony where manifestation of power was spectacular and excessive. It was the objects of power which were in the shade. But disciplinary power is based on invisibility of the subject of power, complemented by the compulsive visibility of its object. Visibility becomes a trap: 'It is the fact of being constantly seen, of being able always to be seen, that maintains the disciplined individual in his subjection' (Foucault, 1975, p. 187).

This permanent visibility becomes an internal feature of the observed in a way which recalls the female self-consciousness of her body and appearance. However, the analogy between the principle of the Panopticon and the operation of the male gaze over the female has to be qualified. Since there is nothing to imply that the inspector who occupies the observing function in the tower is permanently lodged there. On the contrary. As a metaphor, the Panopticon is a dynamic figure because while 'subtly arranged so that *any observer may observe*, at a glance, so many different individuals [it] also *enables everyone to come and observe any of the observers*' (1975, p. 207, emphasis added).

To illustrate this dialectical mechanism I would draw on two films which take the theme of the male gaze literally through a depiction of a male voyeur (for details, see Tseëlon and Kaiser, 1992). These films – *Stakeout* and *Monsieur Hire* – were not produced as feminist films. Even so, both provide examples which demonstrate the dynamic essence of the voyeuristic gaze. In *Stakeout*, police detectives carry out a 24-hour surveillance of a woman's house because her boyfriend is an escaped prisoner. One of the detectives falls in love with the woman. When he meets her accidentally and helps her out, she invites him for dinner. 'I was watching the house – from the inside' he apologises to his partner who had been watching it all from the stakeout point. On another occasion, when he rescues her from an undesirable caller, he yields to his passions and spends the night with her. He wakes up the next morning just too late to 'watch from the inside'. Because in the morning another team has occupied the shift, and he becomes entrapped in the gaze. Unwilling to betray his transgression, the detective tries to leave the house without arousing suspicion dressed in the woman's pink hat and shawl. This scene is symbolically indicative of the easy transformation from the empowerment of the observer to the disempowerment of the observed (typically dressed as a parody of a woman).

Monsieur Hire tells the story of a lonely man who regularly watches a woman who lives across the courtyard from his upstairs apartment. One stormy night, illuminated by the lightning the woman realises that the man is watching her. She is initially startled, but later enjoys and exploits it. She watches him watching her and even self-consciously poses for him. At which point the power/gaze structure is reversed. Being exposed in his gaze, the spectator, too, becomes a spectacle. The end of the unidirectionality of the gaze and the shift in the power structure becomes evident when she comes to visit him. In the beginning he refuses to let her in. Later he does, but when she asks to see the window from where he observed her, and starts inquiring ('What's your favourite moment – when I undress? When I wash?') he drives her away with a scream.

Thus it is not enough to argue that the woman is the object of the gaze. That the power gaze does not inherently belong to the man is best illustrated in the context of courtly love, where the lady is subject to the gaze of two men: her husband and the troubadour. The gaze of the socially superior husband is that of powerful surveillance. The gaze of the troubadour who is her social inferior is that of the powerless unconsummated desire (see Chapter 1). But if the gaze itself is a dynamic concept and implies a two-way direction, why has it become a constitutive element in structuring the female self-conception? In what follows, I will address this question (see also Tseëlon, 1991a).

In the literature which deals with gender construction, the public–private dimension appears to be a key construct. This construct was introduced into anthropology by Lévi-Strauss (1962/1966), both as a dynamic concept implying transformation, and as an essential feature of the universal unconscious structure. But in fact the opposition between nature and culture regarding society in general, and men–women in particular – which gained prominence during the eighteenth century Enlightenment – was introduced by Rousseau (Bloch and Bloch, 1980). Following Lévi-Strauss, Rosaldo (1974a, b) and Ortner (1974) note that there is a cross-cultural dichotomy between nature and culture. Women are perceived as closer to, and are identified with nature, while men represent culture. The natural sphere is then designated as the private domain, the home, with the cultural sphere as the public domain, the outside world.

The general framework can be reduced to two sets of oppositional terms: *nature–private–women* versus *culture–public–men* which are based on three principles: action (nature/culture), space (private/public), actors (women/men). The division is not just analytical, it is argued, but ideological: the private realm is devalued, while the public is invested with prestige. This can be clearly seen, for example, in patrilineal kinship systems where it is the mother who gives life to the offspring but not social identity. The invisible contribution of the father contrasts sharply with the clear and indispensable contribution of the mother. Yet, it is through their father that the children derive legitimacy (Dube, 1986, p. xxv).

Most social analyses which use the public/private division rely on activity combined with space as an organising principle. For example, Ortner (1974) distinguishes between reproduction versus production; Yeatman (1984) focuses on collective versus individual types of sociality; Saegert (1980) talks about aggressive, intense cities versus relaxing suburbs; while Hansen (1987) refers to interpersonal versus impersonal spheres of action. Ardener's muted group theory (1975) designates sphere without space. Here private and public are used only metaphorically. Public refers to the public discourse, or to patriarchal symbolic order, and private refers to the voice of the subordinate group. The muted group is not actually silent. On the contrary: women are talking constantly but produce chatter, gossip, and foolishness (Gallop, 1988). Their muting is a *social invisibility*, exclusion from the symbolic order – *not silence*. The essence of the argument of the muted group theory is that the language of a particular culture does not serve all its speakers equally. Women are not as free to say what they wish because the available linguistic models do not reflect their experiences. Dominant groups determine the dominant communication system of a society. Subordinate groups are made 'inarticulate' because the language they use is derivative. Public discourse in most societies appears to be controlled by men, and appropriate language registers seem to have been 'encoded' by males. Women may be at a disadvantage when wishing to express matters of peculiar concern to themselves in a form which is unacceptable to men (Ardener, 1975). 'Their speech, not conforming to male rules of logic, clarity, consistency, deemed nonsense' (Gallop, 1988, p. 71). While most typologies are not constructed as gender-based, they often overlap with a gender distinction. This pattern brings feminists Imray and Middleton (1983) to propose that since we repeatedly confound gender with sphere, we should use the term private to refer to anything women do, and public to anything men do. Hence, they suggest the use of *actors*, rather than *activity* or *space* as the organising principle for defining public and private.

A structuralist distinction between public and private ignores the contextual, relational aspect of any such division. As Ardener (1981) noted, behaviour and space are mutually dependent: space defines the people in it, but is similarly defined by them. For example, the entry of a stranger may change a private area into a public one, alternatively, access to a particular space may define one as an insider rather than an outsider. Goffman (1959) pointed out that while regions tend to become identified as a front or back region of a performance, many regions function at a particular time and in one sense as a front region, and at a different time and in another sense as a back region. Thus private, or muted, is always in relation to something or someone else. For example a woman may be muted relative to her husband and dominant in relation to her children; Gypsy men are dominant in their own culture and structurally muted *vis-à-vis* the Outsiders (Okely, 1975). This notion is poignantly depicted in Heinrich Böll's classic, *The Lost Honour of Katharina Blum* (1975). A young prim and proper woman, Katharina Blum, spends one evening and one night in the company of Gotten, a radical on the run from the police, whom she met during the city carnival, hiding in the private sphere of his mask. This allowed the intimate details of her life to become the focus of police interrogation and the tabloid press. She regards this as a total and brutal invasion of her private life. In the eyes of the police it is a justifiable outcome. The mere fact of 'knowing' Gotten had made her 'public' (1975, p. 61).

Industrial capitalism highlighted another dialectic relationship between public and private. On the one hand the shift of market economy outside the home accorded the *production* processes of the workplace a higher value than the *maintenance processes* of the home. This was expressed, for example, in devaluing women's work in the household and everything women produce – from crafts to biographies (see, for example, Barrett, 1979; Cox and James, 1987). On the other hand, the shift created an opposite process, that of 'an intimate vision of society', or the disappearance of the public space (O'Neill, 1972; Sennett, 1976). Such was the result of the loss of community functions and privatisation of social resources culminating in the emergence of a strong private sector at the expense of a public sector, and a shift of attention from matters of global concern, to matters of private or local concern. This latter development is what Sennett calls 'superimposing the private on the public'. It is an attempt to 'solve the public problem by denying that the public exists' (1976, p. 27), by 'working out in terms of personal feelings matters which properly can be dealt with only through codes of impersonal meaning' (p. 5). The same confusion exists with regards to community activities and caring for the sick and needy. These activities, Hansen (1987) argues, are private to the extent that they deal with individuals and performed by women, but are public to the extent that they take place outside the home.

The conceptions of privacy referred to in the previous section are very much tied up to the industrialised West where privacy (a historically new phenomenon) is identified with individualism. Evidence from cross-cultural research shows that the very meaning of privacy as well as the links women/private/nature/inferiority and men/public/culture/superiority are not invariable. For example, Sciama found (1981) in a study of Greek shepherds that different definitions of privacy categorised women as outsiders. As Sciama explains, for Mediterranean people little value is attached to personal privacy, while family privacy and even secrecy are thought to be of paramount importance. Among the Sarakatsani shepherds living in continental Greece, north of Corinth

> the most important feature of relationship between families is their mutual competition, lack of trust and hostility . . . the most significant dividing line in their conception of society is that between kin and non-kin, and if kin are associated with all that is good, holy, comfortable and reassuring, non-kin are competitive, hostile and deceitful. (1981, p. 97)

Thus Sciama interprets a distrustful attitude towards wives within the context of 'wife as a non-kin', and not as a derogatory attitude towards women qua women. Ridd (1981) studied a community of coloured people in Cape Town and found a reversal of the nature/culture dichotomy. Here, the public sector was controlled by the whites and reflected the humiliation of apartheid. In contrast the home symbolised refuge and dignity. Women still depended on men for their position in the community, but once married they took complete control of household maintenance and finance, and enjoyed a great deal of power and respect. Finally, in Islamic society women are relegated to the private sphere not because they are considered as inferior. As Mernissi points out 'the whole system is based on the assumption that women are powerful and dangerous beings' (1987, p. 19), and sexual segregation, either physically through space, or symbolically through the veil, 'is a device to protect men, not women' (p. 31).

Having questioned the adequacy of a structuralist public/private framework as an explanation of the conception of the female, I would now like to substitute an interactionist stage/backstage distinction for a structuralist public/private one. My preference of a symbolic interactionist framework is ideological: such a framework is non-essentialist, not based on an image of antagonism, or on the notion of an inherent oppression. And it is more optimistic in that it provides a way of transcending the paradigm of difference. In this framework, doing or being, activity or passivity, public or private become styles of action that represent a continuum rather than a dichotomy. Thus symbolic interactionism offers the tools of a true redefinition because of the ad hoc nature of its categories. It offers a conception of public and private which is both dynamic, relational, and is not tied up to particular locale or participants. Rather, it refers to the experience of feeling exposed. It replaces a structural definition of public and private with a metaphorical notion of what Goffman (1959) calls *front* and *back regions* or *stage* and *backstage*. Stage is then defined not as a particular place or role but through an audience. The presence of an audience which creates self-consciousness is denoted as *front region* or *stage*, the presence of an audience which results in unself-consciousness denotes *back region* or *backstage*.

A symbolic interactionist definition of privacy is similarly space-free.

> Privacy is the possession by an individual of control over information that would interfere with the acceptance of his claims for an identity within a specified role relationship . . . Privacy covers withdrawals from others as well as situations in which individuals remain in the physical presence of one another . . . [Such a definition] clearly distinguishes privacy from such things as seeking a quiet, distraction-free environment for activities . . . [that] would be best referred to . . . [as] 'solitude' or 'seclusion'. (Foddy and Finighan, 1980, pp. 6–7)

The principle of the regions, then, is the actor's ability to control the information that is being displayed to the audience.

According to Goffman relationships in public operate on a similar principle. 'At the centre of social organization' says Goffman 'is the concept of claims', in particular claims regarding territories of the self (1971, p. 51). These are provided by *private regions* and *information preserves*. Information preserve is a set of facts about oneself 'to which an individual expects to control access while in the presence of others' (ibid., p. 63). Since there is a lot of information that can be directly perceived from one's body and behaviour, such a claim can be respected through 'the right not to be stared at or examined'. This phenomenon first appeared when in the eighteenth century women started wearing black masks outdoors. The practice of masquerading, which accompanied the adoption of the concept of privacy, enabled the wearers to keep their privacy in the public domain. It allowed them to observe without being exposed to the dangerous look of a stranger (Heyl, 1994).

Within this framework I would like to argue that women are always on a stage, always observed, always visible: they lack a back region both literally and symbolically. Literally females are 'somewhat vulnerable in a chronic way to being hassled' (Goffman, 1977, p. 329) since men in their dealings with women constantly violate their information preserve through ogling, staring or whistling. Symbolically, women are always on stage because in their mind they are always performing for the male audience. John Berger writes:

> A woman must continually watch herself. She is almost continually accompanied by her own image of herself. Whilst she is walking across a room or whilst she is weeping . . . she can scarcely avoid envisaging herself walking or weeping. She has to survey everything she is and everything she does because how she appears to others, and ultimately how she appears to men, is of crucial importance. (1972, p. 46)

In an interview given in 1994 when she was 60, Brigitte Bardot who had left the public world to become a virtual recluse among her animals said: 'I want to grow old and I'd rather leave behind a pretty image' (*Hello*, 17 September 1994, p. 61). Writing about actresses, Juliet Blair (1981) suggests that the actress's situation is unique in our culture in that it reverses the usual association of women with the private domain. My argument is that an actress is in fact a metaphor not for the exception but for the common situation of the woman in Western culture; culturally invisible yet physically visible – always on a stage.

The question may be asked: is conception of the self in the light of the look of the Other a uniquely female condition as feminist theory argues? By way of answer I would like to contrast two kinds of social theories: feminist and symbolic interactionist. For symbolic interactionism following Mead (1934) there is no self without self-consciousness. We become selves by virtue of our reflexive capacity to become objects to ourselves, to view ourselves from the standpoint of the other. Moreover, it is not *specific* others, but *generalised* others whose view towards ourselves we internalise. The generalised other embodies the collective attitude of our reference group. So, in a sense, self and society are inextricably bound: the self is a reflection of the group, and the group provides the integrative force for the self (Aboulafia, 1986). However, this process results not in a mirror representation of the collective attitude of the group, but in a social representation, as filtered through the individual. It is like an internal talk between the 'I' which is the knower, and the 'me' which is the known. This is a different notion of objectification from the one advanced by feminist theory. Feminist positions explain the fact that 'female subjectivity is most fully achieved . . . when it is most visible' (Silverman, 1988, p. 164) as an objectification of the woman which is an oppressive device in her subjugation (see, for example, Kuhn, 1982; Doane et al., 1984; Betterton, 1987). Contrary to feminist theory, objectification here is viewed not as a demeaning state exclusive to women, but as a general state: the essence of reflexive consciousness.

Since men are significant others in the life of most women in hetero-sexual societies, it is the male perspective which the woman internalises. Similarly, men internalise women's perspective. What is uniquely female, then, is not the process of internalising the look of the audience per se, but the content of that look. John Berger (1972) talks about the *surveyor* and the *surveyed* as two constituent elements of the identity of a woman. According to Mead, the same analysis can be extended to include men as well. Once we have internalised the significant others, all of human behaviour can be seen as actors performing for spectators. The theatre director Peter Brook defines the relationship between actors and audience in a way which epitomises the Meadian self:

> It is hard to understand the true function of spectator, there and not there, ignored and yet needed. The actor's work is never for an audience, yet always is for one. The onlooker is a partner who must be forgotten and still constantly kept in mind. (1968, p. 51)

Now it is true that even though men internalise women as significant others, and women internalise men, there are cultural reasons that make *the woman* more concerned about her appearance (see Chapter 4). In my questionnaire study I asked the women whose eyes were judging their appearance, to which the common response was 'mine', and whether there was anything they did not like about the way they looked, to which the common response was some sort of physical flaw. The results look contradictory but in fact they are not: they indicate the identity between *my look*, and the perceived look of the *male Other*.

The use of a non-feminist theory of self to interrogate a process which has been brought to light by feminist theory has some analytic merits. Rather than reiterating the feminist argument of objectification as commodity fetishism or pre-empting it, it highlights a need for a distinction between two conceptions of objectification that get muddled in feminist theories of spectatorship. One is a conception of objectification as a perceptual process which applies to men *and* women, and the other is a conception of objectification as a technology of oppression in patriarchy. The point of my position is to argue, together with some feminists who theorise representation, that: 'To see objectification in essentialist terms is to deny the possibility of any alternative practice within the representation of women' (Myers, 1988, p. 205).

That women *think* looks are so crucial to the way they are evaluated need not indicate that this is *entirely* the case. Evidence (such as is documented here) suggests that this is the way women *experience* their world. It is not a guarantee that this is the way men actually do. In their extensive review of over 50 studies Shrauger and Schoeneman (1979) reported evidence of congruence between *self-judgements* and *perceived* judgements by others. However, there was no evidence of congruence between *perceived* judgements and *actual* judgements by others. In other words, people projected onto others opinions about themselves that they themselves held, but these were different from what the others really thought. A symbolic interactionist or a psychoanalytic perspective would argue that psychic reality is just as real as an 'objective reality'. The ultimate consequence of existing as a spectacle is a permanent dissatisfaction with the visible self. Ample evidence suggests that women (not just prepubertal but as young as little girls, and not just those suffering from eating disorders) have a more distorted body perception than men do. In line with the cultural requirement to be thin, they tend to think of their bodies as heavier than they really are (see for example, Thompson and Thompson, 1986; Collins and Plahn, 1988; Koslow, 1988; Cash and Brown, 1989; Wardle and Foley, 1989; Myers and Biocca, 1992). The collective imagination may perpetuate itself by making people slot into age-old cultural positions unaware. Which is probably why ancient myths continue to live as present-day elements of reality.

Note

This chapter draws on the articles: E. Tseëlon (1991a), 'Women and the private domain: a symbolic interactionist perspective', *Journal for the Theory of Social Behaviour*, 21, 111–24; and E. Tseëlon and S.B. Kaiser (1992), 'A dialogue with feminist film theory: multiple readings of the gaze', *Studies in Symbolic Interaction*, 13, 119–37.

4

THE BEAUTY MYTH:
THE PRINCESS IS A FROG

The floral beauty of this feminine image from the 1992 Dutch flower show thinly veils ancient symbolism of the Medusa-like threatening woman.

In the previous chapters I showed how the woman has been simultaneously constructed and condemned as deceitful artifice. In this chapter I would like to use this framework to explain the special relations between women and beauty. This analysis is based on social and psychological theories, as well as historical material. Further, I will argue that the paradox which runs through this topic is that the requirement of the woman to be beautiful masks a fundamental ugliness (such as the notion of 'the prostitute in every woman'), which operates like a potential stigma. And that once again, the fear of the woman is projected onto the woman and defended against by glamorising her.

My starting point is the symbolic interactionist notion of the self. As the empirical evidence in Chapter 2 shows, this notion of the self – as a dynamic product of communication and not as a fixed entity – seems to be at the core of the female sartorial identity. Goffman (1959, 1963a) defined the presentation of self as a claim to a certain identity, as a cooperative activity of actor and audience. The claim for an identity is taken on faith so long as it can be sustained (that is, if neither audience nor actor provide evidence which makes it untenable). When discrediting evidence appears, identity is spoiled. Beauty, for the woman, is an identity claim, except that it is a conditionally spoiled identity. It is only through hard work that the woman can avoid being shown up as ugly.

Gregory Stone extended this interactive analysis to identification through clothes. In his formulation the process consists of *programme* and *review*. Programme is a claim for an identity made by the wearers on the basis of dressing cues. Review is a response of the audience. If programme and review coincide – that is, if the wearer's claim is endorsed by the audience – the self of the person who appears is established. If the identity claim is not endorsed by the audience, the self of the one who appears is challenged (Stone, 1962). The process of negotiation of identity is like a series of mirrors, each validating the other. It runs counter to the dualist position which regards appearance and substance, or clothes and person, as separate entities. Yet symbolic interactionism does not claim its vision to be exclusively female. The thesis I would like to propose here though is that *the material me*, as William James referred to it – that aspect of the self which is constituted by one's clothes and possessions – while important for every self is paradigmatic of the female self. This is not to make an essentialist argument. There is nothing inherent in the woman which makes her material self so fundamental to her social existence. But there are cultural practices, traditions, and a centuries old legacy which still encodes and echoes the present-day conceptions of Western woman (Tseëlon, 1992b).

From a very early age, gender is socially constructed through appearance. A positive relationship between physical attractiveness and self-concept throughout the life span is reported consistently for both men and women (see for example, Adams, 1985). Yet beauty appears to be a gender-related category. Looks are important but inconsequential for the man, but they are a defining feature for the woman: both in terms of how others respond to her, and how she experiences her own self (for example, Bar-Tal and Saxe, 1976a, 1976b; Unger, 1985; Mazur, 1986).

I would now like to foreground my argument with the social psychological view. I do not intend to give an exhaustive account but to outline a few central themes, particularly those that pertain to the self concept.

Beauty: the making of a princess

The existence and operation of appearance-based stereotypes in both adults and children are very well established (for a review see Graham and Kligman, 1985; Patzer, 1985; Hatfield and Sprecher, 1986). Research in this area has typically focused on personal characteristics and social consequences of being attractive. Ample empirical evidence confirms that in research hypothetical attractive people (adults and children) are preferred as friends, and are perceived as more competent. Attractiveness is associated with better professional outcomes, while lack of attractiveness is related to perceptions of social deviance. There is also evidence that appearance is emphasised and valued more highly in females than in males. The interpersonal consequences of physical attractiveness are unequivocally stronger for women. Women are more critically judged for attractiveness, and more severely rejected when they lack it, and these judgements have real consequences for them (Jackson, 1992).

The empirical evidence documents the following sex differences: that women have a lower body image than men (for example, Berscheid et al., 1973; Fallon and Rozin, 1985; Franzoi et al., 1989), lower body satisfaction (for example, Koff et al., 1990; Jackson, 1992), that for women body image is related to psychological health (for example, Graham and Jouhar, 1983), romantic relationships (for example, Coombs and Kenkel, 1966; Berscheid et al., 1971; Koestner and Wheeler, 1988), and femininity (for example, Deutsch et al., 1986): both experienced and perceived by others.

The woman is placed in a no-win situation. She is expected to embody a 'timeless' cultural phantasy, but she is not really naturally more attractive than the man. Her special beauty is at best a temporary state, and it takes hard work and concerted effort to maintain. That the stigma associated with unattractiveness and obesity can become self-fulfilling prophecy was demonstrated in a number of studies. These studies showed how the *physically* (un)attractive learn to play the role of the *socially* (un)attractive. One such study employed a method of simulated acquaintance by phone. Snyder et al. (1977) recorded telephone conversations of dyads where the males were led to believe that their female phone partners were either beautiful or not. The females were not aware of this designation. Analysis of the tapes was done by naïve judges. Females who were believed to be beautiful were found to present the behaviour stereotypical of the physically attractive: friendly, likeable, and socially desirable. Similar results were obtained in a double-bind condition with either attractive/ unattractive (Goldman and Lewis, 1977), or obese/non-obese female phone partners (Miller et al., 1990).

The paradox of preserving female beauty, in her race against the hour-glass, is captured by the duchess in Lewis Carroll's *Through the Looking Glass* where she explains to Alice that: 'Now, *here*, you see, it takes all the running *you* can do, to keep in the same place. If you want to get somewhere else, you must run at least twice as fast as that' (1865/1971, p. 145). The essence of the paradox is that however fast she runs in an attempt to control her body, the woman can never confidently master it. Yet because 'A woman is made to feel continually insecure about her physical appearance, and simultaneously so dependent on it' (Chapkis, 1986, p. 140), she is willing, more than men, to go to dangerous lengths to improve her appearance and fight ageing through endless diets and unsafe, unnecessary surgery (Finkelstein, 1991; Wolf, 1991).

Cosmetic surgery is fast becoming a popular and acceptable way of 'improving upon nature'. It has democratised beauty and is no longer the privilege of the rich and famous. In Britain, according to a recent report, 60,000 every year submit themselves to the dangers and promises of the plastic surgeon's scalpel. They go for a variety of procedures including reduction (of breasts and chin, fat and abdomen), augmentation (of breasts, lips, cheeks and calves), wrinkle smoothing, as well as reshaping every bit of face and body (*Observer Life*, Keeping up appearances, 28 November 1993). In his critical essay *America*, Baudrillard observes that in the US, the dedication to the cult of the body is 'utopia achieved', and that 'the only physical beauty is created by plastic surgery' (1986/1989, p. 32). And in California in particular, plastic surgery has become not only part of life, but a badge one wears to flaunt membership in the club of those who take control over their body. It has come to represent, like so many status symbols in American life, a sign of entrepreneurship, and success (*The Times*, Style and Travel, A scar is born, 26 June 1994). A feature in the *Observer Magazine* (23 December 1990) quoted a Los Angeles plastic surgeon saying that the idea of a 'nose job' as a birthday present or a Christmas present is not uncommon among Californian teenagers. And a Santa Monica doctor, formerly chief of plastic surgery at UCLA said 'people here consider cosmetic surgery almost as casually as getting their hair done . . . Attitudes have changed. . . . In the past it would have had to be a pretty God-awful nose, but now we are seeing any teenager who doesn't like their nose'. In an interview, Cher, a world champion of cosmetic surgery expresses concern about losing her looks: 'The idea of not being this way, of losing it all and somehow being less of a person just because I no longer look the same . . . that's kind of scary . . . So I'd like to look as good as I can for as long as I can' (*Daily Express*, 8 June 1992). What epitomises this social phenomenon is not the celebrities, but the ordinary people. A man and a woman who were interviewed for an *Oprah Winfrey Show* admitted to feeling too ugly to leave the house. In fact they felt so ugly that they could swear people were staring at them in public. When they appeared on the show they certainly did not look great beauties, but nothing like the monstrous self-perception that they read into other people's eyes.

What can the study of cosmetic surgery illuminate about gender differences in the role of beauty? Although females are far the biggest client group, male surgery is increasing too. In Britain, one in five operations on facial improvements is on male noses, and one in ten liposuction operations is performed on men. In America men account for one in three of all procedures – an increase of 18 per cent in ten years. Does this trend indicate that men are closing the gap? Not necessarily. There is a fundamental motivational gender difference. For men the common incentive is professional pressures. Looking more youthful and fit is like wearing a fashionable suit. In Britain 'cosmetic surgery is particularly popular with men in marketing or sales jobs, where they are on show for a large part of the time' (*TV Quick Yorkshire*, Cosmetic surgery for men, 25–31 July 1992). Similarly, a spokesperson for the American Academy of Facial Plastic and Reconstructive Surgery confirmed that the emphasis on youth in the workplace is by far the primary reason men undergo surgery (*The Times*, Style and Travel, The new cutting edge, 26 June 1994). For women it is about shaping a new identity, about coming out of the closet, about transforming themselves with a magic wand. It is a thematic variation on the Cinderella motif. Since relationships are so central to their concept of self, feeling good about themselves is bound up with being attractive to others. This is captured well in a telling anecdote of a woman who had spent her father's inheritance, some £25,000 on a series of operations that helped her to rid herself of a family resemblance to a domineering father:

> I knew I would never be popular and successful because I wasn't pretty. I wanted a new face and a new body. And I got it. My partner's very happy with the new me. I no longer have to dress to disguise problems with my figure or use make-up to disguise my nose. (*Observer Life*, Keeping up appearances, 28 November 1993)

The professional/interpersonal gender difference seems to be supported by physical attractiveness research which has shown that physical attractiveness is universally important in mate preference, but more so in female selection. This research has also documented that perceptions of attractiveness deteriorate with age – and again, the trend is stronger for women. In contrast, on the professional scene attractiveness is linked to perceptions of competence and persuasiveness, and seems to benefit both sexes (Jackson, 1992). So, while some men in some occupations are subject to one set of pressures (professional) to preserve their looks, all women are subject to two sets of pressures, professional and interpersonal – where the latter is constitutive of their identity.

What helps promote the ideology of the construction of sexual difference through appearance is a certain climate of opinions created by the media on the one hand, and the scientific community on the other. The first is the propagation of the 'new woman' myth. The second is scientific research which reinforces 'the physical attractiveness myth'. I will discuss each in turn.

The 'new woman' myth made its first appearance in the media in the 1990s. Its message was that the woman's movement managed to prolong the shelf-life of women in the public sphere. As evidence, examples of remarkable middle-aged women (most often public figures and film stars) who managed to keep exceptional looks (most often without really trying) were offered as role models. An unsystematic survey of a handful of newspapers and magazines yields the following harvest. A feature from the women's magazine *Lear's* describing *the face of the 90s* starts with the 'interesting woman', whose beauty comes from within – then goes on to portray a series of outstandingly youthful and attractive middle-aged women (January 1990). A feature in *The Times* headed 'Sexy and sassy at seventy' tells the story of the founder of *Cosmopolitan* who at 70 still has a taut unwrinkled face (which owes much to artifice), and a slim body (which owes much to a daily exercise routine of 80 minutes). And she still believes that 'if she, just a little girl from Little Rock, Arkansas, could get rich, famous, glamorous and marry well, any girl can' (12 October 1992). Next, a feature about top model Lauren Hutton who – at 50 – looks thin, tanned and perfect proves that there is an upside to any age. And the essence of her spectacular looks is that 'she looks precisely her age – albeit with exclamation marks' (*Sunday Express Magazine*, 28 December 1993).

Such features signal a dual message. First, that the woman is supposed to live up to a with phantasy out leaving traces, to conceal her efforts behind an appearance of 'naturalness'. Second, that ageism is a thing of the past. That the probationary status of 'honorary youth' is extended to her provided that she is able to sustain her looks. Her social visibility, however, is still entered on the ticket of attractive physical visibility. And while it can be argued that drinking from the fountain of youth has been a long-standing desire of both men and women, the argument presented here deals with the specific female predicament illustrated in 'the double standard of ageing' (for example, Deutsch et al., 1986). While both sexes dread ageing, it is the woman who is expected to prevent it. This is evidenced, for example, by anti-ageing creams targeted exclusively at her. She is also penalised if she fails: she simply becomes invisible. Research confirms that ageing has more negative effect on perceptions of facial attractiveness of females. Their decline of looks is more precipitous and rapid (Jackson, 1992).

But not everybody seems to buy into the rhetoric of the 'new woman'. For example, Lynn Barber writes in the *Sunday Times* in a column entitled 'The catch: women can never get it right' that for her, the promise of being glamorous at 50 is a burden, not a blessing. Because it means that there is no cut off point to the tiresome exercise of trying to look for ever young and pretty. She goes somewhat towards defying the ideology by claiming that, however unpopular it sounds, this 'media conspiracy' does a dis-service to woman. And that to protest against Isabella Rossellini being sacked as a make-up model at 41 for being too old does not indicate that women above 41 are useless. Rather, it reminds women that they are valuable for many more things than selling cosmetics, or parading their looks. But even she falls into the trap of accepting the terms of 'the beauty system'. Speaking from the perspective of a veteran of the beauty system, she considers it her right to look her age even if it spoils the illusion of everyone else, only because *she* has already served her term 'on the treadmill of attraction' (*Sunday Times*, Style and Travel, 29 May 1994).

Another ideological device that perpetuates the construction of sexual difference is a scientific grounding of a cultural practice. Psychological theories serve the seal of legitimacy on the ideology of 'fitting in' with the norms (of gender construction) by providing a rationale for the psychological benefits of complying. For example, research on physical attractiveness heavily documented the cognitive developmental basis of appearance stereotyping, the personal characteristics, and the social advantages of being attractive (for example, Graham and Kligman, 1985; Patzer, 1985; Dion, 1986; Hatfield and Sprecher, 1986). Only occasionally have researchers studied the negative consequences of attractiveness. For example beautiful women were found at times to be perceived as intimidating (Stokes and Bickman, 1974) and egoistic (Dermer and Thiel, 1975), and to suffer from 'visible handicap' (Foltyn, 1989). Similarly on traits connoting vanity and self-centredness attractive individuals were rated less positively than unattractive persons (Dermer and Thiel, 1975; Bassili, 1981).

And plastic surgeons, eager to protect the integrity of their practice provide another source of support for 'improved body production'. In a survey of two decades of breast augmentation surgery, three plastic surgeons noted that: 'since the purpose of all aesthetic surgery is to improve the quality of life of the patient through an enhancement of her or his own self image . . . this surgery is worthwhile and should be continued' (Biggs et al., 1982, p. 449). But although the psychological message appears to be of psychological well-being, the metamessage is of sexual desirability. And the long-term success of such operations seems to hinge on how sexually appealing, acceptable, or marriageable a woman becomes. Indeed incidence of cosmetic surgery peaks at two periods which mark anxieties of securing entry into the sexual world (adolescence) and fears of an untimely exit (middle age). Thus summarising emotional reactions in patients after cosmetic surgery Bernstein noted that:

> statistics indicate that most men who divorce after 40 remarry, while most women over 40 do not. It may be for these reasons that there is a host of women who feel economically and socially disadvantaged by their divorces and who seek to restore themselves to a more appealing condition. (1980, p. 10)

The 'psychological benefit' factor sounds rather convincing. It is easy to harp on the theme of personal insecurity. It is, however, important to note that the overall picture that comes out of psychological research is rather different. All the advantages of beauty notwithstanding, it is not the case that people benefit *much* by turning from average to beautiful. Rather it is the case that the unattractive suffer because of their appearance (Jackson, 1992).

But in the name of the 'feel good' factor the benefits of beauty procedures are played up, while the dangers are played on a low key. Only recently have features and reports in the media begun to alert people to the dangers inherent in procedures that go wrong. On 13 September 1991, Dr David Kessler, the head of America's Food and Drug Administration, urged women to consider the risks of breast implants. A Granada television programme *World in Action* made current and future customers aware of the dangers of leak or bleed caused by the silicone implanted in the body. On 6 January 1992, the FDA stated its dissatisfaction with the research provided by the manufacturers and called for a halt to the use of silicone breast implants until an expert panel examines complaints (from 2,500 patients) that the implants can cause rupture injuries and auto-immune disorders.

Later that year, disaster stories of harmful beauty procedures began to appear more often. On 13 September 1992, *News of the World Magazine* for example, told of a woman, a Beverly Hills estate agent, whose life and looks have been ruined following silicone injection in the face. The injections – designed to give her face a sculptured cheekbones look – have permanently disfigured her face, and required a series of 34 operations which did not solve the problem. On the same day the *Sunday Times* also published a plastic surgery horror – this time of liposuction. It told the story of a husband and wife who had both attended the same London clinic for liposuction. The feature recounted very different stories. In a moralistic tale headed 'Suckers?' with overtones of the Garden of Eden story, a young couple (38 and 43 year olds) – who describe themselves as slim, fit and interested in their appearance – wanted to look even better. It was the wife who got interested in the idea, and she persuaded the husband. The testimonials of the couple although sounding medically similar are psycho-logically very different. When the bruises cleared, the husband was pleased with the treatment, while the wife was bitterly disillusioned. The pain, the healing time and the results took her by surprise. Although the story is not accompanied by pictures, her evidence that 'it looks awful' is countered by her husband's who thinks that 'My wife is disappointed with her operation, but I don't think she looks as bad as she thinks. She may be a little over-sensitive . . . but I still think she looks fine'. Ironically, in this Eve-genre tale, it is only the wife who gets punished. What is left ambiguous is the 'vanity factor': whether or not it is a case of a worse result, or of greater, more fantastic expectations. Anyway, this story was followed up the following week (20 September 1992) by a feature about the risks of liposuction.

Physical attractiveness research is based on two implicit assumptions. The first assumption is that beauty is a prediscursive given, a fixed quality that individuals either possess or not. This conclusion is reinforced by such references to the distribution of attractiveness as 'there has been no systematic study of the distribution of physical attractiveness levels in the general population' (Berscheid, 1986, p. 295). Or by interpreting current dismissal of Miss Americas of the 1940s as 'a little plump' as evidence not of the changing criteria of beauty, but of the reassuring truism that 'even unattractive people can perhaps hope to be in vogue in the future' (Jones et al., 1984, p. 56). The second assumption can be traced to the Victorian belief that a person's character can be seen through their appearance and that physical beauty reflects spiritual beauty (Sennett, 1977; Finkelstein, 1991). On the whole, research repeatedly affirmed the Victorian belief that beauty of body signals beauty of character 'what is beautiful is good' (Dion et al., 1972). Thus the beautiful were reported to experience greater social power, to be attributed more favourable characteristics and to be better liked (Patzer, 1985, p. 42). Physical attractiveness research tended to focus on a cognitive approach (for example, Frable et al., 1990), or a social learning approach. This approach was supported by evidence for the operation of appearance-based stereotyping, and its roots in socialization of infants and children into stereotypical role expectations (Dion, 1986).

These two assumptions set the scene for treating physical attractiveness as a self-evident category, and for failing to realise that cultural categories are not just an object of study. But that the study itself is a cultural act which reifies certain categories as 'natural'.

Stigma: the beast behind the beauty

Research on stigma refers to a phenomenon where a person bears a mark or sign of deviance (physical, psychological or social) by departing noticeably from norms of appearance or behaviour. A stigmatising label that is applied to the deviant initiates attributions (by self and others) to dispositions that discredit the bearer. The major dimensions of stigma appear to be related to its salience (how visible, concealable, ugly, removable) and disruptiveness (how threatening to others, relevant to the interaction, or the bearer's fault) (Elliott et al., 1982; Jones et al., 1984). While there are some exceptions, ugly or physically deviant people are regarded as clearly disadvantaged. The stigmatising process has disruptive effects both on relationships, and on self-evaluation because self-knowledge and self-validation are so inextricably bound with others' responses. The bearers of stigma may find even a simple interaction troublesome. According to Elliott et al. (1982) possessing a stigma questions the person's claim to legitimacy and leads to a loss of the protection of social norms which sustain the encounter.

The stigmatising process can result in linking the mark to a central aspect of the make-up of the person's identity. If the stigma is minor it is unlikely to engulf the entire self-concept; if it is major, as in the case of physical attractiveness, it is likely to be pervasive and acquire a 'master status'

(Jones et al., 1984, pp. 122–39). However, the way in which a master status stigma influences self-esteem is not clear. Crocker and Major (1989) reviewed research conducted over a period of more than two decades and concluded that self-esteem is not lower among stigmatised people. They noted that some stigmatising conditions lead to low self-esteem, and some do not. They pointed out that very little research has actually investigated the influence of centrality of a stigmatising condition on the resulting self-protective strategies.

Some experimental evidence illuminates an important aspect of this phenomenon, particularly in women. In a recent review of research on physical appearance and gender, Jackson (1992) pointed out three important findings. Contrary to laboratory research findings, she says, real life research provides little evidence that attractive people have more friends, or that unattractiveness is related to criminal behaviour among women. Physical attractiveness was found to be important for both males and females in the workplace and, contrary to expectations, no conclusive gender differences were found in the relationship between body weight and self-esteem. But two findings emerged consistently. First, females are more concerned about their body attractiveness than are males. Second, females are more dissatisfied with some aspect of their appearance. Even normal weight women are unhappy with some part of their body and with their weight (Cash et al., 1986). Recent evidence suggests that this dissatisfaction factor starts with girls as young as six and nine years old (Hill et al., 1992; Ohtahara et al., 1993). Studies also suggest that the distortion of body image is higher among women than among men. In other words: women perceive themselves as heavier than they really are (for example, Thompson and Thompson, 1986; Cash and Brown, 1989). These findings seem to confirm the symbolic interactionist model of self. They indicate that the perceived reality, even if it differs from 'objective' reality can still structure central parts of one's self-concept.

Stigma and beauty: an ideological critique

Physical attractiveness psychologists emphasise the social advantages that are gained by the physically attractive, while stigma social psychologists talk about the social prices paid by those belonging to degraded groups. Both share the belief that *stigma* and *beauty* are self-evident qualities of an almost essentialist kind. Further, they assume that only an extreme position on the scale from normality to deviance (that of the unattractive, obese, disfigured, or the exceptionally beautiful) is constitutive of self-concept, behaviour and others' responses. Finally, both theories treat the experience of attractiveness as inherently positive, and the experience of stigmatisation as inherently negative.

Both approaches form a status quo model which works within a product oriented binary paradigm of beauty/ugliness, stigmatised/stigma-free. It treats 'beauty' and 'stigma' as 'a thing', a feature, and it documents stereotypes and their consequences. It provides informed accounts on the mechanics of the relationship between stigma variables, and by implication advises on how to avoid their adverse consequences. (Some fairy-tales present an epistemology where the true vision of beauty is seen through the ugliness of the frog. But the beast who needs the kiss in order to break a spell is always an enchanted prince, never a princess.) Thus stigma research is uncritically individualistic and it perpetuates a picture of the particular categories employed within an ideological system of gender construction. By failing to examine the roots, conditions of production and implications of the categories themselves, such discourse affirms their 'natural' and 'self-evident' status, and reproduces the power relations that sustain them. For example, omitting to study sex differences systematically, deflects gender relations into individual differences.

An uncritical approach to stigma and beauty also fails to notice that the stigma experience is ambivalent, and not unidimensional (Katz, 1981). It also fails to question the uniformity of the beauty experience. Foltyn (1989) showed in her research that beauty is a role, and perceiving the self as beautiful is contextual, and not constant throughout the life cycle. Indeed, as everyday experience confirms, even in the course of a single interaction people may appear to us more or less beautiful depending on how they move and smile, how animated or tired, happy or angry they feel at any given moment, or how lively they are when they talk or listen.

Admittedly, some critical doubts are occasionally voiced. They include challenges to the exclusivity of the positive nature of attractiveness (for example, Stokes and Bickman, 1974; Dermer and Thiel, 1975; Bassili, 1981; Jones et al., 1984, p. 56; Foltyn, 1989), or the negative nature of stigmatisation (Jones et al., 1984, p. 65), acknowledgement of the political nature of stigmatisation (ibid., pp. 97, 224), and awareness that even possessing a stigmatising trait or quality is no guarantee that the possessor will be marked because of it (ibid., p. 89). In her article on the stigma of excellence Judith Posner (1976) articulated the 'just right' principle. According to this principle, excellence is a mixed blessing since it is as problematic for sustaining the social order as incompetence.

However, such critical notes are not taken up either in theorising (cf. Bobys's critique (1984) of Elliott et al., 1982), or in practice. For example, in a recent article, Frable et al. (1990) define 'master status' deviance both positively (for example, brilliant, rich, gorgeous) and negatively (for example, gay, obese, Hispanic, terminally ill). But in their own study they operationalise deviance with the traditional (negative) concept of stigma. Their subjects included 'positively valued . . . physically attractive women' and 'stigmatized . . . women who indicated that they were Black . . . more than 60 pounds overweight . . . or had severe facial acne scars' (p. 142). Another psychologist openly provides an ideological rationale for perpetuating the existing conceptions:

Goffman still maintains 'that a language of relationship, not attributes is really needed' [to describe stigma] . . . From this basis it would appear that stigma can just as easily attach to the Queen, doctors, clergymen, mothers, children . . . as it can to groups such as the disabled, homosexuals, or ex-prisoners. However, *such contentions squeeze the useful life out of the concept of stigma.* Accordingly, it is maintained here that *the term should be used exclusively in connection with inferior* as opposed to normal or superior attributes. (Page, 1984, p. 8; emphasis added)

Finally, a product approach excludes the possibility that, as I will argue later, *women are stigmatised by the very expectation to be beautiful*, and they are always potentially deviant if they are not careful. The patriarchal regime of the woman defines and judges her through a phantasy model of beauty, which essentially regards her natural body as a stigma. It is for this reason that the physical self becomes the centre of her conception of herself. My argument is that for women physical attractiveness takes on a 'master status' *not only when they occupy an extreme position on the attractiveness scale, but even when they inhabit a middle position.* Further, this kind of stigma is *not* constantly negatively reinforced. On the contrary: the experience of being or becoming beautiful can be very rewarding. Rather, this kind of stigma is evident from the anxiety experienced by women in case they 'don't measure up' or are 'caught in the act'. More on that later. The 'master status' is not a function of the nature of the stigma, or the personal characteristics of the individuals involved. It is an inevitable consequence of the power structure that sustains the ideology of gender construction. It situates the woman as spectacle, the man as spectator, and naturalises the process by making it appear, like any ideology, obvious, inevitable and common sense.

My argument that physical attractiveness functions as stigma departs from the approach taken to physical attractiveness and stigma in social psychological literature. It draws instead on the Goffmanesque notion of stigma as a perspective, and the psychoanalytic notion of femininity as masquerade. And so it is to Goffman's insightful analysis of stigma that I now want to turn.

Stigma and beauty: a Goffmanesque analysis

For Goffman (1963a) stigma is a state of being discredited because of falling short of identity norms, by deviating from expectations. He acknowledges that some attributes are likely to be generally discrediting throughout our culture – and they can be either embedded in one's body, personality, behaviour, history or group membership. But his emphasis is on the relationship between discreditable attributes and the stereotype. The difference between Goffman's account of stigma and the social psychological accounts lies in the nature of the distinction between manifest and latent deviance. Psychological accounts regard stigma as an attribute *of the person* and make a clear distinction between the stigmatised and the normal. Goffman's distinction between the *discreditable* and the *discredited* is dynamic, however, and implies that 'the occasionally precarious and the constantly precarious form a single continuum' (1963a, p. 127). In other words, on the dimension of normality and deviance we do not occupy permanent, but transitory positions. These positions are, therefore, not persons but perspectives. Thus in the normal-deviant drama 'every individual participates in both roles, at least in some connections and in some phases of life' (1963a, p. 138). And it is not the specific stigmatising attributes which determine the nature of the normal/ stigmatised roles: but the frequency with which each is played.

These differences between social psychology and Goffman explain why psychology cannot provide an adequate framework for analysing the stigmatising role of physical attractiveness for women. From its perspective, psychology can only designate attractiveness attributes as inherently discrediting or not, and deal with the consequences of possessing them or not. Psychology cannot accommodate the possibility of treating beauty simultaneously as a positive experience and as a discreditable perspective. In other words, it does not allow for treating women who appear attractive as occupying the normal and the deviant positions at the same time. In contrast, Goffman's position allows to treat physical attractiveness for women as a stigma by virtue of two characteristics. The first is the public existence of women, the fact that they experience their existence as being 'on stage': self-conscious about the impression they are making (1963a, p. 14). The second is the fact that uncertainty is built into the construction of beauty as defining social and self-worth. It is expressed by a permanent insecurity of becoming ugliness unless rigorous discipline is exercised. In Goffman's words: 'The fear that others can disrespect a person because of something he shows means that he is always insecure in his contact with other people' (1963a, p. 13).

To be beautiful is to pursue a picture perfect moment framed by expectation and fear. Therefore 'minor failings or incidental impropriety may . . . be interpreted as a direct expression of his stigmatized differentness' (Goffman, 1963a, p. 15). Beauty for women is a temporary state which only underlines the fact that their value is measured in how well they succeed in the role of a spectacle, and would be more appropriately considered a *stigma symbol* than a *prestige symbol* (1963a, pp. 43–4).

To the extent that the beauty model defines and values the woman through her appearance, it doubly situates her in a stigmatised position. First, she is evaluated according to an idealised criterion she usually falls short of and is ultimately destined to transgress, and second, her natural, bare and uncontrolled body is unacceptable. Like a stigma, it is something to disguise, to alter, to control.

And how is the fact that women typically take part in the beauty system without realising its stigmatising effect to be explained? Psychological theories typically assume that the stigmatising experience is conscious. Their answer would be in terms of cognitive mechanisms or coping strategies (for example, Jones et al., 1984; Frable et al., 1990). According to Goffman, and in accord with ideological analyses (for example, Althusser, 1970/1976) the 'beauty system' is naturalised by the ideology of sexual differences, and is made to feel essential to femininity. In Goffman's words 'we construct a stigma-theory, an ideology to explain his inferiority' (1963a, p. 5). But what this ideology implies is that, like a stigma, the unadorned and unimproved female body is a source of shame and negative feelings. While this is true in general for the status of the body in modernity (for example, Shilling, 1993), for the woman it has an added meaning. This last point is illustrated by an example from a study on the psychology of clothes from the beginning of the century. This study reported that in response to the question about hiding defects with clothing, the dread of being found out and shown up 'reveals in an almost pathetic way the degree to which our worth estimate of ourselves is dependent on the general social currency. This seems to be especially true of women.' A characteristic answer to this question admitted ' "I feel as though eyes were piercing through and noticing it" ' (Flaccus, 1906, p. 77).

   The devalued position of the female body is illustrated, for example, through comic portrayal in popular culture of the carnivalesque grotesque body, and the Christmas pantomime dames. In Bakhtin's reading of Rabelais's novels as a carnivalesque text (1965/1968) particular emphasis is placed on the grotesque body. It is contained in the most varied types of comic folklore of medieval Europe, and the female body plays an indispensable part in it. The grotesque caricatures the negative, the inappropriate: protruding body parts, gigantic dimensions, and fanciful anatomy. It is contrasted with the classical body which is smooth, proportionate and controlled. And like the stigmatised, the woman always has to be on her guard not to let herself go (inadvertently revealing signs of ageing), and not to make a spectacle out of herself (inadvertently disclosing un-beauty: exposing bits of uncontrolled and undisciplined body, failure of diet or grooming). A contemporary form of the grotesque body is contained in a peculiarly British theatrical tradition: the Christmas pantomime – a comic staging of a children's story in which the principal boy is played by a woman, and the leading dame by a man. Cross-dressing is not always comic. It is not funny when a woman is dressing in man's clothes: only the reverse is funny, because of the loss of status displayed. But the pantomime dame is not just a female impostor. He enacts his disguise, and goes out of his way to parody and undermine his disguise. He is a man pretending to be a man pretending to be a woman. In films, cross-dressing belongs to the genres of thriller and comedy (Kuhn, 1985a). In a thriller it acts as deviance, in comedy as grotesque. In both cases it does not destabilise gender coding and identity since the audience knows what the true identity is. This is why transvestites who dress genuinely to pass as women are doubly threatening. They give up a privileged position by crossing over to the devalued realm of femininity, and by so doing they challenge the system of sexual difference (Woodhouse, 1989).

As a response to the devalued status of her body, Western woman regards her body as 'unfinished work' (Wax, 1957, p. 591): 'When she looks in the mirror and sees ugliness reflected back upon herself, what she is actually experiencing is the value that her society has placed upon her gender category, that she has no value' (MacCannell and MacCannell, 1987, p. 214). And the approved cultural response is to erase the original face with a cleanser and skin-colour foundation, and paint a new face made-up to look 'naturally' beautiful. Thus, according to the MacCannells, a woman who relates to men through a set of practices designed to make her more attractive (the beauty system) 'is always fundamentally stigmatized, or seen by herself and others as a half-person, if seen as a person at all' (1987, p. 218).

The balance between doing and overdoing

As MacCannell and MacCannell pointed out, a close examination of the beauty system reveals it to be an *ideology*, in the Althusserian sense: a way of living a contradiction as if it were not a contradiction (1987, p. 208). The implications of this position are that a paradoxical existence is inscribed into the construction of the woman through appearance. For example:

- *The paradox of mental health*: This paradox implies that to be a woman is incompatible with being a well adjusted adult person. If she rejects the feminine model she is diagnosed as having gender identity disorders (such as anorexia nervosa), but if she embraces the model of femininity she is narcissistic, and does not have a mature healthy personality (for a dramatic illustration, see Broverman et al., 1970).
- *The paradox of authentic femininity*: This paradox implies that neither the feminine model of beauty, nor the 'natural' one are authentic. If the woman tries to live up to a phantasy of timeless beauty she is a fake. But if, instead, she embraces the natural look, she is committed to just as much effort of control. The only difference is that by accepting a definition of the natural, healthy and fit look as desirable, she is not yielding to a model of strength but to a model of beauty. And those who doubt it should observe the fact that the models for this 'strong' beauty are film stars (like Jane Fonda) rather than athletes (Chapkis, 1986, p. 12).
- *The paradox of worth*: This paradox implies that even when she succeeds, she fails. If she refuses to join the beauty system, or if she is not capable of sustaining her looks, she is devalued and feels worthless. However, if she succeeds she reaffirms that her value is legitimised through appearance, her non-identity.
- *The paradox of power*: This paradox implies that even when she exercises control over her body she is powerless. For she can never be powerful as long as she operates within a system that judges her

through her looks, and she is always insecure either for not having beauty or for fear of losing it.

Whose responsibility?

From the psychoanalytic perspective of femininity as masquerade there is no feminine essence. According to Lacan, sexual identity is not a prediscursive given (that is, it does not exist independently of language and culture), but is a product of a system of differences (that is, a symbolic system such as language) – the symbolic order. In this system, every element acquires meaning by being what the other is not – ugly is what is not beautiful, dark is what is not light, and so on. Since power and privilege in the symbolic order are symbolised by the phallus, the female sex is defined negatively as that for which *not all the attributes* are a function of the phallus. Thus the woman is left with two positions she can assume. She can either side with the phallus and appear masculine (castrating), or she can side with the no-phallus and appear feminine (castrated). The nineteenth-century Victorian woman adopted the feminine strategy and yielded to the beauty regime in order to attract, to please and to get married. Her twentieth-century counterpart – the career woman – adopts the masculine strategy and yields to the contemporary beauty regime (a model of strength rather than frailty). But neither of them transcends the paradigm: they are two sides of the same coin. Both assume physical attractiveness to be an essential requirement for her position and worth. The only difference is in the locus of responsibility for looking good. An advertisement for Nike sports shoes which appeared in *Cosmopolitan* (September 1991) shows two images: a soft frail image of Marilyn Monroe and a picture of a bronze-coloured sporty woman during workout. In between, the text reads

> A woman is often measured by the things she cannot control. She is measured by the way her body curves or doesn't curve, by where she is flat or straight or round. She is measured by 36–24–36 and inches and ages and numbers, by all the outside things that don't ever add up to who she is on the inside. And so *if a woman is to be measured*, let her be measured by the things she can control, by who she is and who she is trying to become. Because as every woman knows, measurements are only statistics. And statistics lie. (emphasis added)

This message, while appearing to liberate the woman from the imposition of an arbitrary standard of her physical features, ties her to the same standard *but places the responsibility on her*. This message is telling her that she can really achieve the required standard if only she tries hard enough (Wolf, 1991). By implication, both the modern, strong, independent woman who controls her body and her destiny, and Marilyn Monroe – a cultural icon of the traditional, vulnerable and exploited woman – ultimately 'have to measure up'. The social requirement is still there, only the means of achieving it are different. And the social requirement is that the woman is evaluated (and comes to evaluate her self) according to the yardstick prescribed by the dimension of visibility (see Chapter 3). The woman's success is a result of her visibility, her failure results in her invisibility (evidenced, for example, by the taboo placed on menopause; Greer, 1991). The importance of visibility is inherent in the nature of phantasy itself. As Cowie noted, the word derives from the Greek term meaning 'to make visible' and has come to mean 'the making visible . . . of what can never directly be seen' (1984/1990, p. 154). A Marxist argument has been put forward in *The Beauty Myth* (1991). Its author, Naomi Wolf, argues that since its inception in the post industrial period the beauty myth waxes and wanes to counter women's advance. She views the current backlash of the beauty myth (even where only meritocracy seems to operate) as a response of the employers to feminism's achievements on the job front (*Spare rib*, Dec/Jan 1991). But we need not locate the ideology of sexual difference in any specific 'conspiracy' theory. It is a cultural practice produced by the structure of power relations, as well as internalised mythologies. And the mythologies are foreshadowed by the primordial fear of the woman.

Fear of the ageing woman

Susan Deri (1990) points to an unconscious link between the aged and women. Both feature in destructive phantasies about the powerful pre-Oedipal mother who is the source of nourishment and destructive phantasies. Those phantasies return as a fear of retaliation. Freud emphasises that the fear which governs sexual development is the father's retaliation which forms the core of the Oedipal complex. Deri suggests instead that this is a cop-out – that the castration fear is overlaid upon an earlier fear of the life threatening mother. It is the maternal threat, and not the threat of castration, which links the fear of death to the woman. The aged, on the other hand, represent death by their very being.

But why is female ageing more threatening than ageing in general? The ageing woman serves as the memento mori to that which the beauty system is trying to defend against. An empirical support for this notion comes from an unexpected direction. In their study, Snyder and Miene (1994) looked at the motivational foundations of attitudes towards the elderly. The subjects in the study were presented with stories describing the experiences of someone like themselves who volunteers to work with old people. In the course of their work these fictitious characters gain insight into the function of their own stereotypes. The insight was based on one of three approaches to stereotyping: cognitive, sociocultural or psycho-dynamic. Each group of subjects was presented with one version. The cognitive version suggested that stereotypes provide cognitive economy. They help to simplify a complex world. The sociocultural vignette portrayed the social function of stereotyping as helping people identify with their own social and cultural in-groups. The psychodynamic story viewed stereotypes as self-protective devices. The second part of the study measured the shift in stereotyping of the elderly among the subjects. Snyder and Miene found that a negative shift occurred only in the condition of the psychodynamic version, and only among male subjects. This study confirms the ego-protective functions of men's fear of ageing.

The ageing woman portrays an unashamed undisguised ugliness that society has placed on the category of woman. And she is beyond the control of the beauty system. Yet even here she is caught up in a paradox. She is threatening if she has given up the fight for beauty and failed to defeat the inevitable. But she is equally threatening if she tries to do just that: defy the inevitable. Such was the case following the scientific discovery that women can have babies after menopause. On a BBC *Horizon* programme on the matter (11 January 1993), Dr Stevenson of King's College Hospital said that menopause in women is one of 'nature's design faults'. He explained that while in other species the menopause occurs close to the time of death, only in humans the female spends about a third of her life 'in a hormone-deficient state'. The meanings of such a development are quite complex. On the one hand it represents liberation from the constraints of 'natural motherhood', and natural menopause which renders her vulnerable to what one doctor defined a sexist 'colossal bit of biological sabotage on women'. On the other hand it is one move in the patriarchal project of controlling nature in which she is an incidental pawn on the road to medical glory. A patriarchal project which brings her back under the control of 'the beauty system' through the back door.

Female responses reflect this ambivalence. An American grandmother, Jonie Mitchell, who had undergone the treatment that allowed her to conceive at the age of 52 was interviewed on the programme. Exuding this American healthy, fit, well groomed look that unites the 22-year-old with the 52-year-old, she said that the experience is a victory to the American entrepreneurial myth that if you want something hard enough and work hard at it all is in your hands. The writer Germaine Greer represents a more spiritual conception, one that is willing to admit that the desire to conquer nature is simply another aspect of the denial of death and the illusion that by sophisticated technology mortality can be conquered (see Chapter 5). She recommended acknowledging that things have their internal timing and logic, and coming to terms with the process of ageing, with change and mortality. Once such recognition is truthfully embraced, this is the real liberation. But it was Polly Toynbee, writing in the *Radio Times* (9–15 January 1993) who admitted that she does not particularly care about the argument of doing things naturally. Yet she finds the sight of 'beaming pensioners displaying little newborns' rather unseemly.

The making of a frog

Finally, I would like to end this chapter with highlighting the case of the prostitute. The prostitute provides a paradigmatic illustration to my general thesis about the stigma of beauty. She is an attractive but dangerous woman. Her sexual independence makes her necessary but threatening. While society tolerates her, her essence is denigrated and she is clearly marked out of decent company. Metaphorically, therefore, she represents the woman. And she also represents the spoiled identity that awaits the woman who fails to keep up the mask of virtue, the veil of beauty. Such a Fallen woman then simply lapses back and reaffirms her essential nature – that of ugliness, with a face of a prostitute.

The notion of the woman as a prostitute at heart has been laid down by religious teachings. In the Hebraic tradition the reference to female non-marital sexuality as adultery was introduced by the prophets and the Talmud. Israel's history is seen as the story of a married woman who betrayed her husband. Her betrayal confounds acting promiscuously and worshipping the Canaanite gods of Palestine (baalim) (Setel, 1985; Halbertal and Margalit, 1992). Both adultery and idolatry are marked by a woman's love of finery which becomes part of the scene of the sin.

The prophet says:

> I will visit upon her the days of baalim, wherein she burned incense to them, and decked herself with earrings and her jewelry, and she went after her lovers and forgat me, saith the Lord. (Hosea, Ch. 2: 13)

and

> Though thou clothest thyself with crimson, though thou deckest thee with ornaments of gold, though thou rentest thy face with painting, in vain shalt thou make thyself fair. (Jeremiah, Ch. 4: 30)

Condemnation of the sexually active woman has been part of European traditions from Roman literature, which argued that within every respectable woman there lurked a whore, to medieval Christian misogyny (Anderson and Zinsser, 1988, pp. 46–9). The Christian doctrine of the original sin made the association between the archetypal woman (Eve) and the prostitute a particularly straightforward one. The love of finery in itself, or personal adornment constituted sufficient grounds to regard a woman as a prostitute as is amply demonstrated in the teachings of the church fathers:

> if one withdrew the veil of the temple – I mean the head-dress, the dye, the clothes, the gold, the paint, the cosmetics . . . with the view of finding within the true beauty, he will be disgusted . . . For he will not find the image of God dwelling within . . . but instead of it a fornicator and adulterous has occupied the shrine of the soul. And the true beast will thus be detected – an ape smeared with white paint. And that deceitful serpent, devouring the understanding part of man through vanity . . . this pander of a dragon has changed women into whores. (Clement of Alexandria, 1867, Vol. 4, p. 276)

> the distinctions of dress and ornaments are more suited to prostitutes than to virgins . . . while so many things are offensive to God, more especially are the sumptuous ornaments of women. (Cyprian, Bishop of Carthage, 1868, Vol. 8, p. 333)

> The characteristics of ornaments, and the garments, and the allureness of beauty, are not fitting for any but prostitutes and immodest women. (ibid., p. 343)

Tertullianus distinguishes between dress which is 'womanly gracing', and ornament which is 'womanly disgracing'. 'Against the one we lay the charge of ambition, against the other of prostitution' (1869, p. 309).

This legacy of the equivalence between a woman and a prostitute is indicated through contemporary linguistic usages (metaphors, jokes, curses and popular narratives), especially those which do not appear to be targeted against women. Those that are grounded in such common assumptions need no explanations. In his critique of 'thoughtless communism' which seeks to universalise private property, Marx uses woman as a signifier of private property which travels from exclusivity to universality:

> Just as woman passes from marriage to general prostitution, so the entire world of wealth (that is, of man's objective substance) passes from the relationship of exclusive marriage with the owner of private property to a state of universal prostitution with the community. (1844/1964, p. 133)

On a different note in January 1995 a high-ranking Israeli officer who addressed high school teenagers about to join the army said, among other things, that men have always been warriors, and women have been whores. The public outcry that ensued in the media and the parliament, his condemnation and his prompt apology testified both to the ubiquity of the metaphor and to the sensitivity to its usage.

What is the secret of the power of the prostitute metaphor? A historical clothing analysis reveals that one of the early reasons for creating distinctions in dress was the desire to mark the respectable from the unrespectable woman and set her apart (Ribeiro, 1986). In Rome prostitutes were forbidden to wear a respectable matron's dress. Antagonism between wives and high-class whores was as much a feature of Roman life as it was in Greece. One group existed as the inseparable shadow of the other. Apparently the wives openly envied the courtesans who prided themselves on their education, wit, beauty and independence. The antagonism between these two groups of women was to persist throughout history in different guises. Its contemporary manifestations are embodied in the tension between the wife and the 'other woman' (Richardson, 1985). Only recently an actress writing in the *Observer Magazine* criticised 'those "other women" who regularly screw other people's husbands'. She accused those woman who are 'taking a sort of timeshare in a husband, or just having a man out on loan' of doing it purely 'for their own sexual gratification' in a total disregard for the woman they are betraying – and get off too lightly (13 September 1992). On the other side of the fence, a woman writing from her own experience 'In defence of the other woman' urged her readers to see her side of the story, and to consider that 'no one – not even a wife – is ever one hundred per cent innocent' (*Options*, November 1992). What both groups seem to overlook is the responsibility of the husband in the equation. The accusatory tone of the one, and the apologetic tone of the other which frame the debate demonstrate how the 'discourse of sinful Eve' has been internalised by its victims even in a cultural context that no longer views women as victims. The basis for the historical tension between the virtuous wife and the disreputable prostitute can be explained by the fact that prostitution was a conscious and positive choice in the face of grinding poverty and lack of opportunity. It was a choice which offered better pay, easier conditions and greater autonomy than other forms of female work.

In the Roman economy no stigma or shame was associated with prostitution. In the ancient Near Eastern cultures sacred prostitution in fertility cults was a common practice (Brooks, 1941). In the Hebraic tradition not all prostitution was condemned. Taking vows was a common female religious practice. In order to pay them back, women often resorted to prostitution. Yet prostitution for the sake of paying vows for the Temple was seen as a sacrificial act of communion between God and worshipper. Only prostitution as part of fertility rituals (which was not a Hebrew custom) was seen as betrayal (Van der Toorn, 1989). Christianity brought into prostitution the notion of sin.

Prostitution was marked first sartorially, and later morally. It was achieved by making prostitutes easily identifiable by their clothing or some signal of costume. The justification for such measures was that it would protect respectable women. But in fact it served two other purposes: the sexually independent woman embodied all of male fears of female sexuality. Demarcation rendered her mythical quality containable, and the institution of female prostitution allowed society to make money off their transgressions. In Greece prostitutes were distinguished by flowered robes. They were forbidden precious materials such as scarlet or purple or jewels, and prescribed cheap robes with flowers or multicoloured stripes. In some cities light, transparent garments were unlawful, whereas in others, like Sparta, they were the badge of the virtuous woman (Sanger, 1859/1972, p. 46). Roman high-class prostitutes were not allowed to wear the female chaste stola. They were forbidden to wear signs of virtue such as purple robes, jewels or shoes. Instead they wore gilded sandals and floral dress. Many prostitutes ostentatiously flaunted their status by wearing filmy silk and gauze Oriental dresses – that displayed what they were intended to cover (Sanger, 1859/1972, p. 75). In the Middle Ages wearing a veil was a sign of a chaste woman and was not allowed to prostitutes (Otis, 1985, p. 67). But while the dress code was not enforced on high-class prostitutes, it was imposed on lower-class prostitutes in an attempt to regulate their movements. In Leipzig she was required to wear a yellow coat, trimmed with blue; in Vienna to tie a yellow kerchief across her shoulder; in Augsburg to wear a green sash, and in Berne and Zurich red caps. At Mantua prostitutes were ordered to wear a short white cloak over their clothes. At Bergamo, the cloak was yellow, in Parma white, and in Milan black (Sanger, 1859/1972, p. 162). Bristol and London decreed striped hoods. In Avignon furred cloaks were banned. Also outlawed were silk, gold, silver and precious stones. Legal records of the period show that habitual disregard of these rules resulted in heavy fines being imposed by many municipal authorities (Roberts, 1992). According to Otis (1985) the general status of whores in medieval society was comparable with the position of Jews in that period: both essential to the economy but despised for the role they were allocated to fulfil within it; indispensable but despicable (pp. 69–70). The most striking similarity was the dress code requirement, in which the authorities attempted to compel both groups to wear distinguishing markers on their clothing.

As a result of the feudal crisis at the end of the medieval period a surplus of urban workers was created. Women were among the groups most affected. They began to be excluded from the crafts and trades they had participated in equally with men during the Middle Ages. Once again, prostitution offered the only bearable means of subsistence. In the Renaissance the high-class courtesan enjoyed rather high power. She was rich and independent; her profession provided her with the financial and social ability to live in sumptuous homes, and to participate in the masculine world of education and culture. Like the Renaissance, the Reformation in the sixteenth century defined any independent female sexuality as threatening and therefore evil. But it was the Puritan movement in the seventeenth century which condemned all forms of pleasure as sinful. The moral decadence of the aristocracy during the eighteenth century allowed prostitution – and to a lesser extent the stage – to continue to offer the woman of talent and ambition the only career. At the same time the Societies for the Reform of Manners peaked in the eighteenth century with the aim of eradicating prostitution.

Even the French Revolution did not bring prostitutes any liberation. The political triumph of bourgeois morality and values, with its insistence on the sexual purity of its women, led to regarding prostitutes as criminal. In the nineteenth century moral reform became central to the discourse of public health. As a result the state played a greater role in the regulation and control of sexual behaviour through legislation and police registration. This move increased the social isolation and stigmatisation of the prostitutes. Consequently many whores and other independent women were being made into outcasts in their own communities. Social purity extended beyond sanitary supervision of venereal diseases. By tapping deep seated anxieties it drew a clearer boundary between the respectable and the disreputable woman (Weeks, 1981/1989).

The Victorian era had brought in another classical age of the courtesan, while pathologising low-class prostitution. True to his values of middle-class morality, middle-class man created a split between the respectable chaste wife, and the oversexed prostitute. Even the chastity of the good wife, as I have shown in Chapter 1, was nothing but an image. It signified the essential nature of the woman, the threatening prostitute, while at the same time creating a defense against her. As old as the tradition of respect for the good wife was the tradition of disgust – and desire – for the woman who broke the rules and had sex with more than one man. Both the Victorian Madonna and the Victorian whore were projections of man's own phantasy. Here, in the logic of Freud's 'epistemology of disgust', the intensely desired pleasure that cannot be allowed into experience undergoes repression and hysterical conversion from pleasure to disgust.

Because of his fear of independent female sexuality, man stigmatised it as characteristic of a prostitute no matter how high the woman's social rank. Cultural legends are sometimes more persistent than rational explanations. As I noted in Chapter 1, the threat of being considered a prostitute is not absent even from contemporary dressing concerns. In fact, the fear of communicating such suggestion united women across age and marital status. Popular culture continues to offer motifs which depict the fascination/fear with the sexually independent (potentially whore) woman. In the film *Fatal Attraction* an independent career woman embarks on a casual affair with a married man, but soon discovers herself to be more involved than she intended to. Her demonisation in the film reaches such proportions that the only way to contain it is to kill her. In the recent film *Indecent Proposal* a financially struggling architect who married his teenage love agrees (with his wife's encouragement) to an offer by a very rich man of a million dollars if he lends him his wife for a night. The logic underlying this tale is the old cliché that every woman is a whore, the difference between them is the price.

Could the fear of the ugliness of the woman be explained, once more, as a projection of the ugliness of the man? In his witty analysis of the philosophy of clothes *The Eternal Masquerade*, Bradley (1922) defines the essence of women's dress as an 'artistic draping to illusion'. Beauty, he explains, is an evolutionary development. Man in his primitive state was ugly. Clothing was invented to conceal this ugliness. Hence 'when man, tired of beauty, seeks a fresh emotion in destruction, woman strips herself to lure him back to creation' (1922, p. 8). More on that in Chapter 5.

Note

This chapter draws on the article, E. Tseëlon (1992b), 'What is beautiful is bad: physical attractiveness as stigma', *Journal for the Theory of Social Behaviour*, 22, 295–309.

5

THE BEAUTY MASQUE OF DEATH

The Semiotic Cycle of the Woman: fairy princess daughter and black
death mother at Halloween in California.

In this chapter I would like to examine the role that female beauty and
decorativeness plays in the cultural imagination. Constructing the woman
as beautiful, adorned, made-up and disguised with finery seems to be
central to her conception. At the same time she also represents death. She
is not the exclusive symbol of death. The image of the man in the black

cloak and the scythe springs to mind more immediately than a woman's. Yet, while the icon of the angel of death does not extend to *men* as such, *women* are implicated in the collective symbolism. Drawing on psychoanalytic notions, I would account for the paradoxical observation that the woman appears both as signifying attractiveness and adornment, and as signifying death. I argue that death and beauty are two sides of the same coin. And that the woman serves the dual function of signifying a fear and the defence against it at the same time. As Freud observed, some phenomena cannot be explained away simply on rational grounds. Deep seated fears, that appear to be more collective than personal, and that have currency beyond their time, require explanations that would address themselves to the intense and insistent quality of the emotion. They require explanations at a different level from rationality. They require explanations at the mythical level. He argued that the fear of castration which is also echoed in the fear of losing one's eyes or eyesight is one such example. The 'peculiarly violent and obscure emotion' it commands goes beyond a simple logical explanation having to do with the importance of the organ. Another example is the cultural fear of death (and the woman). It cannot be explained away in rational terms. The manifestation of disproportionately strong emotions is interpreted in a psychoanalytic logic as evidence of repression. Freud (1919) termed this kind of repressed fear the uncanny. The uncanny is the opposite of all that is familiar, tame, intimate, friendly, comfortable, arousing a sense of agreeable restfulness and security as one feels inside one's home. And it is more than intellectual uncertainty. It originates in familiar things becoming defamiliarised through repression. According to psychoanalytic reasoning every affect belonging to an emotional impulse which is repressed is transformed into anxiety. The uncanny is nothing new or alien, but something which is familiar and old-established in the mind, but has become alienated in the process of repression.

Feelings of uncanniness are clearly distinguishable from ordinary fear. And the conditions under which these feelings arise are unmistakable. They arise in situations which seem to confirm an animistic system of beliefs in realities of wish-fulfilments, secret powers, omnipotence of thoughts, animation of inanimate objects, the return of the dead, the phantasy of being buried alive, and spirits and ghosts – the stuff of which fairy-tales are made. There is another kind of uncanny which originates from repressed infantile complexes – castration complex, womb phantasies etc. – but this is not very frequent:

> What is involved is an actual repression of some content of thought and a return of this repressed content, not a cessation of belief in the reality of such a content . . . an uncanny experience occurs either when infantile complexes which have been repressed are once more revived by some impression, or when primitive beliefs which have been surmounted seem once more to be confirmed. (Freud, 1919, p. 249)

When does something acquire the quality of the uncanny? Freud locates the main source of the experience of the uncanny in the return of the repressed:

> it is possible to recognize the dominance in the unconscious mind of a 'compulsion to repeat' proceeding from the instinctual impulses and probably inherent in the very nature of the instincts – a compulsion powerful enough to overrule the pleasure principle, lending to certain aspects of the mind their daemonic character. (Freud, 1919, p. 238)

It is this uncanny fear to which female decorativeness seems to be the answer. Drawing on Elias and Ariès one can see that as suppression of emotions increased so did the role of the imaginary. The more repression operates, the more the role of phantasy increases. The more the fear of death becomes sublimated, the more the woman (as representing death) needs to be idealised, phantasised. This is indeed what happened to women's dress in the nineteenth century. But I will return to this later. The uncanny position of the woman would also seem to follow from the fact that themes that construct her as a 'demonic' being keep recurring and gaining currency regardless of the sophistication of the general discourse. A case in point is the current craze of vampire films and the motif of the deadly woman, for example in films (*Thelma and Louise*, *Nikita*, *Kiss of the Spider Woman*, *Basic Instinct*) which adopt a kind of inverted feminism: where the women is no longer just a victim of horror, but also a perpetrator of one. Such phenomena when seen together with the resurgence of the theme of vampires, Dracula and Frankenstein in the nineteenth century Gothic novel, testify to the uncanny role death and the maiden occupy in our culture. What might have unleashed them may be purely incidental: the Aids scare in the case of Dracula and the vampires as some propose, or the achievements (and the backlash) of feminism, as others argue. The important issue seems to be what Freud points out in his analysis of the uncanny – that a rational explanation is not enough if only because of the timeless appeal of such themes.

Students of comparative mythology have identified an almost universal misogyny in the Creation and Fall stories in various cultures. Remarking on the apparent universality of linking women with evil and death Schwarz notes:

> What these myths from high cultures have in common with the narratives from primitive cultures . . . and with the biblical story . . . is on the one side the loss of the benefits of paradise, and on the other the connection of the calamity with woman. (Schwarz, 1973, quoted in Phillips, 1984, p. 74)

In what follows I want to explore the cultural identity between woman, death and beauty that pervades the Western collective consciousness. I will examine the thesis that relates the aestheticisation of both the woman and death to the process of repression of emotions in the civilising process in general, and fetishism in particular.

Attitudes to death and the civilising process

I would now like to illustrate Elias's thesis (1939, Vols 1 and 2) of the civilising process by reference to Ariès's study of Western attitudes towards death (1976, 1977/1981). I would then like to extend this framework to explain attitudes towards the woman – in particular to her appearance.

The model of the 'civilising process' is based on an analysis of the development of the courtly behaviour in European history. It links two processes – the establishment of the Absolute monarchies, and the development of economy of drives – through a process of increased interdependencies resulting from increased globalisation. In his analysis, Elias noted two corresponding historical processes: transformation of social structure and personality structure. One process resulted in a gradual transition from a society of chivalrous duels and battles to a court society of manners and political intrigue. The other process resulted in a development in the structure of emotions. The 'civilising process' transformed the affect economy. It created the private sphere where the naked body, emotions and instincts were suppressed from public life thus advancing the shame frontier, and it changed patterns of pleasure. What had been suppressed in the real became a dream image. What was denied immediate gratification emerged in dreams and phantasies. Since the civilised person was denied by socially instilled self-control from spontaneously touching what she or he desires, active pleasure gave way to the passive pleasure of spectating.

Attitudes towards death throughout history

The transition of emotions from an open expression to a gradual restraint, ritualisation of bodily functions, and displacement of instinctual urges from acting out to phantasy, parallels Ariès's analysis of Western attitudes towards death. In his account, the increased estrangement of death was accompanied by a shift from an open display of the dead body to its concealment, but was counteracted with an obsessive phantasmic visibility. According to Ariès, until the early Middle Ages death was tame and was treated with familiarity and resignation. Familiarity with death was a form of acceptance of the order of the universe in which the boundaries between the natural and the supernatural were indefinite.

In antiquity the dead were considered impure, and their return was feared – hence they were relegated to cemeteries outside the town. In contrast, early Christianity (from the sixth century) fought the pagan fear of the dead with a veneration of the dead. The dead were brought into the community and were buried inside the church. Communal graves were common. Graves were anonymous. Bones were dug up to make room for new ones and stacked visibly in the charnel. Beginning with the eleventh century a formerly unknown relationship developed between the death of each individual and her or his awareness of being an individual: 'In the mirror of his own death each man would discover the secret of his individuality' (Ariès, 1977/1981, p. 51). Starting in antiquity the attitudes to death were undergoing a transition from being an event in the life of the collective, to the emerging notion of individual death. With this increased awareness of the individual, and individual death, the dead body started getting concealed. It was placed in a coffin or under a monument, and it was replaced by an image mounted on the coffin, known as *representation*. Thus familiarity was maintained by means of the artifice of camouflage and representation. Gradual concealment of the body from the thirteenth century onwards was accompanied by a series of representations from the wax effigy which signified the social body, through the death mask, which was an exact reproduction, to embalming, which was an actual preservation of the physical body.

In order to appreciate the civilising process of attitudes towards death, one needs to consider the three registers of psychic functioning: the real, the symbolic and the imaginary. And here we find support for the Freudian notion (1930) that civilisation blocks instinctual discharge. As a result, the suppressed instinctual libido finds alternative expression. It is repressed onto a defence mechanism. Failing that, it returns in the form of a neurotic symptom. This is just what seems to have happened according to Ariès's account. As death became a stranger and emotions repressed, the fear of death found expression through the practice of death masks and embalming in the register of the real, and through macabre eroticism in the imaginary. At the end of the fifteenth century, the themes concerning death began to take on erotic meaning. In the new iconography of the sixteenth century, death raped the living. From the sixteenth to the eighteenth centuries, countless scenes or motifs in art and literature associated death with love, Thanatos with Eros (even the word for 'orgasm' in some languages literally means 'small death'). Like the sexual act, death was increasingly thought of as a transgression which tears the person from daily life, from rational society, from monotonous work, plunging them into an irrational, violent and ecstatic world. From the sixteenth century the notion of break was introduced. It was born and developed in the world of erotic phantasms. It then passed into the world of the real and acted-out events (Ariès, 1977/1981, pp. 56–8). The Socratic detachment and Stoic acceptance of death during the Renaissance and the Baroque (sixteenth and seventeenth centuries), while leading to humility and simplicity in funerals, was complemented by a shift of death from the real to the phantasmic. Death became an ecstatic imaginary phantasy.

During the Enlightenment (seventeenth and eighteenth centuries) the dead body became a source of curious and morbid fascination. But even in a society which thought it controlled death through rational and restrained approach, currents of scientific discourse failed to cover undercurrents of phantasy. A savage and dangerous skeleton hitherto repressed in the cupboard came out to bring to the collective consciousness the same old fears. The imaginary register was dominated by macabre eroticism through phantasies and repressed fears of the kind which makes up the experience of the uncanny. This time the macabre was not only eroticised as in the sixteenth century, but also violent. The dead body became a site of conflicting attitudes: desire and horror; ecstasy and sadistic pleasure. Necrophilia which made the dead body an object of desire became common, and its counterpart in fictional fantasies – from the baroque theatre to the Gothic novel – was the common motif of the reawakened corpse (the vampire), apparent death (being buried alive), and the Double. In the Age of Reason scientific curiosity and calm acceptance reflected a control of emotions expressed, for example, in a passion for anatomy, a fashion for dissection, and a renewed taste in preservation through embalment. On another level, however, it betrayed fear in the form of a re-established need for a physical separation between the dead and the living. Burial came back to the cemetery. This time it was rationalised with a rhetoric of a concern with hygiene and public health.

The nineteenth century saw another revolution in feeling. The century of Romanticism indulged in emotional excess. The private sensibility was born – and emotions that once belonged in the traditional community and the individual of the late Middle Ages/early modern times were transferred to the family. Separation and loss became more unbearable, and death became an assault on the emotional cohesion of the family (Ariès, 1977/1981, p. 67). In an era marked by hysterical mourning survivors accepted the death of another person with greater difficulty than in the past (Ariès, 1977/1981, p. 67). Appropriately, it was expressed in uncontrolled dramatic emotionality. Mourning claimed to have no obligations to social conventions but to be the spontaneous expression of a very grave wound. People cried, fainted, languished and fasted. It was a return to the excessive, exaggerated and spontaneous demonstration of the early Middle Ages (twelfth century). Such extravagance of emotions soon demanded some form of defence from the naked fear. This was expressed in two forms. One was the fear of apparent death which invaded reality and fiction. The other was the creation of the 'beautiful death'. Death was exalted and luxuriously displayed in ostentatious funerary processions, cults of remembrance, tombs and memorial statues, mummification of bodies, public funerals, pompous monuments and extravagant tombstone sculptures. Characterised as wild and terrifying but also sublime it was treated with fascination, idealised as a desirable stage, a final rest and reunion with loved ones.

Once again, a growing alienation from death brought about an increase of the dramatic element. As dead bodies became an affront to good taste, they were covered and idealised. Death was transformed into an illusion of art. It began to hide under a mask of beauty. Finally, towards the end of the century the thin veneer broke down. Death ceased to be beautiful and became ugly, hidden, shameful and improper – like the body's biological functions. In the second half of the nineteenth century those surrounding the dying person had a tendency to hide from them the gravity of their condition. The first motivation for the lie was the desire to spare the sick person, to ease the burden of their ordeal. But this sentiment very rapidly was taken over by a different sentiment characteristic of modernity: one must avoid the disturbance and the overly strong and unbearable emotion caused by the ugliness of dying and by the very presence of death in the midst of a happy life. The procedure of hushing-up began not for the sake of the dying but for the sake of the living, for society's sake. Between 1930 and 1950 the evolution accelerated markedly. This was due to the displacement of the site of death. One no longer died at home in the bosom of one's family, but in the hospital, alone (Ariès, 1977/1981, pp. 86–7). The moral duty and the social obligation were to contribute to the collective happiness by avoiding any cause for sadness or boredom, by appearing to be always happy, even if in the depths of despair. By giving in to sadness, one infringes on the veil of happiness society desires to pull over its face. It seems that the modern attitude towards death, that is to say effacing death in order to preserve happiness, was born in the United States around the beginning of the twentieth century. Death and mourning have been medicalised, delegitimised, become a problem, a failure, an embarrassment, a disruption (Bauman, 1992).

Twentieth century attitudes towards the sight of the dead body are ambivalent: both denial and indulgence. In the register of the imaginary, the culture has a morbid penchant with dead bodies. News reports abound with images of mutilated, disfigured and tortured human bodies, and the genre of horror films is experiencing a nostalgic resurgence of vampire and Dracula films. In the register of the real, the culture sometimes protests a display of the dead body as being tasteless and insensitive. In a recent air crash of a plane heading to Kathmandu, the Nepalese authorities displayed the bodies of the 167 victims for the relatives to identify. This practice which is customary in Nepal aroused quite different feelings in Britain. The *Daily Telegraph* headed its news item with 'Sightseers queue to gaze at the remains of the Airbus victims. Nepal air crash relatives face parade of the dead' (1 October 1992). Meanwhile *The Times* headed its report with a more explicit 'Display of bodies provokes outrage' and quoted British diplomats who complained about 'the grotesque peep-show'.

In the register of the symbolic the culture betrays a preoccupation with death masked by acts that celebrate life. It created the 'health cult' and the perception of death as a shameful defeat, as an error of nature. As Bauman says 'death does not come now at the end of life: it is there from the start, calling for a constant vigil . . . Fighting death may stay meaningless but fighting the causes of dying turns into the meaning of life' (1992, p. 140). This health cult, however, represents the upmarket end of the social matrix. It coexists alongside a growing presence of a destructive drug culture.

From Ariès's survey of Western attitudes to death it emerges that the more society tries to deny death the more it returns to colonise its consciousness. From antiquity to the present death has gradually been constructed as less tame and more violent. It was expressed by concealing its face, ritualising mourning, and finally banishing it altogether from public sight. Strategies of defence included *denial, representations* (eleventh to eighteenth centuries), *aestheticising* (nineteenth century), *ignoring* and *attacking* (twentieth century).

All these strategies are currently evident to some extent. By far the most common is the strategy of denial. It is performed by creating a substitute that serves like a shield or a veil from the reality of finitude. It either denies its finality or defers it by inventing the 'beyond' or the concept of the mortal soul. Beauty is one such strategy. Death is ornamented in a way which disguises its original ugliness or horror. Beautification of death is found in solemn serene funeral services surrounded by hymns and flowers, and formally attired people whose every trace of crying or emotional upset are kept under the strictest check. Graves are adorned with flowers, with stylised tombstones and memorial sculptures. Making death beautiful is also found in a method that is enjoying a comeback in the UK and the US: embalment of the dead. That this strategy is gaining in popularity can be illustrated by an example from a recent feature in the *Observer*. It glamorises the practice by linking it with art ('The art of embalming'), and with a trendy image of an embalmer: young (25-year-old) and yuppie (with a mobile phone and a Porsche) whose lifetime ambition has been to 'work with the dead' (*Observer Magazine*, 28 November 1993). 'Most embalmers', reads another feature, 'see themselves as artists combining the steady hand of a surgeon, with an artist's eye for naturalness' (*Independent*, 7 January 1992). Another defence strategy – ignoring, pretending that death does not exist – characterises present-day norms of polite conversation and customs. The dying are shunned from sight to hospitals, cemeteries are tucked away out of sight, and the dying body in its natural state is typically seen only by those whose job it is to deal with it. The final strategy, attacking, marks the cult of high-tech medicine, and the research on ageing which constructs mortality as a pathology to be tackled. So much so that as Bauman puts it: 'people no longer die of mortality but of some identifiable cause'.

Thus it is possible to articulate a number of principles that explain attitudes towards death. One principle is that the civilising process yields to a dialectic. The more estranged people become from death, the more death turns from a familiar misfortune to a fearful intruder. The more they try to control it, the more they betray their obsession with it. And while denial is exercised on the level of the real, the repressed returns on the level of the imaginary. Both macabre eroticism and romantic excess were manifestations of the return of the repressed. What was not allowed in social conventions was expressed in imagination and phantasy. When emotions were suppressed the uncanny fear of death expressed itself in phantasies of the living dead, being buried alive, and the effaced boundaries between ecstasy of death and love. When emotions were unrestrained – as in the nineteenth century Romanticism – the fear of death expressed itself in the logic of fetishism: concealing the disturbing reality behind a mask of beauty, preserving the dead bodies (mummification), and indulging in ceremonial burials and memorials.

That the strategies of dealing with death are closely tied in with the European brand of a socio-emotional experience, the civilising process, can be appreciated by a brief glimpse of another culture whose mode of operation privileges the ambivalent over the unilateral. The Mexican culture, for example, produces a different set of sensibilities and of attitudes to death. Octavio Paz in *The Labyrinth of Solitude* (1967) contrasts the American and the Mexican way of life by highlighting the love of fairy-tales and detective stories of the Americans, compared with the love of myth and legend characteristic of the Mexicans. Americans, he says, negate aspects of reality that are not happy, while Mexicans are willing to contemplate horror. This explains the difference between the Mexican and American approach to the dead. (What is true for Americans is also true for the British, as Gorer's research (1965) revealed.) Death is not hidden away but is present in the fiestas, games, loves and thoughts. The Mexicans are familiar with death. They joke about it, caress it, celebrate it and are seduced by it. They face death with contempt, irony and nostalgia. Fascination with death is, for them, a gravitational force. The traditional feast of *The Day of the Dead* captures this complex attitude in all its nuances. This holiday, celebrated on the first and second of November combines Spanish and Indian origins. On this day the spirits return to dine with their living relatives. The graveyards turn into picnic grounds, the tombs are turned into tables, the food is laid on beds of flowers. The feast includes daily dishes such as beans, rice and fruit as well as specialities of the season. For the children there are candy skulls, pastry coffins, and bone shaped bread. Markets overflow with papier mâché skeletons depicted as performing various tasks. The mood is not melancholic but rather joyous (Brenner, 1970). The Mexican's dialectical attitude to life and death means that the two are inseparable: a concern with death marks passion for life 'a civilization that denies death ends by denying life' (Paz, 1967, p. 51). Life flows into death: its opposite and complement.

How can the changes in the affective structure with regard to death be explained by Elias's thesis of the civilising process? I will first review the civilising process (1939, Vols 1 and 2), before proceeding to apply it to the study of attitudes towards death. The principle of the civilising process is a correspondence between transformation of social structure and personality structure. The warrior culture of the Middle Ages (tenth to twelfth centuries) which was characterised by autarkic economy, and undeveloped division of labour and economic infrastructure, featured a high degree of instability and a low degree of interdependence between regions. Consequently, there was a low degree of regular drive control. The structure of society that favoured centralisation in the Age of Absolutism (seventeenth and eighteenth centuries) contrasts with the instability of the central authority characteristic of the feudal phase. The gradual formation of the Absolutist courtly society was accompanied by a transformation of the drive economy. The change in drive control and conduct that we call 'civilisation' is closely related to the growing interweaving and interdependence of people. The change from barter economy to money economy, the increase in the division of labour, the development of towns and of courts of the greatest feudal lords increased integration in a network of interdependencies. The state of the division of functions resulted in greater dependence of individuals on each other, and on the technical apparatus. Correspondingly, the pressures of court life, the necessity to distinguish oneself from others and to fight for opportunities (and the favour of the prince) with relatively peaceful means, through intrigue and diplomacy, enforced a constraint on the affects, a self-discipline and self-control. With the rise of the middle classes and the gradual displacement of the social and political centre of gravity from the court to the nation-states (since the mideighteenth century), the civilising process transformed the affect economy in a number of ways. First, as more constraints were placed on instinctual uninhibited behaviour the shame frontier advanced. Fear of social degradation – exposure to the superiority of others – was converted into individual anxiety, instilled as self-compulsion, whether in the form of modesty (embarrassment, shame, guilt), or a sense of humour. Second, alongside the social division of labour, the emotional private sphere emerged. The naked body and all its functions was relegated to the private and concealed. Instincts were privatised, suppressed from public life, enclosed in the nuclear family. Social prohibitions were internalised and became part of the affective and drive control even in private. Third, the civilising process changed patterns of pleasure. What had been suppressed (like the naked body) in the real became a signifier of wish-fulfilment. What was denied impulsive gratification was shifted to dreams and phantasies. Denial through socially instilled self-control of the urge to touch whatever the heart desired, meant that the eye took on a very specific significance: it became a mediator of pleasure. Active pleasure of touching had been transformed into the passive pleasure of looking. This last point corresponds to what Lowe (1982) describes as a shift in the hierarchy of sensing quite apart from the dynamics of the civilising process. According to Lowe, a transformation occurred from the chirographic medieval culture, based on the priority of hearing and touching, to a typographic Renaissance culture and photographic bourgeois culture based on the primacy of sight. These developments followed the technological advances of print culture and photographic culture which privilege the visual sense.

Elias's thesis provides a handle on understanding the development of attitudes towards death in Western culture. Two modes of dealing with death emerge which correlate with modes of affect control. When affect control is low, and people are in touch with their emotions, there is less need to defend against death in the imaginary and symbolic registers. Death is dealt with in the real. It does not have the dramatic quality that characterises the more controlled periods. For example in antiquity and the Middle Ages death was treated with resignation, almost indifference. In antiquity the dead were feared, therefore they were separated from the living and buried outside the town. In medieval times the dead were no longer feared but they became increasingly less visible. In contrast, in the nineteenth century Romanticism's indulgence in expressive emotions evidences dramatisation in the real, but also fear in the imaginary (such as the fear of apparent death). Why is there a difference between the attitudes to death in these two periods of similar patterns of affective control (the Middle Ages and Romanticism)? From Elias's model we might conclude that the degree of affect control in the nineteenth century was greater than in the tenth to the twelfth centuries, certainly from the point of view of interdependencies. But there is another difference between these two periods, and one which does not feature as prominently in Elias's theory. His theory deals more with the interrelations between structural transformations and personality transformations, and less with inter-relations between systems of thought and belief. Yet as Ariès makes clear, there is a fundamental difference between the sensibility of the Middle Ages and Romanticism. The Middle Ages mark the beginning of the notion of 'death of the self'. Romanticism, on the other hand, marks the beginning of the notion of 'death of the other'. Moreover, while the former is embedded in a sensibility which treats death with intimate familiarity, the latter is rooted in a sensibility which regards death as violation and intrusion. Consequently, the greater fear of death generated by the Romantic conception is translated into both sublimation and horror phantasies – both of which are absent from the medieval counterpart. And in periods where emotional control was operating – such as the Renaissance, Baroque and the Enlightenment – it was indeed accompanied by fears acted out as phantasies. In fact the civilising process is more complex than it seems. It is not just about self-restraint. It is about a dialectic process operating on simultaneous but conflicting levels. While growing restraint dominated one level of social consciousness, imagination dominated another.

The civilising process becomes even more complex when applied to women, both as subjects and as objects. As Elias himself points out the compulsion man placed on himself was less than that placed on his wife. Constraints were only exercised towards one's peers, less so towards social inferiors. And women were considered inferior in medieval society. The relationship between the sexes was based on power, and women's major function was seen as that of gratifying basic drives, providing physical pleasure and sensual satisfaction. The knights of the ninth and tenth centuries did not behave particularly delicately towards their own wives, or women of lower rank. Wife-beating and rape (inside or outside of marriage) was not uncommon. Women in the castles, especially when their husbands were away on battles, were constantly vulnerable to the advances of other men, familiar or passersby. At the same time women's own restraint was regulated and guarded by men. The pressures on the libidinal life of women throughout Western history, with the exception of the great absolutist courts, were considerably heavier on women than on men of equal birth (Elias 1939/1982, p. 82).

Indeed, as I discuss in Chapter 1, the pervasive image we have of the 'courtly love' tradition is the exception that proves the rule. It is only the relation of a socially inferior and dependent man to a woman of higher rank (troubadour to a lady) that leads to the restraint and consequent transformation of drives. Courtly love needs to be seen against the power structure characterising all the actors in the drama. It was not a paradigm of how men treated women at that time. Rather it reflected a minority élite behaviour. But it was a paradigm of what was to come. The troubadours were a special kind of knight. They were poor knights without land who placed themselves at the service of a greater knight.

According to Elias, just as in the course of the civilising process fears of physical attack are increasingly replaced by anxieties of social embarrassment, open expression of emotions was replaced with a ritualised acting out. Real battles were transformed into tournaments, and the desire to have the woman transformed into a desire in looking (Elias 1939/1982, pp. 121–2).

A similar principle emerges here as is operating in attitudes to death. With regard to death we saw that uninhibited emotions generated defences in the real. At the same time, repressed emotions generated phantasies in the imaginary. As for women, traditional fear of the woman in the pre-civilising process (up to the eleventh century) was expressed in medieval misogyny. But in the course of the gentrification of society the woman was transformed into a phantasy object of desire, an idolised spectacle. It is then that the gaze started playing a central part in her construction and self-conception (see Chapter 3).

The anxiety of loss and the defences against it

Having related the idealisation of the woman and death in the course of repression of emotions in the civilising process, I now want to examine my thesis of the woman as a defence against, and a symbol of death anxiety.

How can an object which defends against a fear represent that very fear? In order to see the connection between the two apparently contradictory concepts, it is helpful to examine the concept of a transitional object. Introduced by Winnicott (1953/1986), it refers to soft clingy objects of attachment (like a teddy bear or a blanket) that in the first year of life eases the transition from the symbolic union with the mother, to separation. It helps the child to ward off separation anxiety by creating an illusory substitute which re-establishes the symbiosis. It is this capacity to substitute the absent object (mother's breast) with an object which symbolises it which helps the child cope with the separation. It does so by creating an illusion of a union. This is how the capacity to symbolise is related to the capacity to separate (Barkin, 1978).

A transitional object may develop into an infantile fetish. In this it shares some characteristics with adult fetishism which is invoked to deal with castration anxiety. In both cases a reality of splitting and absence is denied by creating an illusion of unity and wholeness. The phantasy of unity is maintained at a price. Those instincts which cannot be gratified are then split off from their unity of the ego by the process of repression (Freud, 1920). This split runs through the fabric of our mental life.

The roots of castration anxiety are sexual, according to Freud. The anxiety refers to the discovery of the anatomical difference between the sexes. This gives rise to the phantasy that they both started out the same, but the girl has been castrated. The boy, in turn, fears a similar fate if paternal retaliation is provoked. According to Lacan castration anxiety refers to a linguistic concept. It is a metaphor for the process of entry into language and culture. It consists of two stages: in the mirror stage the child becomes aware of the difference between its own subjective experience of the world (which feels disjointed and uncoordinated) and its unified representation in the mirror. In the second stage upon entering language, the child is confronted with the gap between its subjective experience of itself and the linguistic categories available to her/him to encode this experience (Lacan, 1954/1991a; 1954/1991b; 1955/1991).

The loss of the symbolic fusion with the original object of desire – the pre-Oedipal mother – can never be recovered. It is paradise lost. After that, life is an unending search for this phantasy, and a choice of a series of stand-in substitutes. But they never really fill the lack. Later, in the Oedipal stage the child discovers the castrated mother and loses her again, this time to the father. The absence produced by the maternal lack is replaced with a fetish in the form of a part of her body or clothing – or with her idealisation. The function of the fetish is to adorn the woman with an object which stands in for the absent phallus.

The absence produced by death is replaced with the death mask, effigy or an embalmed body: an image. In her study of representations of woman as death Bronfen noted that 'the beauty of Woman and the beauty of the image both give the illusion of intactness and unity, the obliteration of death's ubiquitous "castrating" threat to the subject' (1992, p. 64). And Freud noted that the desire to preserve the ego by duplicating it (as in the literary theme of the 'double') is also at the root of the ancient Egyptian art of making images of the dead in lasting materials.

Metaphorically the phantasy of the pre-Oedipal mother has been used by cultural theorists to refer to every illusion of unity that protects against splitting and end. And the phantasy of castration refers to every act that threatens the unity of the imaginary whole subject with the real split subject. The connection between castration and death has been made by Freud. He regarded the fear of death, like the fear of conscience as a development of the fear of castration. He has specifically noted that the unconscious does not have representation of its own death and behaves as if it were immortal (Freud, 1923). Death is the most extreme form of castration (Freud, 1926). In the same way that the sight of the female body triggers male anxiety of castration, the sight of the dead body triggers anxiety of mortality. Both anxieties are glossed over by maintaining a phantasy of unity through transitional fetishistic objects.

Through the concept of the uncanny a psychoanalytically informed explanation draws together the anxieties provoked by the female body and the dead body. And by invoking the concept of fetishism an analogy is drawn between the means used to deflect these anxieties. The act of fetishism involves two processes: denial and compensation. It points to what is absent in the act of representing it. The castration-fetishist is disavowing the sight of lack by overvaluating an aspect of the threatening body (that is, a part of the body) or an item of clothing. Applied more broadly the concept is used in feminist theory (and in feminist film theory) to describe the commercialisation of the female body, its manufacturing along desirable lines, the beauty cult and the glamorisation of the film stars. The mortality-fetishist denies the lack by filling it with art. It involves such practices as dressing and embalming the dead but also cremating, staging funerals as 'cultural events' with music and flowers and formal clothes, restraint and decorum, turning cemeteries into flower and sculpture gardens, and creating representation and memorial monuments. At the same time as denying death, the mortality-fetishist is also engaged in practices designed to combat mortality (health regimes, research on ageing) and signs of ageing (cosmetic surgery, workout, diet).

Woman and death share many characteristics. They are both mysterious, ambiguous, unrepresentable, silent and threatening man's sense of wholeness and stability. Both are the eternal Other: a metaphor of disruption and transgression. As men's Other they come to symbolise everything that is desirable but forbidden (the forbidden fruit), compelling and repulsive (desire and disgust), beauty and the beast. They are wild and tame, excessive and disruptive, material and mythic, erotic and dangerous, objects of curiosity to be explored and controlled. In the golden age, male humans lived among the gods. Death and woman sprang up at the same time (in the figure of the first woman). The alignment of death and beauty in the figure of the woman is found in many mythical figures: from Medusa, Pandora and the sirens, through demonic Lilith and temptress Eve (see Chapter 1). The beautiful deadly woman is also common in representations which depict the woman in an image of Venus (the archetypal beautiful, seductive and vengeful woman), holding a mirror and perhaps arranging her hair (the Lorelei, and the mermaid with a comb and glass are versions of her) (Hollander, 1975/1980, p. 400). The deadly beautiful woman is also found in folk-tales. Some of those female characters are inherently beautiful (like Snow White's stepmother), others – like the witches – are inherently ugly but can disguise themselves as beautiful. But all of them use their beauty as a deceptive device. Their beauty is a strategy of seduction luring the man to his destruction. Even in Mexico where the attitude to death is so different from the West, woman is still the signifier of death. In the words of Leonardo Linares, an artist who makes representations of death for *The Day of the Dead*: 'We think of La muerte (death) as a woman. We give her a form, a presence. You can be married, you can be single, but she'll have you in the end. Death will be my last love' (from an exhibition on *The Day of the Dead* at the Museum of Mankind in London).

By the same logic in which woman is equivalent to death, beauty is equivalent to some death rituals. One can easily note that many beauty procedures that are targeted at women (for example, make-up and plastic surgery) share similar features with some funerary rituals (death mask and embalment). In both cases the mask of permanence replaces undesirable temporality while drawing attention to it. Make-up serves two opposite functions. For teenagers it is a way of putting on the signs of adulthood. For the older woman, it is a way of holding on to the signs of youth. In both cases the desire is to lend the living individualised face an idealised timeless mask of beauty. This procedure captures the spirit of the making of death masks practised widely around the fifteenth and the sixteenth centuries. Unlike stylised effigies which reflected the deceased 'social face', death masks were introduced to eternalise a signature of individuality by replicating the deceased 'physical face'. Paradoxically, 'reproducing the features of death was the best way to imitate life' (Aries, 1977/1981, p. 262).

Cosmetic surgery is another example. I have recently observed a documentary of the cosmetic procedure of facelift. The ritual bears a striking resemblance to rituals of mummification. The purpose might appear different in both cases. The facelift is intended for the here and now and mummification is for the beyond. But the desires – to defy mortality and to arrest its visible signs – are similar. And both seek to inscribe the natural body with a cultural stamp. Even the procedures share some similarities: in both of them incisions to the outer skin are made in order to create a more appealing appearance of the outer skin. In the process of mummification the internal organs were removed through an abdominal incision and the body cavity was filled with crushed spices and sewn up again. To recreate the facial features and to preserve the body tissues material was packed under the skin through a series of small incisions made in its surface.

Thus similar treatment of the body signifies seemingly contradictory attitudes: refusal/denial of death – as in modern culture – and its affirmation – as in ancient culture. As we shall see later, they are two faces of the same coin.

The mummy and the enigma of the woman

On 10 June 1975 a large expert team of researchers completed an extensive investigation of 17 human and 22 animal mummies in the Egyptology collection at Manchester Museum. The investigation – carried out by an expert team from the Manchester University medical school – came to a climax with the unwrapping of a mummy. The research was described by the Egyptologist who headed the team in a book entitled *Mysteries of the Mummies* (David, 1978). The project had two aims: first, to find out information about religious and funerary customs, living conditions, the state of physical and dental health, and the process of mummification in ancient objects. Second, to subject the body to the latest radiological, and other post mortem techniques, as well as Carbon-14 and dating methods in order to establish the cause of death, and to date the bones and wrappings. The idea of unwrapping a mummy to satisfy scientific curiosity created some objections. It clashed with the desire to preserve an item of depleting stock of national heritage. It also interfered with the intentions of those who had preserved the body for the after-life, and as such could have been regarded as an act of desecration.

The narrative structure of the report sounds like an adventure book as the following extracts illustrate:

> With the team assembled the next task was to persuade the Museum authorities to allow the unwrapping of a mummy . . . (p. 86)

> The next task was to choose a suitable mummy . . . a mummy with something of a mystery surrounding it would clearly be a very suitable choice . . . (p. 87)

> A suitable room had to be found for the unwrapping, one large enough to give the team an adequate amount of space in which to work and one which would accommodate the large amounts of people who were involved in the project . . . space had to be found for the press and television cameras, for the unwrapping . . . was rapidly becoming newsworthy . . . (p. 88)

> All the preparations being complete, it was an expectant team which gathered under the glare of the arc lights, before a large audience, for the start of the unwrapping . . . (p. 88)

> . . . in the operating theatre at Manchester University medical school, the rapt attention of a large and expectant audience was focused on a group of green-gowned figures clustered round the operating table. The TV lights picked them out with brilliant clarity. An operation was about to begin. But this was no ordinary operation for the 'patient' was already dead. Dead and indeed buried. (p. 7)

Two mysteries surrounded the chosen mummy: first, the lower part of its legs were missing. Second, its gender identity was not established, but there were certain indications that the mummy of a 13-year-old child was of a woman. And although the evidence remained inconclusive, the cover of the book positions it within a particular symbolic cultural juncture. The cover features a picture of three masked medical experts from the investigative team in an operating theatre gear and pose. At the top corner there is a smaller framed portrait of a beautiful Egyptian princess embodying a phantasy of what the mummy might have looked like in real life. The book's title – *Mysteries of the Mummies* – set in big print just opposite the picture creates a graphic and conceptual unity. The mystery ceases to be that of the mummy alone, but is extended to the woman, not a real woman, but the idea of a woman.

I dwell on this example because it provides a link between the conflicting cultural constructs I wish to explore: woman, death and beauty. Constructed as an account of adventure, the mummy whose mystery was to be explored was most probably a woman; the woman whose enigmatic characteristic is one of her defining features in Western cultures. Another part of the mystery is death, her twin enigma. The mummy defies death to some extent due to its timeless preservation of the state in which it was arrested. It enables modern scientists thousands of years later to satisfy a number of desires at once: scientific curiosity about disease, technological mastery over an ancient but awesome relic of nature and faith, as well as the erotic fascination that is contained in the excitement of unveiling and undressing. The voyage of discovery metaphor appropriately underlies the fact that the woman, whom Freud once referred to as the dark continent and the secret of life, is still shrouded in mystery.

The mummy-woman (whose gender identity is more an assumption than a certainty) and death (which already claimed her body) are both in some sense outside the control of even the most sophisticated scientific procedures. Yet in another way they are caught up as a spectacle in the gaze of scientists, audience and television lights. Both woman and dead body become objects of a voyeuristic gaze and curious fascination.

On another level, the research team was concerned with imposing a set of modern values on the mummy as a symbol of a set of beliefs in an afterlife. Because the very act of unwrapping the mummy functions as a cultural sign. It represents the control, or the attempt to control a mystery of nature, by products of the human mind. And every representation, as Freud noted, is a cannibalistic discourse. It effaces the represented object with something that replaces it. In some ways the various coverings of the mummy, and its anthropoid coffin stand in for the person inside.

Finally, the results of the investigation are like a fetishistic enactment of the castration phantasy. Fetishism is a defence strategy employed to preserve the phantasy of the phallic (pre-Oedipal) mother, and to dissimulate the phantasy of castration. Both can be traced to the ambivalent attitudes towards the protective mother. The maternal body combines the phallic (phantasy of wholeness and union) with the castrated (reality of lack and split). Thus her body is the site of ambivalence: comfort (unity) on the one hand, death (separation anxiety and castration anxiety) on the other. Due to the ambivalence inherent in her function, the mother encodes both confirmation and denial. The child soon learns that some instinctual wishes (such as the desire of the mother) are incompatible with others (such as the father's desire), or with society's incestual taboos.

And just as undressing is more arousing than nakedness because it upholds the phantasy (of the pre-Oedipal wholeness), the preparation for the investigation of the mummy at Manchester University, and the process of unwrapping the covering turned out to be more exciting than the findings. The findings actually reveal the reality of lack. In the words of Rosalie David 'they gave rise to certain deductions and much speculation' (1978, p. 92).

The aesthetisation of death and the beautification of the living are defensive strategies. They are designed to protect the person from realisation of some lack by creating an illusion of wholeness and immortality. Death is the lack or cut in the physical and the social body, while castration is a lack that creates the awareness of sexual difference. In a sense both death rituals and feminine beauty function like a symptom. A neurotic symptom is formed out of failure of the pleasure principle. It develops when antagonistic desires are gratified by one and the same act. It hides a conflict between libidinal wishes and the ego (for example, loss of maternal object and threat of paternal retaliation) simultaneously denying and affirming. It articulates as it hides. The protection of the ego works in two ways: defies the castrative laws of culture (which demand renunciation of primal desires and aggressions). It also defies the mortal laws of the real (with images, objects and narratives). One such strategy to ensure preservation against extinction of the ego is by multiplication of the self. (In art and in dreams it appears in the form of multiplying the genital symbol. This, by replacement through opposites represents castration.) Another strategy is simply to live vicariously and safely through imaginary egos: to die with one fictional hero, and die again with another (Freud, 1915b).

But the position of the woman is even more complex: first, constituted as a symptom she is doubly inscribed as death. She is a signifier for it (lack, castration) and her beauty is a veil for it (the illusion of wholeness lost to the infant, regained to the fetishist). This paradox is best illustrated by the religious requirement of muslim woman to veil herself in public. The veil is not required to protect her. Rather it protects the man from *her* sexuality and *his* inability to control his own. Here, female attractiveness is literally and metaphorically defended against with the veil (Mernissi, 1987). The veil has both erotic connotations and chaste ones. It hides and it reveals, and it reveals as it hides.

Freud articulated another way in which female beauty simultaneously represents and defends against death. First, in *On the Theme of the Three Caskets* (1913), he relies on evidence from folk and myth of all early cultures where fate is conceived as three women controlling destiny and necessity, life and death. The fates were often engaged in spinning and cloth making. The Greeks personified the fates as Clotho (spinner), Lachesis (disposer of the lots) and Atropos (inevitable), who, with an inversion of the common female activity of weaving, cut the thread of life. Freud observed a common motif where the protagonist is faced with the choice of one of three women (sometimes sisters). The typical choice of the youngest, loveliest and quietest of the three often coincided with the choice of death. Applying the technique of dream analysis, in particular replacement by opposite, he deduced that the youngest, fairest and loveliest was the goddess of death represented as the goddess of love. Thus death is replaced with its contrary, beauty, while the passive submission to the inevitability of the fate of death is replaced with choice. The function of beauty on this account is to lend an illusion of choice to the inevitable.

Second, beauty itself has an elusive quality and as Freud pointed out in *On Transience* 'the idea that all this beauty was transient [gives] a foretaste of mourning . . . and since the mind instinctively recoils from anything that is painful . . . enjoyment of beauty interfered with by thoughts of its transience' (1916, p. 306). 'The creation of beauty allows us to escape from the elusiveness of the maternal world into an illusion of eternity (a denial of loss), even as it imposes on us the realisation that beauty is itself elusive, intangible, receding' (Bronfen, 1992, p. 64).

If the cultivation of beauty and fashion signifies, on one level, the vanity of the living which defies death, on another level it signifies death itself, because signification is always simultaneously denying while highlighting that which it signifies. This dual signification is amplified in the case of the woman. Fashionable woman represents both an affront to death (which is at the heart of fashion) and a destructive temptation (which is at the heart of Woman). The artist Bianka Eshel-Gershuni creates images of womanhood out of materials of beautiful, romantic Kitsch. These images, however, are underlined by themes of pain and suffering. Severed heads, dead animals, and funerary artefacts are arrayed alongside colourful flowers, golden bits of jewellery, and images of dolls and angels. Apart from the ambivalence inherent in flowers which signify both life and death (especially artificial flowers which she uses), sometimes a perfectly serene and innocent beauty bears only traces of death, like the piece entitled 'Everything contains at least an eighth of death'. This inevitability of some kind of identity (beyond the signifying one) between woman and death is echoed in 'The dialogue of fashion and death', where the nineteenth century philosopher Giacomo Leopardi describes how fashion brags of the way she afflicted humankind with sacrificial pains. In the dialogue, fashion reminds death that they are both daughters of decay, and both aim to destroy and change all things albeit by different methods. Fashion's way is 'to cripple people with narrow boots; to choke their breath and make their eyeballs pop with the use of tight corsets' and in general to 'persuade and force all civilized people to put up every day with a thousand difficulties and a thousand discomforts, and often with pain and agony, and some even to die gloriously, for the love they bear me' (1827/1983, p. 51). But her greatest achievement she considers, is to transform life itself into some kind of death.

> And whereas in ancient times you had no other farmlands but graves and caverns, where in the darkness you sowed bones and dust, seeds that bear no

fruit; now you have estates in the sunlight; and people who move and go about on their own feet are, so to speak, your property and at your disposal from the moment they are born, although you have not yet harvested them. (1827/ 1983, p. 53)

Perhaps fashion's real victory is not just to transform life to death but to make the people who practise this believe that they are choosing life. A case in point is the recent popularity of tattooing (Sanders, 1989) and piercing. The current craze is not practised as a tribal sign of belonging, but as an individual sign of celebrating identity and claiming the body. Interviewed in a TV documentary *Feminism in the 90s* (Channel 4, July 1994) one woman adorned with pierced ears, nose, tongue, lip, nipples and navel, and a large tattoo on her hip and shoulder, said that for her piercing and tattooing was not about masochism and suffering, but about self-expression through wearing artwork and stating control over her body: 'You are making a conscious choice of adding something to what you were born with which you had no control over'. She added that 'the navel piercing was to celebrate being flat again having given birth to my daughter'. And a woman who does body piercing explained that this motivation is not uncommon, and that she has pierced women's nipples after they breastfed as a kind of symbolic act of taking back that part of the body they have given to their child.

Note

This chapter is based on papers presented at two conferences: Death, Dying and Disposal, Oxford, April 1993; and the British Psychological Society, London, December 1993.

6
POSTMODERNISM AND THE CLOTHED MEANING

A punky icon, with bright yellow and fuchsia coloured hair, enclosed in an academic gown during the Oxford degree ceremony, July 1994. End of meaning, or tongue in cheek statement?

There is nothing new about a woman submitting her face and/or body to the sculpting hands of a cosmetic surgeon. An advert for a cosmetic surgeon Keith Wahl in San Diego shows a surgeon in operating theatre uniform holding a framed picture. In the picture a model poses in a bikini in a clothes shop. She is reflected in mirrors giving a multiple image of her from three different angles. The text refers to cosmetic surgery as to a work of art, and urges the audience to choose '*the* artist'. The small print says 'cosmetic surgery requires a portrait painter's eye, an engraver's precision and a sculptor's touch'. Such advertisements are standardly used to argue the case of patriarchal culture reshaping the woman to fit its narrowly defined moulds. (Ironically, the surgeon refused to grant me permission to reproduce his advertisement here.)

But there is something new when the artist is the patient instead of the doctor. An art video recently made shows Orlan, a French performance artist and professor of fine arts, during her cosmetic surgery. The operation, the first in a series of 16 is designed to transform her into a self-made self-portrait combining such features as the chin of Venus and the brows of Mona Lisa. In a television interview (*Eurotrash*, Channel 4, September 1993) Orlan explains that she mixed some images from mythology together with her own face on the computer, until she came up with the image she wanted for herself. For her, the work is no different from traditional work on self-portrait. 'My idea was not to become more beautiful, or to look younger. I just wanted to change my face to a completely different image' she says. And she explains the difference between her and women who commonly use the services of cosmetic surgery. According to her, by reshaping herself she is not submitting to the pressures of society. Rather, she is actually breaking free from tradition: 'It's a case of art and life taken to the extremes. In the art world women have always been seen just as objects or models. In my case I am really using my body as my material. I am the one who is completely in charge.'

A similar challenge to the victimisation view of various aspects of women's appearance comes from the new veiling movement in Cairo. Caught up between cultural colonialism of Western values and traditional patriarchal values, educated, working and modern middle-class women started a movement 'to abandon Western clothes in favour of some form of covered Islamic dress' (MacLeod, 1992). Despite its traditional appearance, the new veiling has new connotations. It represents a voluntary choice, not a form of dress imposed on the woman against her will. Using a complex reading of the Gramscian hegemonic relations, MacLeod views the new veil as a space where ideological positions compete, rather than as a sign of ideological domination. The struggle indicates the dilemma faced by modern Islamic women regarding their role and identity:

> I argue that women, even as subordinate players, always play an active part that goes beyond the dichotomy of victimization/acceptance, a dichotomy that flattens out a complex and ambiguous agency in which women accept, accommodate, ignore, resist, or protest – sometime all at the same time. (MacLeod, 1992, p. 534)

What is common to both examples I have opened with is the claim of a new meaning for old symbols. Both subvert traditional meaning assigned to traditional cultural signs. Both illustrate the notion that the dress or appearance code is not an overdetermined language. Rather, it is a dynamic site of struggle for control of the power to define selves and situations. And both can be said to represent postmodern fashion. One of the hallmarks of postmodernity, or late Capitalism, is according to social theorists, a preoccupation with a refashioning of personal identities out of cultural materials (Gergen, 1991; Giddens, 1991). The essence of this process is the inventive use that is made of the cultural materials. Features are borrowed from one context and appropriated into another together with a whole new set of meanings, and style becomes a substitute for identity. Jameson (1984) defines this process as pastiche. One of the first social theorists to link dress with identity, Gregory Stone, defined dress as a mode of identification, by which the person 'announces his identity, shows his value, expresses his mood, or proposes his attitude' (1962).

Sartorial gender coding

An examination of the development of sartorial gender signification reveals a consensus between fashion theorists (for example, Flügel, 1930/1971; Bell, 1947/1992; Davis, 1988) about the sartorial revolution at the end of the eighteenth century that overturned the traditional relationship between power and splendour.

In her analysis of fashion, costume historian Lois Banner (1992) notes that from the eleventh to the nineteenth centuries in late medieval and early modern Europe young male bodies were just as much eroticised as female ones. This was evidenced from the elongated pointed shoes of the eleventh century, through the short jackets and leggings of the fourteenth century which featured a codpiece designed to protect while drawing attention to the genitals. It was also evidenced in 'feminised' features of garments from the sixteenth to the eighteenth centuries in the form of petticoat-like breeches, powdered wigs, coats of velvet and satin, embroidered and trimmed with gold or silver lace, shoes and hats decorated with ribbons. In fact, as Bradley (1922) points out in his treatise on the philosophy of clothes, it was the men, more than the women who were the fashionable, eroticised sex. And he puts forward the idea that female fashions were always the antithesis of male ones: 'Woman displayed no originality or individuality in her costume; she was content to adapt her dress from the existing fashions of the man' (1922, p. 96). For example, the revolution in male dress in the fourteenth century – where the loose wrapping was discarded in favour of a short tunic over body-tight garments and a codpiece fastened with ribbon – had no female counterpart. Rather the opposite. In the 'subtle intuition of the allurement of the antithesis' the woman draped herself in voluminous skirts and hid her feet. The 'age of style' of the seventeenth century was marked by a graceful male fashion, while female fashion was neither as graceful, nor as extravagant as man's. It was inclined towards greater simplicity. The 'age of design' of the eighteenth century found the lady 'unable to keep pace with the elegance of the gentleman of the period'. 'In the history of any civilised nation' Bradley notes 'the story of its development in art, dress, and manners forms a truer record of its progress than a dreary catalogue of its wars, pestilences, and famines' (1922, p. 41).

It is in this spirit that I proceed to examine the revolution in dress that marks the end of the eighteenth century and the beginning of the nineteenth century. Flügel, writing on *The Psychology of Clothes* (1930/ 1971) summarises the difference between the fashion of the sexes in the following manner:

> From the fall of the Roman Empire to the end of the eighteenth century, there was little to choose between the decorativeness of the two sexes, except perhaps that, whatever style of dress was in vogue, the skirt always conferred a certain dignity that was lacking from the bifurcated nether garments of men. (p. 106)

Then, towards the end of the Middle Ages the introduction of the décolleté established a difference in the male and female principle of attraction. While man 'continued to stake all his attractiveness upon his clothing', the woman used exposure and concealment. And while man symbolised his genital libido in his clothes, the woman symbolised her more diffuse libido, where the whole body is sexualised, in other parts as well. For example, as early as the fourteenth century she realised the asset of her hair and adorned it in elaborate modes and arranged it in bags of gold nets studded with precious stones. In the fifteenth century she played with her head-dress and crowned it with horns some 30 inches from end to end, covered with gold tissue and coloured draperies. Towards the end of the seventeenth century her hair towered to such heights that it needed to be arranged on a frame and was likened to a steeple – trimmed with lace and ribbons. By the mid-eighteenth century, women's hair rose to new heights, and a scented paste was needed to hold the increasingly tall construction of hair (including false) and feathers together.

And just as the woman mastered the use of erotic exposure, a sartorial revolution in male dress occurred. In what Flügel terms 'the great masculine renunciation' man gave up his right for beauty and ornamentation in dress: 'Men's fashions, splendid as they had been before, rose, during the eighteenth century, to an apex of perfection, only to crash during the next century to a level of ugliness never before conceived in history' (Bradley, 1922, p. 196). At the same time occurred what Bradley calls 'the female revolution in dress'. For centuries, however elaborate, fantastic or grotesque she was, artistically she failed to vie with man:

> Almost to the beginning of the nineteenth century woman's inventive powers were dormant. She simply adapted or elaborated man's designs. Man puffed out his shoulders and bagged his breeches; woman swelled her sleeves and hooped her skirt. Thus throughout the ages she copied her lord and master, but never attaining his grace nor his symmetry and form. (1922, p. 192)

During the nineteenth century, as Veblen (1899/1912) showed us, woman's decorativeness was one aspect of conspicuous consumption which conferred status on her husband. Like Nora in Ibsen's *A Doll's House* her role was to be as much an ornamental asset as a chaste wife and a devoted mother. In the graceful simplicity of the Empire gown Bradley sees the beginning of 'the woman's emancipation in dress'. From 'towering absurdity' she moved to 'a height of simplicity'. The sleeping beauty, awakened from a centuries-old sleep leaped ahead, and her creativity soon outstripped man's. A Paris couturier once said that modern woman's freedom in dress owes much to Isadora Duncan. Isadora's free spirit ushered in the modern expressive dance inspired by the Greek ideals of beauty and simplicity. She also introduced the flowing, unconstrained tunics worn over bare arms and barefoot legs. Her ideals of personal liberty, free love and freedom of bodily movements were ahead of her time and earned her much criticism. It was Simmel who observed that individualisation in dress is related to power, and that fashion served a peculiar function for women. Because of her lack of power, fashion served as a valve through which woman's desire for some conspicuousness and individual prominence finds an outlet, when its satisfaction is denied her in other fields (1904/1957).

The case of postmodern fashion

In the first five chapters I presented various kinds of evidence for a relationship between essence and appearance. In terms of a semiotic language I showed a link between male notions of female *essence*, and their translation into *appearance* expectations. It has been suggested by fashion theorists (such as Davis, 1988; Evans and Thornton, 1991) that postmodern fashion is characterised by ambivalence, fragmentation and freedom from signification. In other words, that postmodern fashion does not mean anything other than itself. Other theorists like Wilson criticised the simplified notion that views postmodern fashion as characterised by fragmentation and loss of identity, as well as freedom to choose one's identity through inventing a series of appearance identities: 'Just as we oversimplify if we see Victorian women's fashions as *only* operating to restrict women, so we are equally mistaken if we see the rise of twentieth-century fashion as representing *only* increased freedom and liberation' (1992, p. 10).

If this is the case, one may further ask if it still makes sense to talk about a connection between a *construction* of the woman and a *presentation* of the woman. To some extent this is an open question. However, in the remainder of this chapter I would like to go some way towards addressing the broader question of whether postmodernity marks the end of signification in fashion in its traditional sense. To this end I will explore, through a historical analysis, whether as Baudrillard argues, postmodern fashion is a carnival of signs with no meanings attached to them, or whether it falls prey to its own rhetoric.

A historical analysis of the signification of dress

Dress is a form of social control and social categorisation. Throughout European history it was a way of defining people's roles, status and gender; a mechanism of inclusion as well as exclusion. It drew demarcation lines along social hierarchies and moral roles. The respectable woman was distinguished from the prostitute, the man from the woman, the noble from the peasant. Up until the seventeenth century there were certain forms of organised control through legislation. The laws of apparel were not really enforced, except with regard to the most vulnerable members (such as prostitutes or Jews). But their importance is in the fact that they provide signposts for values that were at stake and required state regulation (Harte, 1976).

Clothes have mirrored social hierarchy, sexual division and moral boundaries. Hierarchy was regulated by how scarcity of materials determined their use in each class. From the Greek and Roman periods, through Byzantine and medieval eras, but particularly since the fourteenth century which marks the beginning of fashion (for example, Laver, 1969/1985; Wilson, 1985), the costliness of materials or workmanship involved in the production of garments distinguished courtly from common. Throughout the history of dress it was the principle of scarcity of resources which symbolised rank in dress. Natural scarcity provided 'guarantee of exclusivity' (Goffman, 1951). Scarcity took either the form of rarity in nature (as in the case of the furs of certain animals, or of gold and precious stones), or in the man-made resources (as in the case of silk which up to the fifteenth century was imported from the East). All the above meant that economic constraints effectively guarded the social order since those expensive materials were only within reach of the nobility. Servants and workmen wore more wool, no silk or dyed cloth, and less ornamentation than their masters (Black and Garland, 1975). Coarse and common furs were used by the lower classes, while finer, smaller and more rare ones were worn by the wealthy (Ewing, 1981). Sexual division in dress was regulated by distinctly different styles for each sex. Moral boundaries defined the difference between a respectable and unrespectable woman, married or single. For example, in Roman times prostitutes were marked by fancy and ornamented clothes, and in Victorian times married women were allowed greater licence to expose their skin than unmarried women.

An examination of the symbolic aspect of dress within a historical context (see also Tseëlon 1992c, 1994), shows it to fall into three major stages: classical, modern and postmodern.

Classical stage

In the fourteenth century the expansion of trade, and the prosperity of the wool and weaving industries made previously expensive materials available to the emerging urban middle classes. This development threatened to blur and to break down the hierarchical society of feudal times. In the Middle Ages where class order was rigid and appeared ordained, dress reflected the God-given subordination of the lower orders to their superiors. As long as the class system was stable and undisturbed there were few fashion changes among the lower classes. The system was challenged when 'the urban patricians began to manoeuvre into positions of equality with the old feudal nobility' (König, 1973, p. 111), and more so since the end of royal absolutism (in the French Revolution) (König, 1973, pp. 139–45). A petition to King Edward III from the House of Commons complaining that common men had begun to wear fabrics which did not fit their rank or income resulted in the legislation of the first Sumptuary law defining precisely the type and quality of fabrics which could be worn by various classes. Similar laws continued to be passed until the sixteenth century with severity but little success. The Sumptuary laws which attempted to regulate clothing practices along status lines, did not relate to style since rank was manifested in the quality of fabric, in the details and the choice of decoration rather than in different styles (Baldwin, 1926; Harte, 1976).

Up to the fourteenth century the shape of the garments remained almost unchanged. It was in the second half of the fourteenth century that clothes began to take on new forms. Since styles were not sanctioned by law, servants imitated their masters in dress and manners. After 1600 when the nobility began to allow its servants to follow the fashion more closely it became impossible to tell 'who was the mistress and who was the maid' (de Marly, 1986, p. 41). But if styles were not a class marker, the aristocracy could only distinguish itself by the speed with which it adopted new styles. A cycle of differentiation and emulation developed. The wealthy were the first to take on the new styles. The lower classes who could not afford them, caught up with them only later, in less luxurious materials, or with cast-off garments from their masters. As soon as the new style was copied by the lower classes, the upper classes adopted a new one (Simmel, 1904/1957).

Modern stage

Industrial capitalism was marked by technological developments such as the invention of the sewing machine and wash-proof dyes. These developments democratised fashion by reducing the price of materials and making coloured fabrics (once an aristocratic preserve) available to the mass market. The Industrial Revolution created the modern city, the mass society, the anonymity and the distinction between public and private zones unknown in the Middle Ages (Elias, 1939/1982). This separation between the public and the private spheres resulted, in turn, in a distinction between a private self and public personae, and in a need to keep the private self secret behind an 'art of dissimulation and disguise' (Wilson, 1985). Technological advances increased mobility and pace of life and multiplied social roles. A new order was created in which work rather than lineage determined status. At the workplace rank was denoted by uniforms, and outside work dress took on other signifying roles. Fashion kept pace with the increasingly fragmented multi-role life of the bourgeoisie. It defined time of day (daywear, eveningwear), type of activity (work, leisure), type of occasion (formal, informal), gender – even an individual mood (Black and Garland, 1975).

These developments threatened the traditional social order. They gave rise to an alternative, more subtle system of demarcation. In an attempt to distinguish the aristocracy by lineage from the nouveaux-riches, this system grounded certain sartorial practices in moral values. This ethical code of Noblesse Oblige was encapsulated, for example, in the concept of *gentility*, developed in the nineteenth century by the landed gentry to distinguish the *genuine* from the *pretend*. This code held that to be a *lady* was a standard of conduct which included rules of etiquette, elegance and subtlety which 'those of birth and education learned to discriminate between good taste and sham' (Steele, 1985, p. 139). Bright tints and clashing combinations were considered vulgar due to their breach of certain rules of harmony and propriety. Such sensibility frames, for example, Bernard Shaw's flower girl in *Pygmalion*. Eliza Doolittle who comes to discuss her elocution lessons with Professor Higgins, turns up for a morning appointment clad in her best clothes, and wearing a hat decorated with a garish combination of orange, sky-blue and red ostrich feathers: 'The knowledge of . . . manners, language, and dress, became an artificial dividing-line, separating the Ins from the Outs' (Steele, 1988, p. 93).

Postmodern stage

Postmodernism appeared to reflect a radical break with the dominant culture and aesthetics (Back, 1985). In architecture, where it has been most acutely addressed it represented romantic subjectivity, plurality of forms, fragmentation of styles, diffuse boundaries. Thus it substituted disunity, subjectivity and ambiguity, for the modernist unity, absolutism and certainty (Jencks, 1978). In the sciences it was evidenced in a Western *crisis in representation*, its authority and its universal claims. This challenge to the *correspondence theory of truth* resulted in replacing the *master narratives* which mirror the world, with a plurality of *narrative truths* which reflect, instead, the conventions of discourse (Owens, 1983; Lyotard, 1984). The postmodern cultural shift has left its mark on the fashion world through its rejection of tradition, its relaxation of norms, and its emphasis on individual diversity, and the variability of styles (Back, 1985), resulting in diminishing shared agreed meanings of styles (Tseëlon, 1989).

Fashion and postmodern simulation

In structural linguistics meaning is carried out through a system of signs. According to de Saussure the meaning of signs is made up of two elements: *signifiers* (sound-images) which index the *signifieds* (concepts) (1916/1959). The structural linguistics of de Saussure is based on two principles: a principle of depth and a principle of surface. The metaphysics of depth refers to meaning as based on the link between the signified which underlies the signifier (for example, in fashion imagery, the colour pink stands for the feminine). A principle of surface implies a relational concept of meaning. It is the notion that signs do not have inherent meaning but gain their meaning through their relation to other signs (for example, in fashion the 'soft' gains meaning against the 'severe', the 'elaborate' against the 'austere', and the 'feminine' against the 'masculine'; cf. Barthes, 1967/ 1983).

For Baudrillard the meaning of clothes is a transition from a semiology where meaning resides in 'natural' signs, through a semiology where meaning resides in arbitrary (structuralist) signs, to a new (post-structuralist) semiology where signs transcend meaning. It is a change from *dress* whose function is to regulate ceremonial distance between bodies – that is, to create discrimination from nature – to *fashion* which creates social distinctions – to *post-fashion* which is 'a deconstruction of both the form of the sign of fashion and the principle of signification itself' (1976/ 1993, p. 133).

According to Baudrillard, in primitive societies the presentation of signs is linked to the symbolic order. Rituals of conspicuous waste such as the potlatch serve to reaffirm the social order. In modernity, excess of signs is linked to the referential order. It is an arbitrary and aesthetic spectacle whose function is ornamental as well as representational. It mirrors the social order. In postmodernity, the transgression of signs is linked to pure pleasure: 'the passion for futility and the artificial . . . plays the role of transgression and violence, and fashion is condemned for having within it the force of the pure sign which signifies nothing' (1976/1993, p. 129).

In his *orders of simulacra* Baudrillard (1983) identified three orders of sign value. The first order, that of *imitation* characterising the classical period, presupposes dualism where appearances disguise reality. In the second order, *production*, appearances create an illusion of reality. In the third order, *simulation*, appearances invent reality. No longer concerned with the real, images are reproduced from a model. And it is this lack of a reference point which threatens the distinction between true and false. It is a reality captured by the following lines from a recent article in the *Independent on Sunday* about MTV (music video): 'Rock videos give you a sense that you could switch off the real world with your TV remote control: reality is just another channel' (6 January 1991, p. 8).

Baudrillard's tripartite model can be superimposed on the stages of development of sartorial signification that I identified above. Analysis of the three stages of sartorial representation in terms of signification relations produces the following model:

- *classical stage*: direct signifier–signified links (Baudrillard's order of imitation).
- *modern stage*: indirect signifier–signified links (Baudrillard's order of production).
- *postmodern stage*: signifier–signifier links (Baudrillard's order of simulation).

The first order of simulacra (*imitation*) which characterises the classical stage is based on the religious belief in transcendental value (Sennett, 1977). In sartorial terms, clothes would be seen to reflect the order of nature without ambiguity. Thus, for example, medieval dress recreated the social order by assigning the more elaborate and rich garments to the élite. The second order of simulacra (*production*) characterises the (industrial) modern stage. Its shift to secularism is based on a code of the immanent rather than the transcendent. Thus according to Sennett, Victorians believed appearances to have personal meaning that can be revealed involuntarily. Therefore their desire was to disclose as little as possible through their own (while learning as much as possible about others). At the same time the onset of machine production made available mass-produced clothes, and encouraged a taste for anonymity in cosmopolitan life: 'and behind uniform fronts the road was open to create illusions' (Sennett, 1977, p. 176). The cosmopolitan city was a world in which physical appearance had no certainty. For this reason it became important to establish whether people unduly transform economic achievement into the social category of a 'gentleman', and whether a respectable looking woman was not in fact 'loose'. Thus when clothes ceased to be indexical of status due to homogeneity of style, a subtle expert system of status differentiation through appearance accessed only to initiates has evolved. This system coded the minutiae of appearance, and commodity fetishism, a term assigned by Marx to the process of mystifying material objects of consumption by investing them with human qualities, turning use value into exchange value. Clothes were attributed symbolic meanings that reflected the person's character or social standing. In both *imitation* and *production* the signifier indexes an underlying meaning, either inherent, or constructed. In contrast, the third order of simulacra (*simulation*) refers to the principle of the postmodern dress which problematises the notion of a correspondence theory of representation. Hence it makes no reference to an outside reality, and is indifferent to any traditional social order. Rather, it is based on coded similarities and differences.

Last, the reading of each kind of signifier is also different: *imitation* marks an obliged sign which refers unequivocally to a status. It signifies 'the natural order of things'. *Production* references not 'the law of nature' but 'the law of exchange'. Its meaning is not fixed to a particular signified but is open to struggle (for example, when environmental awareness to

Green issues turns fur, once a symbol status of sumptuous refinement, into a symbol of the morally inadequate and environmentally insensitive). *Simulation*, by virtue of its being referent-free invites a reading of a different order: it is a perpetual examination of the code.

The question is, can we argue that fashion in a postmodern era has lost its signifying function? I wish to examine this question from two contrasting perspectives. On the one hand, fashion theories identify a move from élitism to democratisation in sartorial representation. On the other hand, Baudrillard's Marxist theory of consumption, espoused in his *For a Critique of the Political Economy of the Sign* (1972/1981), argues that power relations are always inscribed into the very production of objects.

Early modern theories of fashion viewed the fashion process as reifying the social hierarchy, and as a site of struggle for social supremacy. They assumed the élite's desire to preserve the social order to be the single point of origin for fashion. Thus, in *The Theory of the Leisure Class* Veblen (1899/1912) developed the notion that the increasing wealth of the leisure class gave heed to display conspicuous consumption of leisure and waste. Conspicuous consumption is coded into clothes through their superfluousness, decorativeness and non-functionality.

The notion of fashion change as a dynamic of the upper classes' desire to keep a clear demarcation line between the classes, and an opposite desire of the lower classes to emulate the upper classes, was first put forward by Simmel (1904/1957). In his 'trickle down' model of fashion Simmel postulated an upward spiral in which the upper classes adopt a style that differentiates them, and as soon as this is copied by the lower classes, the upper classes discard it in favour of a new style. And along similar lines the conspiracy theory of fashion assigned the authoritative voice of fashion to its creators (designers) and manufacturers (industry) (see for example, Gibbins, 1971; Sproles, 1985).

In the 1960s this early conception was contested by the assumption of a 'trickle across' process (King, 1963). According to this formulation the emulation of the upper classes has broken down in the twentieth century because mass production made similar styles available simultaneously to all classes. Other democratisation theories argued that fashion styles were not dictated by the fashion houses. Rather they originated in a mass movement (Blumer, 1969), in the high street (Field, 1970), or in subcultures (Hebdige, 1979), whereupon they were appropriated into mainstream fashion. Thus modernist analysis regarded fashion as reflecting social movements or social change.

In contrast, Baudrillard argues that when products move from the referential to the representational order they acquire social meaning because: 'objects never exhaust themselves in the function they serve, and in this excess of presence they take on their signification of prestige' (Baudrillard, 1972/1981, p. 32). Drawing on Marx's notion of products as 'instruments' (reflecting a functional logic of use-value), and 'commodities' (reflecting an economic logic of exchange-value), Baudrillard extends the framework of the ideology of consumption to include 'objects' (reflecting the logic of sign-value). He argues that the political function of regulating objects by sign-value is to homogenise desires and reproduce the power structure of the political economy (Kellner, 1989, pp. 21–5). Thus the transition from use-value and exchange-value to sign-value creates *symbol* (reflecting the logic of a gift) and *sign* (reflecting the logic of status). This transformation involves two levels. First, the change from a product to a symbol is commodity fetishism: a mystification of the product which conceals a signifying function (such as, status) with a utilitarian gloss (such as, need fulfilment). Second, the change from a symbol to a sign involves what Baudrillard calls *semiological reduction* whereby an ambivalent symbolic object becomes a univocal flat image. Thus the ideology of consumption is expressed in appropriating the product as a sign, while masking the labour, exploitation and power relations that go into its production.

Baudrillard's position is antithetical to fashion theory which views postindustrial fashion as reflecting a democratisation process. From his perspective democratisation theories fall into the trap of confusing the ideology of consumption with consumption itself. This ideology creates the illusion of democratisation. It promotes the myth of the universal meaning of fashion – right down the social scale – and masks the social inequalities behind a democracy of leisure. The ideology of consumption is a *theatrical sociality*. It creates the appearance of a social change while being in fact a game of social change. It is subversive, recycling past models in new forms, yet it is controlled by the fashion industry and does not really change the essential order (Baudrillard, 1976/1993).

However, the Marxist analysis of signification is not Baudrillard's last word on the matter of fashion. In his later writings – *Fatal Strategies* (1983/ 1990) and *Seduction* (1979/1990) – he extends the paradigm of simulacra to a paradigm of seduction. The notion of the seductive attraction of signs operates in two ways. On the one hand it is an elaboration of postmodern simulation (including fashion). On the other hand it is an alternative metaphysics which replaces the Marxist power principle and the Freudian pleasure principle. It substitutes symbolic (seductive) power for real power. It also replaces the psychoanalytic psychic economy of drives, desires and the unconscious with a different libido – one which feeds on competition, challenge, risk, provocation. This is a libido which is secretive but not repressed, a 'catalystic impulse', a 'deeper energy' of fission, rupture and vice, a compelling energy which is enigmatic, luring, hypnotic and enchanted. It is not a passion for desire, but a passion for games and rituality; one which is dual but not polarised, reversible but not dialectical.

Thus if in *For a Critique* he defines fashion as 'a kind of meaning drive' to innovate signs (1972/1981, p. 78), in *Seduction* (1979/1990) he talks about a system where reversibility puts an end not just to the stability of the sign. It also marks the end of the principle of opposition itself as a basis for meaning. Seduction is based on the attraction of the void. Presence which hides absence. As a metaphysics it is a feature of modern as well as postmodern fashion. It is a feature of modern fashion both historically (since it was a common courtly game from the Renaissance to the eighteenth century, 1983, p. 103) and metaphorically. For it substitutes an *appearance* of democracy for *absence* of real social change. Seduction is also applicable to postmodern fashion where signs are used randomly, playfully – and where an *attempt for meaning* (which is evidenced both in fashion magazines and in fashion analyses such as Lurie's, 1981/1992) masks a *meaning void*.

So in a postmodern culture where the signifier is not fixed to a particular signified, and the same fashion item can be read in any number of ways, can the fashion sign still be said to have meaning, or is it, as Baudrillard argues 'beyond meaning'? By way of an answer, postmodern theory offers two contrasting visions: *postmodernism of reaction* and *postmodernism of resistance* (Foster, 1983). The former characterises fashion theory, and the latter characterises Baudrillard's position.

Postmodernism of reaction is strategic: it repudiates modernity and exploits cultural codes only to reaffirm liberal individualism. From the perspective of fashion theory, postmodern fashion with all its playful nihilism of styles still alludes to a reality of signification. Within this framework the very concept of postmodern fashion becomes a status marker, as can be illustrated by two paradigmatic features of postmodern fashion: fake jewels and nostalgia clothes. In the world of jewellery, a conscious and deliberate use of non-precious materials is made, without the low status connotations associated with such materials: quite the contrary. This is exemplified by a fashion article in the *Independent on Sunday* which plainly talks about an addiction to 'fabulous fakes' but points out that:

> It is never a matter of not being able to afford the real thing. We actually prefer the non-precious. Costume jewellery, unlike most real gold and real jewels, is shaped by fashion, designed to complement the clothes of the moment. (23 December 1990, p. 32; emphasis added)

Another hallmark of postmodernist fashion is imitation and integration of an eclectic mixture of styles and periods into a new discourse (or montage, or collage, or bricolage) (see for example, Jameson, 1984; Newman, 1986). Despite its seeming uprootedness such nostalgic fashion need not be taken at face value. Alternatively it can indicate that fashion does not cease to signify even when it removes itself from the market forces. For Jameson imitation of bygone styles lends historical depth to a world of surface signifiers, and shows 'a desperate attempt to appropriate a missing past'. For Baudrillard (1972/1981), bygone objects derive their value from affirmation of craft-value and repudiation of the stigmata attached to industrial production. And according to McRobbie (1989), second-hand fashion is used by those who can risk looking poor in a stylised way which marks out their distance both from conventional dress and from real poverty. In different ways, the above examples show how repudiation of the stylistic values of representation expresses yearning to these values.

Postmodernism of resistance, however, is engaged in a different project: it deconstructs modernity and questions cultural codes in order to critique liberal humanist values. Moving away from the logic of consumption Baudrillard's postmodernism of resistance (1983) points to a 'deconstruction of the principle of signification': a breakdown of the notion of objects as an index of differentiation. For him simulation replaces signification: it is a playful spectacle, a carnival of appearances. It empties traditional signs of their signification (for example, the use of religious symbols as ornaments, or expensive materials in common contexts), and is completely self-referential 'fashion for its own sake'. For him, the effacing of 'real history' as referent leaves us nothing but empty signs and marks the end of signification itself.

Baudrillard articulates in a single stroke two contradictory accounts of fashion representing two stages of development. Modern fashion as a signifier of a wider social process within industrial capitalism which reproduces the power relations of industrial capitalism. And postmodern fashion where fashion loses its signifying function as an emblem of a social process.

The argument for a fashion which is a stage 'beyond meaning' suffers from a number of weaknesses. Baudrillard's assumption of the indeterminacy of the code and the instability of signifier–signified relationship brings him to doubt the possibility of a referential function. This need not be the case. From a theoretical viewpoint, a looser signifier–signified relationship can simply mean fragmentation of society into smaller units of relevant frames of reference, with less rigid boundaries, rules and membership requirements. It may also imply shorter and faster cycles of change of what a relevant reference group regards as the appropriate code – but it does not necessarily indicate the abolition of a code. From an empirical viewpoint, there is ample evidence, both experimental and anecdotal to suggest that signification in fashion is far more resilient than some postmodern thinkers would have us believe (for a review and critique see Tseëlon, 1989). Perhaps the best example comes from the professional dress code which signals that even in the 1990s, the ethos of 'dress for success' is still the prevailing code. In a recent in-flight magazine of AirUK, targeted to business people on short commuting flights between UK and Europe, I read a handful of tips from a corporate image consultant, such as

inconsistency in your standard of dress leads others to believe that you are inconsistent in other respects.

The thinner the briefcase the more status and power the businessman commands . . . a huge suitcase . . . is a real credibility breaker.

a professional man should not have . . . a tie which is too short . . . socks that do not match the shoes or trousers . . . plastic looking belts.

women should choose only three or four colours to work into their business wardrobe. (*Flagship*, June/July 1993)

In fact in an interview given by John Molloy who has just updated his 1977 classic *The Women's Dress for Success Book* he claims that the changes are minor, and the basic guidelines are the same. As in the heyday of the 'tailored suit' he still recommends the knee-length skirted suit in dark colours and blouses in contrasting light colours as the most effective business-woman gear (Ha'aretz, 6 January 1995). Thus the reality of the traditional professions is indeed a far cry from a floating carnival of signs! In terms of body appearance, for example, the tyranny of the models of thinness, and the aesthetic, medical and moral onslaught on fat is heavily documented (cf. Hughes, 1992). The evidence suggests that the meanings of body shapes are not as free floating as the postmodern idea of 'freedom to shape one's embodied identity' would imply.

Even resistance to fashion is still defined within the order of fashion but fails to acknowledge that fashion as a whole (whatever the authority of its signs) is locked into a broader signification system. In other words, the very participation in the playful carnival of fashion with its floating signs is already inscribed in signification. It is a form of cultural capital. Paradoxically, the act of subverting signification itself becomes a signifier. It is a status marker of the rich and famous, those powerful enough or distinguished enough to flaunt conventions, those creative enough and confident enough to invent, or those marginalised enough not to care.

The self-referentiality of fashion (the fact that fashion is produced from models, and does not represent anything) does not in itself herald the end of meaning either. Reference in the outside world (whether or not fashion corresponds to anything outside itself) is not the only source that confers meaning. Even a closed system can generate its own signifying chains. Perhaps the best example for this can be seen in the most self-referential ritual of the fashion world: on the catwalk – the seasonal fashion show where top designers display their new collections. A BBC programme *The Look* which gives a behind-the-scene view of the fashion world (produced by Jeremy and Gina Newson, first broadcast in October 1992), describes the event as a rite-of-passage, an annual pilgrimage where the high priests of the fashion shrines present a new set of commandments of colour, cut, fit and fabric to a congregation of the fashion faithful. The temple of fashion, though, is not open to everyone and only a carefully scrutinised set of fashion editors, photographers, buyers, distinguished clients and celebrities are allowed into the inner sanctuary. Access to such an event and the seating plan draw a political map of social success and a complex web of interests. The cycle of competition, prestige, ingratiation and intrigue that is set in motion by each such event testifies to its ceremonial qualities and signifying function – which are not confined to the fashion world alone.

Finally, postmodern fashion like any fashion reflects at least one level of meaning: that of countering death. And almost like the Freudian fetish the seduction of absence (of meaning) by presence (of artifice) is 'the only existing form of immortality' turning even death into 'a brilliant and superficial appearance' (Baudrillard, 1979/1990, p. 97). One of its most cynical manifestations is an increasing use by fashion houses of motifs from the Second World War including Nazi symbols, and even Auschwitz prisoners' striped uniform. This last item was displayed in January 1995 at a collection of the Parisian House Comme des Garçons on the 50th anniversary of the liberation of Auschwitz. 'This is the despair that nothing lasts, and the complementary enjoyment of knowing that beyond this death, every form has always the chance of a second coming' (Baudrillard, 1976/1993, p. 119).

Note

This chapter draws on the articles: E. Tseëlon (1992c), 'Fashion and the signification of social order', *Semiotica*, 91, 1–14; and E. Tseëlon (1994), 'Fashion and signification in Baudrillard', in D. Kellner (ed.), *Baudrillard: A Critical Reader*, Oxford: Blackwell.

BIBLIOGRAPHY

Aboulafia, M. (1986). *The Mediating Self: Mead, Sartre, and Self-Determination*. New Haven: Yale University Press.

Adams, G.R. (1985). Attractiveness through the ages: implications of facial attractiveness over the life cycle. In J.A. Graham and A.M. Kligman (eds), *The Psychology of Cosmetic Treatments*. New York: Praeger.

Althusser, L. (1970/1976). Ideology and ideological state apparatuses. In *Essays on Ideology*. London: Verso.

Anderson, B.S. and Zinsser, J.P. (1988). *A History of Their Own: Women in Europe from Prehistory to the Present*. Vol. 1. London: Penguin.

Aquinas, T. (1932). *The Summa Theologica of St. Thomas Aquinas*, part 2, vol. XIII, trans. by the fathers of the English Dominican Province, London.

Ardener, E. (1975). Belief and the problem of women. In S. Ardener (ed.), *Perceiving Women*. London: Malaby Press.

Ardener, S. (1981). Ground rules and social maps for women: an introduction. In S. Ardener (ed.), *Women and Space*. New York: St. Martin's Press.

Arendt, H. (1958). *The Human Condition*. Chicago: University of Chicago Press.

Ariès, P. (1976). *Western Attitudes Toward Death from the Middle Ages to the Present*. London: Marion Boyars.

Ariès, P. (1977/1981). *The Hour of Our Death*, trans. H. Weaver. New York: Oxford University Press.

Arkin, R.M. (1980). Self presentation. In D.M. Wegner and R.M. Vallacher (eds), *The Self in Social Psychology*. Oxford: Oxford University Press.

Arkin, R., Appleman, A.J. and Burger, J.M. (1980). Social anxiety, self presentation and the self serving bias in causal attribution. *Journal of Personality and Social Psychology*, 38, 23–35.

Askew, M.W. (1965). Courtly love: neurosis as institution. *Psychoanalytic Review*, 52, 19–29.

Back, K.W. (1985). Modernism and fashion: a social psychological interpretation. In M.R. Solomon (ed.), *The Psychology of Fashion*. Lexington, MA: Lexington Books.

Bakhtin, M. (1965/1968). *Rabelais and His World*, trans. H. Iswolsky. Cambridge, MA: The MIT Press.

Baldwin, F.E. (1926). *Sumptuary Legislation and Personal Regulation in England*. Baltimore: John Hopkins Press.

Banner, L. (1992). The fashionable sex, 1100–1600. *History Today*, 42, 37–44.

Barkin, L. (1978). The concept of the transitional object. In S.A. Grolnick and L. Barkin (eds), *Between Reality and Fantasy: Transitional Objects and Phenomena*. New York: Jason Aronson.

Barrett, M. (1979). Introduction. In *Virginia Woolf, Women and Writing*. New York: Harcourt Brace Jovanovich.

Barrett, W.P. (1931). *The Trial of Jeanne d'Arc*. London: Routledge & Kegan Paul.

Bar-Tal, D. and Saxe, L. (1976a). Perceptions of similarly and dissimilarly attractive couples and individuals. *Journal of Personality and Social Psychology*, 33, 772–81.

Bar-Tal, D. and Saxe, L. (1976b). Physical attractiveness and its relationship to sex-role stereotyping. *Sex Roles*, 2, 123–33.

Barthes, R. (1967/1983). *The Fashion System*, trans. M. Ward and R. Howard. New York: Hill and Wang.

Bassili, J.N. (1981). The attractiveness stereotype: goodness or glamour? *Basic and Applied Social Psychology*, 2, 235–52.

Baudrillard, J. (1972/1981). *For a Critique of the Political Economy of the Sign*, trans. C. Levin. St. Louis: Telos.

Baudrillard, J. (1976/1993). *Symbolic Exchange and Death*, trans. I. Grant. London: Sage.

Baudrillard, J. (1979/1990). *Seduction*, trans. B. Singer. New York: St. Martin's Press.

Baudrillard, J. (1983). *Simulations*, trans. P. Foss, P. Patton and P. Beitchman. New York: Semiotext(e).

Baudrillard, J. (1983/1990). *Fatal Strategies*, trans. P. Beitchman and W.G.J. Niesluchowski. New York: Semiotext(e).

Baudrillard, J. (1986/1989). *America*, trans. C. Turner. London: Verso.

Bauman, Z. (1992). *Mortality, Immortality and Other Life Strategies*. Cambridge: Polity.

Baumeister, R.F. (1982). A self presentational view of social phenomena. *Psychological Bulletin*, 91, 3–26.

Baumeister, R.F. (1986). *Public Self and Private Self*. New York: Springer.

Baumeister, R.F. (1987). How the self became a problem: a psychological review of historical research. *Journal of Personality and Social Psychology*, 52, 163–76.

Belk, R.W. (1988). Possessions and the extended self. *Journal of Consumer Research*, 15, 139–68.

Bell, Q. (1947/1992). *On Human Finery*. London: Virgin.

Bereshith Rabbah (Midrash Rabbah Genesis) (1939). Vol. 1, H. Freedman a•d M. Simon (eds) (trans. H. Freedman). London: Soncino Press.

Berger, J. (1972). *Ways of Seeing*. London: BBC and Penguin.

Bergler, E. (1953). *Fashion and the Unconscious*. New York: Brunner.

Bernstein, N.R. (1980). Emotional reactions in patients after elective cosmetic surgery. In R.M. Goldwyn (ed.), *Long-term Results in Plastic and Reconstructive Surgery*. Boston: Little and Company.

Berscheid, E. (1986). The question of the importance of physical attractiveness. In C.P. Herman, M.P. Zanna and E.T. Higgins (eds), *Physical Appearance, Stigma and Social Behaviour: The Ontario Symposium, Vol. 3*. Hillsdale, NJ: Erlbaum.

Berscheid, E., Dion, K.K., Walster, E. and Walster, G.W. (1971). Physical attractiveness and dating choice: a test of the matching hypothesis. *Journal of Experimental Social Psychology*, 7, 173–89.

Berscheid, E., Walster, E. and Bohrnstedt, G. (1973). The happy American body: a survey report. *Psychology Today*, 7, 119–31.

Betterton, R. (ed.) (1987). *Looking On. Images of Femininity in the Visual Arts and Media*. London: Pandora.

Biggs, T.M., Cukier, J., and Worthing, L.F. (1982). Augmentation mammaplasty: a review of 18 years. *Plastic and Reconstructive Surgery*, 69, 445–50.

Black, A.J. and Garland, M. (1975). *A History of Fashion*. London: Orbis.

Blair, J. (1981). Private parts in public places: the case of actresses. In S. Ardener (ed.), *Women and Space*. New York: St. Martin's Press.

Bloch, H.R. (1992). *Medieval Misogyny and the Introduction of Western Romantic Love*. Chicago: University of Chicago Press.

Bloch, M. and Bloch, J.H. (1980). Women and the dialectics of nature in eighteenth-century French thought. In C.P. MacCormack and M. Strathern (eds), *Nature, Culture and Gender*. Cambridge: Cambridge University Press.

Blumer, H. (1956). Sociological analysis and the 'variable'. *American Sociological Review*, 19, 3–10.

Blumer, H. (1969). Fashion: from class differentiation to collective selection. *Sociological Quarterly*, 10, 275–91.

Bobys, R.S. (1984). Understanding another stigma: comment on Elliott, Ziegler, Altman, and Scott. *Deviant Behavior*, 5, 97–9.

Böll, H. (1975). *The Lost Honor of Katharina Blum. Or: How Violence Develops and Where It Can Lead*, trans. L. Vennewitz. New York: McGraw-Hill.

Bondi, F. and Mariacher, G. (1979/1983). *If the Shoe Fits*, trans. J. Chisholm. Venice: Cavallino.

Bradley, D.H. (1922). *The Eternal Masquerade*. London: Werner Laurie.

Brenner, A. (1970). *Idols Behind Altars*. New York: Beacon Press.

Bridenthal, R. and Koonz, C. (1977). *Becoming Visible: Women in European History*. Boston: Houghton Mifflin.

Brissett, D. and Edgley, C. (1975). Introduction. In D. Brissett and C. Edgley (eds), *Life as a Theater: A Dramaturgical Sourcebook*. Chicago: Aldine.

Bronfen, E. (1992). *Over Her Dead Body*. Manchester: Manchester University Press.

Brook, P. (1968). *The Empty Space*. Harmondsworth: Penguin.

Brooks, B.A. (1941). Fertility cult functionaries in the Old Testament. *Journal of Biblical Literature*, 60, 227–53.

Broverman, I.K., Broverman, D.M., Clarkson, F.E., Rosenkrantz, P.S. and Vogel, S.R. (1970). Sex-role stereotypes and clinical judgments of mental health. *Journal of Consulting and Clinical Psychology*, 34, 1–7.

Brown, P. (1986). The notion of virginity in the early church. In B. McGinn and J. Meyendorff (eds), *Christian Spirituality: Origins to the Twelfth Century*. London: Routledge & Kegan Paul.

Buck, R. (1988). Nonverbal communication: spontaneous and symbolic aspects. *American Behavioral Scientist*, 31, 341–54.

Burns, J.E. (1985). The man behind the lady in troubadour lyric. *Romance Notes*, 25, 254–70.

Buss, A.H. and Briggs, S.R. (1984). Drama and the self in social interaction. *Journal of Personality and Social Psychology*, 47: 1310–24.

Calderon De La Barca, P. (1636/1958). *Life is a Dream* (La Vida es Sueño), trans. W.E. Colford. Woodbury, New York: Barron's Educational Series.

Cameron, D. (1990). Introduction: why is language a feminist issue. In D. Cameron (ed.), *Feminist Critique of Language*. London: Routledge.

Carrazé, A. and Oswald, H. (1990). *The Prisoner: A Televisionary Masterpiece*, trans. C. Donougher. London: W.H. Allen.

Carroll, L. (1865/1971). *Alice in Wonderland* and *Through the Looking Glass*. London: Oxford University Press.

Cash, T.F. and Brown, T.A. (1989). Gender and body images: stereotypes and realities. *Sex Roles*, 21, 361–73.

Cash, T.F., Winstead, B.A. and Janda, L.H. (1986). The great American shape-up: we're healthier than ever, fitter than ever . . . but less satisfied with how we look. *Psychology Today*, 20, 30–7.

Chapkis, W. (1986). *Beauty Secrets: Women and the Politics of Appearance*. Boston: South End Press.

Cheek, J.M. and Hogan, R. (1983). Self-concepts, self presentations and moral judgements. In J. Suls and A.G. Greenwald (eds), *Psychological Perspectives on the Self*, Vol. 2. Hillsdale, NJ: Erlbaum.

Chodorow, N. (1971). Being and doing: a cross-cultural examination of the socialization of males and females. In V. Gornick and B.K. Moran (eds), *Women in Sexist Society: Studies in Power and Powerlessness*. New York: Basic Books.

Chodorow, N. (1978). *The Reproduction of Mothering: Psychoanalysis and the Sociology of Gender*. Berkeley: University of California Press.

Chua, B.H. (1992). Shopping for women's fashion in Singapore. In R. Shields (ed.), *Lifestyle Shopping: The Subject of Consumption*. London: Routledge.

The writings of Clement of Alexandria (1867). Ante-Nicene Christian Library. Translations of the writings of the fathers down to AD 325, ed. by A. Roberts and J. Donaldson, Vol. 4. London: Hamilton.

Cohen-Alloro, D. (1987). *The Secret of the Garment in the Zohar*. Research projects of the Institute of Jewish studies, The Hebrew University of Jerusalem.

Collins, J.K. and Plahn, M.R. (1988). Recognition accuracy, stereotypic preference, aversion, and subjective judgement of body appearance in adolescents and young adults. *Journal of Youth and Adolescence*, 17, 317–34.

Cooke, E. (1678) trans. a treatise by an anonymous papist *Just and Seasonable Reprehension of Naked Breasts and Shoulders*, prefaced by Riched Baxter. London: Jonathan Edwin.

Coombs, R.H. and Kenkel, W.F. (1966). Sex differences in dating aspirations and satisfaction with computer-selected partners. *Journal of Marriage and the Family*, 28, 62–6.

Cowie, E. (1984/1990). Fantasia. In P. Adams and E. Cowie (eds), *The Woman in Question m/f*. London: Verso.

Cox, J. (1993). *The Functions of Clothing and Clothing Deprivation: A Gender Analysis Among Students*. Unpuplished BA (Hons) thesis, University of Sussex.

Cox, S. and James, B. (1987). The theoretical background. In S. Cox (ed.), *Public and Private Worlds*. Wellington, New Zealand: Allen & Unwin, Port Nicholson Press.

Crocker, J. and Major, B. (1989). Social stigma and self-esteem: the self-protective properties of stigma. *Psychological Review*, 96, 608–30.

Csikszentmihalyi, M. and Rochberg-Halton, E. (1981). *The Meaning of Things: Domestic Symbols of the Self*. Chicago: University of Chicago Press.

Curtin, M. (1985). A question of manners: status and gender in etiquette and courtesy. *Journal of Modern History*, 57, 395–423.

The writings of Cyprian, Bishop of Carthage (1868). *On the Dress of Virgins*. Ante-Nicene Christian Library. Translations of the writings of the fathers down to AD 325, ed. by A. Roberts and J. Donaldson, trans. R.E. Wallis, Vol. 8. London: Hamilton.

David, R. (ed.) (1978). *Mysteries of the Mummies. The Story of the Manchester University Investigation*. London: Cassell.

Davis, F. (1988). Clothing, fashion and the dialectic of identity. In D.R. Maines and C.J. Couch (eds), *Communication and Social Structure*. Springfield: Charles Thomas.

Davis, F. (1992). *Fashion, Culture and Identity*. Chicago: University of Chicago Press.

de Beauvoir, S. (1968). *The Second Sex*. New York: Bantam Books.

de Marly, D. (1986). *Working Dress: A History of Occupational Clothing*. London: Batsford.

Deri, S. (1990). The aged and the woman: partners by prejudice. *Psychoanalytic Review*, 77, 519–23.

Dermer, M. and Thiel, D.L. (1975). When beauty may fail. *Journal of Personality and Social Psychology*, 31, 1168–76.

de Saussure, F. (1916/1959). *Course in General Linguistics*, trans. W. Baskin, ed. C. Bally, A. Sechehaye and A. Riedlinger. London: Peter Owen.

Deutsch, F.M., Zalenski, C.M. and Clark, M.E. (1986). Is there a double standard for aging? *Journal of Applied Social Psychology*, 16, 771–85.

Dion, K.K. (1986). Stereotyping based on physical attractiveness: issues and conceptual perspectives. In C.P. Herman, M.P. Zanna and E. T. Higgins (eds), *Physical Appearance, Stigma, and Social Behavior: The Ontario Symposium*, Vol. 3. Hillsdale, NJ: Erlbaum.

Dion, K.K., Berscheid, E. and Walster, E. (1972). What is beautiful is good. *Journal of Personality and Social Psychology*, 24, 285–90.

Dittmar, H. (1989). Gender identity-related meanings of personal possessions. *British Journal of Social Psychology*, 28, 159–71.

Dittmar, H. (1992). *The Social Psychology of Material Possessions. To Have is to Be*. New York: St. Martin's Press.

Doane, M.A. (1982). Film and the masquerade: theorising the female spectator. *Screen*, 23, 74–87.

Doane, M.A. (1988–9). Masquerade reconsidered: further thoughts on the female spectator. *Discourse. Journal for Theoretical Studies in Media and Culture*, 11, 42–54.

Doane, M.A., Mellencamp, P. and Williams, L. (eds) (1984). *Re-vision: Essays in Feminist Film Criticism*. Los Angeles: American Film Institute.

Dube, L. (1986). Introduction. In L. Dube, E. Leacock and S. Ardener (eds), *Visibility and Power*. Delhi: Oxford University Press.

Duby, G. (1992). The courtly model. In C. Klapisch-Zuber (ed.), *A History of Women in the West*. Vol. 2: *Silences of the Middle Ages*. London: Harvard University Press.

Eco, U. (1986). Lumbar thought. In *Travels in Hyperreality*. Orlando, FL: Harcourt Brace Jovanovich.

Edgley, C. and Turner, R.E. (1975). Masks and social relations: an essay on the sources and assumptions of dramaturgical social psychology, *Humboldt Journal of Social Relations*, 3, 5–12.

Elias, N. (1939/1978). *The Civilizing Process*. Vol. 1: *The History of Manners*, trans. E. Jepchott. Oxford: Blackwell.

Elias, N. (1939/1982). *The Civilizing Process*. Vol. 2: *State Formation and Civilization*, trans. E. Jepchott. Oxford: Blackwell.

Elliott, G.C., Ziegler, H.L., Altman, B.M. and Scott, D.R. (1982). Understanding stigma: dimensions of deviance and coping. *Deviant Behavior*, 3, 275–300.

Evans, C. and Thornton, M. (1991). Fashion, representation, femininity. *Feminist Review*, 38, 48–66.

Ewing, E. (1981). *Fur in Dress*. London: Batsford.

Fallon, A.E. and Rozin, P. (1985). Sex differences in perceptions of desirable body shape. *Journal of Abnormal Psychology*, 94, 102–5.

Featherstone, M., Hepworth, M. and Turner, B.S. (eds) (1991). *The Body: Social Process and Cultural Theory*. London: Sage.

Field, G.A. (1970). The status float phenomenon: the upward diffusion of innovation. *Business Horizons*, 13, 45–52.

Finkelstein, J. (1991). *The Fashioned Self*. Cambridge: Polity.

Flaccus, L.W. (1906). Remarks on the psychology of clothes. *Pedagogical Seminary*, 13, 61–83.

Flügel, J.C. (1924). Polyphallic symbolism and the castration complex. *International Journal of Psycho-Analysis*, 5, 155–96.

Flügel, J.C. (1930/1971). *The Psychology of Clothes*. London: The Hogarth Press and The Institute of Psycho-Analysis.

Foddy, W.H. and Finighan, W.R. (1980). The concept of privacy from a symbolic interactionist perspective. *Journal for The Theory of Social Behaviour*, 10, 1–17.

Foltyn, J.L. (1989). *The Importance of Being Beautiful: The Social Construction of the Beautiful Self*. PhD dissertation, University of California at San Diego.

Forsyth, N. (1987). *The Old Enemy. Satan and the Combat Myth*. Princeton: Princeton University Press.

Foster, H. (1983). Postmodernism: a Preface. In H. Foster (ed.), *The Anti-Aesthetic: Essays on Postmodern Culture*. Port Townshend, WA: Bay Press.

Foucault, M. (1975). *Discipline and Punish: The Birth of the Prison*, trans. A. Sheridan. New York: Pantheon Books.

Frable, D.E.S., Blackstone, T. and Scherbaum, C. (1990). Marginal and mindful: deviants in social interactions. *Journal of Personality and Social Psychology*, 59, 140–9.

Frankenburg, F.R. and Yurgelun-Todd, D. (1984). Dressing disorder. *American Journal of Psychiatry*, 141, 147.

Franzoi, S.L., Kessenich, J.J. and Sugrue, P.A. (1989). Gender differences in the experience of body awareness: an experiential sampling study. *Sex Roles*, 21, 499–515.

Freedman, R. (1986). *Beauty Bound*. Lexington, MA: Heath and Company.

Freud, S. (1905). *Three Essays on the Theory of Sexuality, Standard Edition*, Vol. 7, 125–245.

Freud, S. (1913). *On the Theme of the Three Caskets, Standard Edition*, Vol. 12, 291–301.

Freud, S. (1915a). *Instincts and Their Vicissitudes, Standard Edition*, Vol. 14, 117–40.

Freud, S. (1915b). *Thoughts for the Times on War and Death, Standard Edition*, Vol. 14, 273–300.

Freud, S. (1916). *On Transcience, Standard Edition*, Vol. 14, 303–7.

Freud, S. (1919). *The 'Uncanny', Standard Edition*, Vol. 17, 219–52.

Freud, S. (1920). *Beyond the Pleasure Principle, Standard Edition*, Vol. 18, 7–64.

Freud, S. (1923). *The Ego and the Id, Standard Edition*, Vol. 19, 1–66.

Freud, S. (1926). *Inhibition, Symptoms, and Anxiety, Standard Edition*, Vol. 20, 87–175.

Freud, S. (1927). *Fetishism, Standard Edition*, Vol. 21, 152–7.

Freud, S. (1930). *Civilization and its Discontents, Standard Edition*, Vol. 21, 64–145.

Freud, S. (1940). *Medusa's Head, Standard Edition*, Vol. 18, 273–4.

Freud, S. and Breuer, J. (1895). *Studies on Hysteria*, Vol. 2, in *The Standard Edition of the complete psychological works of Sigmund Freud*, edited and trans. James Strachey. London: Hogarth Press, 1953–86.

Fussell, P. (1984). *Class*. London: Arrow Books.

Gallop, J. (1988). The female body. In *Thinking Through the Body*. New York: Columbia University Press.

Gergen, K.J. (1991). *The Saturated Self: Dilemmas of Identity in Contemporary Life*. New York: Basic Books.

Gibbins, K. (1971). Social psychological theories of fashion. *Journal of Home Economics Association of Australia*, 3, 3–18.

Giddens, A. (1991). *Modernity and Self Identity*. Cambridge: Polity.

Gilligan, C. (1982). *In a Different Voice*. Cambridge, MA: Harvard University Press.

Ginzburg, L. (1909/1937). *The Legends of the Jews*, Vol. 1: *Bible Times and Characters from the Creation to Jacob*, trans. Henrietta Szold. Philadelphia: The Jewish Publication Society of America.

Goffman, E. (1951). Symbols of class status. *British Journal of Sociology*, 2, 294–304.

Goffman, E. (1959). *The Presentation of Self in Everyday Life*. New York: Anchor Books.

Goffman, E. (1963a). *Stigma*. Englewood Cliffs, NJ: Prentice Hall.

Goffman, E. (1963b). *Behaviour in Public Places*. Glencoe, IL: The Free Press.

Goffman, E. (1971). *Relations in Public: Microstudies of the Public Order*. Harmondsworth: Penguin.

Goffman, E. (1977). The arrangement between the sexes. *Theory and Society*, 4, 301–31.

Goffman, E. (1979). *Gender Advertisements*. New York: Harper and Row.

Goldman, W. and Lewis, P. (1977). Beautiful is good: evidence that the physically attractive are more socially skilled. *Journal of Experimental Social Psychology*, 13, 125–30.

Gorer, G. (1965). *Death, Grief, and Mourning in Contemporary Britain*. London: The Crest Press.

Gouldner, A.W. (1970). *The Coming Crisis in Western Sociology*. New York: Basic Books.

Graham, J.A. and Jouhar, A.J. (1983). The importance of cosmetics in the psychology of appearance. *International Journal of Dermatology*, 22, 153–6.

Graham, J.A. and Kligman, A.M. (eds) (1985). *The Psychology of Cosmetic Treatments*. New York: Praeger.

Graves, R. (1955/1981). *The Greek Myths*. Vol. 1. Harmondsworth: Penguin.

Greer, G. (1991). *The Change: Women, Ageing and the Menopause*. London: Hamish Hamilton.

Habermas, J. (1974). The Public Sphere: An Encyclopedia Article (1964). Reprinted in *New German Critique*, 3, 49–55.

Halbertal, M. and Margalit, A. (1992). *Idolatry*, trans. N. Goldblum. Cambridge, MA: Harvard University Press.

Hansen, K.V. (1987). Feminist conceptions of public and private: a critical analysis. *Berkeley Journal of Sociology*, 32, 105–28.

Harré, R. (1979). *Social Being*. Oxford: Blackwell.

Harré, R. (1986). Social sources of mental content and order. In J. Margolis, P.T. Manicas, R. Harré and P.F. Secord (eds), *Psychology: Designing the Paradigm*. Oxford: Blackwell.

Harré, R. (1991). *Physical Being*. Oxford: Blackwell.

Harte, N.B. (1976). State control of dress and social change in pre-industrial England. In D.D. Cleman and A.H. John (eds), *Trade, Government and Economy in Pre-industrial England*. London: Weidenfeld and Nicolson.

Hatfield, E. and Sprecher, S. (1986). *Mirror, Mirror . . . The Importance of Looks in Everyday Life*. Albany: SUNY Press.

Heath, S. (1989). Joan Riviere and the masquerade. In V. Burgin, J. Donald and C. Kaplan (eds), *Formations of Fantasy*. London: Routledge.

Hebdige, D. (1979). *Subculture: The Meaning of Style*. London: Methuen.

Helmer, J. (1970). The face of the man without qualities. *Social Research*, 37, 547–79.

Heyl, C. (1994). *Disguise as a Bridge Between Private and Public Sphere in Eighteenth Century England*. Paper presented at a conference 'Mask, Masquerade and Carnival' in Venice.

Hill, A.J., Oliver, S. and Rogers, P.J. (1992). Eating in the adult world: the rise of dieting in childhood and adolescence. *British Journal of Clinical Psychology*, 31, 95–105.

Hollander, A. (1975/1980). *Seeing Through Clothes*. New York: Avon Books.

Horney, K. (1950/1982). The search for glory. In M. Rosenberg and H.B. Kaplan (eds), *Social Psychology of the Self Concept*. Illinois: Harlan Davidson.

Hughes, B. (1992). *Body Sculpture: Eating for the Sake of Appearance*. Paper presented at the Theory, Culture & Society meeting in Seven Springs.

Imray, L. and Middleton, A. (1983). Public and private: marking the boundaries. In E. Gamarnikow, D.H.J. Morgan, J. Purvis and D. Taylorson (eds), *The Public and the Private*. London: Heinemann.

Irigaray, L. (1977/1985). *This Sex Which is Not One*, trans. C. Porter and C. Burke. Ithaca, NY: Cornell University Press.

Jackson, L.A. (1992). *Physical Appearance and Gender: Sociobiological and Sociocultural Perspectives*. State University of New York Press.

James, W. (1890). *The Principles of Psychology*, Vol. 1. New York: Henry Holt.

Jameson, F. (1984). Postmodernism or the cultural logic of late capitalism. *New Left Review*, 146, 53–92.

Jencks, C. (1978). *The Language of Post-Modern Architecture*. London: Academy Editions.

Jones, E.E. and Sigall, H. (1971). The bogus pipeline: a new paradigm for measuring affect and attitude. *Psychological Bulletin*, 76, 349–64.

Jones, E.E. and Pittman, T.S. (1986). Toward a general theory of strategic self-presentation. In J. Suls (ed.), *Psychological Perspectives on the Self*, Vol. 1. Hillsdale, NJ: Erlbaum.

Jones, E.E., Farina, A., Hastorf, A.H., Markus, H., Miller, D.T. and Scott, R.A. (1984). *Social Stigma: The Psychology of Marked Relationships*. New York: W.H. Freeman & Company.

Judaica Encyclopedia (1971). Jerusalem: Keter.

Kaiser, S.B. and Freeman, C. (1989). *Meaningful Clothing and the Framing of Emotion: Toward a Gender-relational Understanding*. Paper presented at a meeting of the Society for the Study of Symbolic Interaction in San Francisco.

Katz, I. (1981). *Stigma: A Social Psychological Analysis*. Hillsdale, NJ: Erlbaum.

Kellner, D. (1989). *Jean Baudrillard: From Marxism to Postmodernism and Beyond*. Stanford, CA: Stanford University Press.

King, C.W. (1963). Fashion adoption: a rebuttal to the 'trickle-down' theory. In S.A. Greyse (ed.), *Toward Scientific Marketing*. Chicago: American Marketing Association.

Koestner, R. and Wheeler, L. (1988). Self-presentation in personal advertisements: the influence of implicit notions of attraction and role expectations. *Journal of Social and Personal Relationships*, 5, 149–60.

Koff, E., Rierdan, J. and Stubbs, M.L. (1990). Gender, body image and self-concept in early adolescence. *Journal of Early Adolescence*, 10, 56–68.

Komarovsky, M. (1946). Cultural contradictions and sex roles. *American Journal of Sociology*, 52, 184–9.

König, R. (1973). *The Restless Image: A Sociology of Fashion*, trans. F. Bradley, introduced by Tom Wolfe. London: George Allen & Unwin.

Koslow, R.E. (1988). Differences between personal estimates of body fatness and measures of body fatness in 11 and 12 year old males and females. *Journal of Applied Social Psychology*, 18, 533–5.

Kramer, H. and Sprenger, J. (1486/1951). *Malleus Maleficarum*, trans. and introduced by Montague Summers. London: Pushkin Press.

Kuhn, A. (1982). *Women's Pictures: Feminism and the Cinema*. London: Routledge & Kegan Paul.

Kuhn, A. (1985a). Sexual disguise and cinema. In *The Power of the Image: Essays on Representation and Sexuality*. London: Routledge & Kegan Paul.

Kuhn, A. (1985b). Lawless seeing. In *The Power of the Image: Essays on Representation and Sexuality*. London: Routledge & Kegan Paul.

Kuzmics, H. (1991). Embarrassment and civilization: on some similarities and differences in the work of Goffman and Elias. *Theory, Culture and Society*, 8, 1–30.

Lacan, J. (1954/1991a). The ego-ideal and ideal ego. In J.-A. Miller (ed.) *The Seminar of Jacques Lacan*, Book 1 (trans. J. Forrester). New York: Norton.

Lacan, J. (1954/1991b). A materialist definition of the phenomenon of conciousness. In J.-A. Miller (ed.) *The Seminar of Jacques Lacan*, Book 2 (trans. S. Tomaselli). New York: Norton.

Lacan, J. (1955/1991) The dream of Irma's injection (conclusion). In J.-A. Miller (ed.) *The Seminar of Jacques Lacan*, Book 2 (trans. S. Tomaselli). New York: Norton.

Lacan, J. (1966/1977). The signification of the phallus. In *Ecrits: A selection*, trans. A. Sheridan. New York: W.W. Norton.

Lacan, J. (1975/1991). The topic of the imaginary. In *The Seminar of Jacques Lacan*, Book 1, trans. J. Forrester, ed. J.-A. Miller. New York: Norton.

Lacan, J. (1982). *Feminine Sexuality: Jacques Lacan and the 'Ecole Freudienne'*, trans. J. Rose, eds J. Mitchell and J. Rose. New York: W.W. Norton.

Langlois, J.H. (1986). From the eye of the beholder to behavioral reality: development of social behaviors and social relations as a function of physical attractiveness. In C.P. Herman, M.P. Zanna and E.T. Higgins (eds), *Physical Appearance, Stigma, and Social Behavior: The Ontario Symposium*, Vol. 3. Hillsdale, NJ: Erlbaum.

Laver, J. (1937). *Taste and Fashion, From the French Revolution until Today*. London: George G. Harrap.

Laver, J. (1969). *Modesty in Dress: An Inquiry into the Fundamentals of Fashion*. London: Heinemann.

Laver, J. (1969/1985). *Costume and Fashion: A Concise History*. London: Thames and Hudson.

Lee, J.S. (1990). *Jacques Lacan*. Boston: Twayne.

Lemoine-Luccioni, E. (1987). *The Dividing of Women or Woman's Lot*, trans. M.-L. Davenpot and M.-C. Réguis. London: Free Association.

Leopardi, G. (1827/1983). The dialogue of fashion and death. In *Moral Tales* (Operette morali), trans. P. Creagh. Vol. 1. Manchester: Carcanet New Press.

Lerner, R.M. and Karabenick, S.A. (1974). Physical attractiveness, body attitudes, and self concept in late adolescents. *Journal of Youth and Adolescence*, 3, 307–16.

Lévi-Strauss, C. (1962/1966). *The Savage Mind*. Chicago: University of Chicago Press.

Lowe, D.M. (1982). *History of Bourgeois Perception*. Brighton: Harvester.

Lowen, A. (1968). In defense of modesty. *Journal of Sex Research*, 4, 51–6.

Lurie, A. (1981/1992). *The Language of Clothes*. London: Bloomsbury.

Lyotard, J.-F. (1984). *The Postmodern Condition: A Report on Knowledge*. Manchester: Manchester University Press.

MacCannell, D. (1983). Erving Goffman (1922–1982). *Semiotica*, 45, 1–33.

MacCannell, D. and MacCannell, J.F. (1987). The beauty system. In N. Armstrong and L. Tennenhouse (eds), *The Ideology of Conduct: Essays on Literature and the History of Sexuality*. New York: Methuen.

MacLeod, A. (1992). Hegemonic relations and gender resistance: the new veiling as accommodating protest in Cairo. *Signs*, 17, 3, 533–57.

McRobbie, A. (1989). Second-hand dresses and the role of the ragmarket. In A. McRobbie (ed.), *Zoot Suits and Second Hand Dresses: An Anthology of Fashion and Music*. London: Macmillan.

Markus, H. and Kunda, Z. (1986). Stability and malleability of the self concept. *Journal of Personality and Social Psychology*, 51, 858–66.

Marx, K. (1964). *The Economic and Philosophic Manuscripts of 1844*, ed. D. Struik. New York: International Publishers.

Mazur, A. (1986). U.S. trends in feminine beauty and overadaptation. *Journal of Sex Research*, 22, 281–303.

Mead, G.H. (1934). *Mind, Self and Society*. Chicago: University of Chicago Press.

Meredith, B.C. (1988). *A Change for the Better: A Guide to Cosmetic Surgery*. London: Grafton Books.

Mernissi, F. (1987). *Beyond the Veil: Male–Female Dynamics in Modern Muslim Society*. Bloomington and Indianapolis: Indiana University Press.

Messinger, S.E., Sampson, H. and Towne, R.D. (1962). Life as theater: some notes on the dramaturgical approach to social reality. *Sociometry*, 25, 98–110.

Miller, C.T., Rothblum, E.D., Barbour, L., Brand, P.A. and Felicio, D. (1990). Social interactions of obese and nonobese women. *Journal of Personality*, 58, 365–80.

Millman, M. (1980). *Such a Pretty Face: Being Fat in America*. New York: Berkeley Press.

Molloy, J.T. (1977). *The Women's Dress For Success Book*. Chicago: Follett.

Mulvey, L. (1975). Visual pleasure and narrative cinema. *Screen*, 16, 6–18.

Musil, R. (1930/1953). *The Man Without Qualities*, trans. E. Wilkins and E. Kaiser. New York: Coward-McCann.

Myers, K. (1988). Towards a feminist erotica. In H. Robinson (ed.), *Visibly Female: Feminism and Art Today: An Anthology*. New York: Universe Books.

Myers, P.N. and Biocca, F.A. (1992). The elastic body image: the effect of television advertising and programming on body distortions in young women. *Journal of Communication*, 42, 108–33.

Nelli, R. (1989). Love's rewards. In M. Feher Naddaff and T. Nadia (eds), *Zone 4*, part 2: *Fragments for a History of the Human Body*. New York: Zone.

Newman, M. (1986). Revising modernism, representing postmodernism. In L. Appignanesi (ed.), *Postmodernism: ICA Documents*. London: ICA.

Nietzsche, F. (1885/1987). *Beyond Good and Evil*, trans. R.J. Hollingdale. Harmondsworth: Penguin.

Ohtahara, H., Ohzeki, T., Hanaki, K., Motozumi, H. et al. (1993). Abnormal perception of body weight is not solely observed in pubertal girls: incorrect body image in children and its relationship to body weight. *Acta Psychiatrica Scandinavica*, 87, 218–22.

Okely, J. (1975). Gypsy women: models in conflict. In S. Ardener (ed.), *Perceiving Women*. London: Malaby Press.

O'Neill, J. (1972). *Sociology as a Skin Trade: Essays Towards a Reflexive Sociology*. New York: Harper & Row.

Ortner, S. (1974). Is female to male as nature is to culture? In M.Z. Rosaldo and L. Lamphere (eds), *Women, Culture and Society*. Stanford, CA: Stanford University Press.

Otis, L.L. (1985). *Prostitution in Medieval Society*. Chicago: University of Chicago Press.

Owen Hughes, D. (1992). Regulating women's fashion. In C. Klapisch-Zuber (ed.), *A History of Women in the West*. Vol. 2: *Silences of the Middle Ages*. London: Harvard University Press.

Owens, C. (1983). The discourse of others: feminists and postmodernists. In H. Foster (ed.), *The Anti-Aesthetic: Essays on Postmodern Culture*. Port Townshend, WA: Bay Press.

Page, R.M. (1984). *Stigma*. London: Routledge & Kegan Paul.

Patzer, G.L. (1985). *The Physical Attractiveness Phenomena*. New York: Plenum.

Paz, O. (1967). *The Labyrinth of Solitude: Life and Thought in Mexico*. London: Allen Lane.

Peirce, C.S. (1931–1958). *Collected Papers*. Cambridge, MA: Harvard University Press.

Perinbanayagam, R.S. (1985). *Signifying Acts: Structure and Meaning in Everyday Life*. Carbondale and Edwardsville: Southern Illinois University Press.

Perniola, M. (1989). Between clothing and nudity. In M. Feher Naddaff and T. Nadia (eds), *Zone 4*, part 2: *Fragments for a History of the Human Body*. New York: Zone.

Phillips, J.A. (1984). *Eve: The History of an Idea*. San Francisco, CA: Harper & Row.

Posner, J. (1976). The stigma of excellence: on being just right. *Sociological Inquiry*, 46, 141–4.

Ribeiro, A. (1986). *Dress and Morality*. London: Batsford.

Richardson, L. (1985). *The New Other Woman: Contemporary Single Women in Affairs With Married Men*. New York: Free Press.

Ridd, R. (1981). Where women must dominate: response to oppression in urban South Africa. In S. Ardener (ed.), *Women and Space*. New York: St. Martin's Press.

Riviere, J. (1929). Womanliness as masquerade. *The International Journal of Psychoanalysis*, 10, 303–13.

Roberts, N. (1992). *Whores in History: Prostitution in Western Society*. New York: HarperCollins.

Róheim, G. (1948). Song of the sirens. *Psychiatric Quarterly*, 22, 18–44.

Rolley, K. (1990). Fashion, femininity and the fight for the vote. *Art History*, 13, 47–71.

Roman de la Rose (E. Langlois (ed.) Le Roman de la Rose par Guillaume de Lorris et Jean de Meun, Paris 1914–24. Begun in about 1230 by Guillaume de Lorris and continued in about 1275 by Jean de Meun.)

Rosaldo, M.Z. (1974a). Introduction. In M.Z. Rosaldo and L. Lamphere (eds), *Women, Culture and Society*. Stanford, CA: Stanford University Press.

Rosaldo, M.Z. (1974b). Women, culture and society: a theoretical overview. In M.Z. Rosaldo and L. Lamphere (eds), *Women, Culture and Society*. Stanford, CA: Stanford University Press.

Rudofsky, B. (1972). *The Unfashionable Human Body*. London: Rupert Hart-Davis.

Russell, J.B. (1972). *Witchcraft in the Middle Ages*. Ithaca, NY: Cornell University Press.

Russo, M. (1986). Female grotesque: carnival and theory. In T. de Lauretis (ed.), *Feminist Studies Critical Studies*. Bloomington: Indiana University Press.

Saegert, S. (1980). Masculine cities and feminine suburbs: polarized ideas, contradictory realities. *Signs: Journal of Women in Culture and Society*, 5, Suppl., S96–S111.

Sanders, C.R. (1989). *Customizing the Body: The Art and Culture of Tattooing*. Philadelphia: Temple University Press.

Sanger, W. (1859/1972). *A History of Prostitution*. New York: Harper & Brothers.

Sartre, J.-P. (1943/1966). *Being and Nothingness*, trans. H.E. Barnes. New York: Washington Square Press.

Schlenker, B.R. (1980). *Impression Management*. Monterey, CA: Brooks/Cole.

Schlenker, B.R (ed.) (1985). *The Self and Social Life*. New York: McGraw-Hill.

Schlenker, B.R. and Leary, M.R. (1982). Social anxiety and self-presentation: a conceptualization and model. *Psychological Bulletin*, 92: 641–69.

Schlenker, B.R. and Leary, M.R. (1985). Social anxiety and communication about self. *Journal of Language and Social Psychology*, 4: 171–92.

Schneider, D.J. (1981). Tactical self-presentations: toward a broader conception. In J.T. Tedeschi (ed.), *Impression Management Theory and Social Psychological Research*. New York: Academic Press.

Schopenhauer, A. (1970). *Essays and Aphorisms*. London: Penguin.

Sciama, L. (1981). The problem of privacy in mediterranean anthropology. In S. Ardener (ed.), *Women and Space*. New York: St. Martin's Press.

Sennett, R. (1977). *The Fall of Public Man: On The Social Psychology of Capitalism*. New York: Vintage Books.

Setel, D. (1985). Prophets and pornography: female sexual imagery in Hosea. In L.M. Russell (ed.), *Feminist Interpretations of the Bible*. Oxford: Blackwell.

Shilling, C. (1993). *The Body and Social Theory*. London: Sage.

Showalter, E. (1991). *Sexual Anarchy: Gender and Culture at the Fin de Siècle*. London: Bloomsbury.

Shrauger, J.S. and Schoeneman, T.J. (1979). Symbolic interactionist view of self-concept: through the looking glass darkly. *Psychological Bulletin*, 86, 549–73.

Silver, M. and Sabini, J. (1985). Sincerity: feelings and constructions in making a self. In K.J. Gergen and K.E. Davis (eds), *The Social Construction of the Person*. New York: Springer.

Silverman, K. (1988). *The Acoustic Mirror: The Female Voice in Psychoanalysis and Cinema.* Indiana: Indiana University Press.

Simmel, G. (1904/1957). Fashion. *International Quarterly*, 10, 130–55. Reprinted in *American Journal of Sociology*, 62, 541–58.

Smith, J.Z. (1978). The garments of shame. In *Map is Not Territory: Studies in the History of Religions*. Leiden: Brill.

Snyder, M. (1974). Self monitoring of expressive behaviour. *Journal of Personality and Social Psychology*, 30, 526–37.

Snyder, M. (1979). Self-monitoring processes. In L. Berkowitz (ed.), *Advances in Experimental Social Psychology*, Vol. 12. New York: Academic Press.

Snyder, M. (1981). Impression management. In L.S. Wrightsman and K. Deaux (eds), *Social Psychology in the 80s*. Belmont, CA: Brooks/Cole.

Snyder, M. (1987). *Public Appearances Private Realities: The Psychology of Self-Monitoring.* New York: W.H. Freeman and Company.

Snyder, M. and Miene, P.K. (1994). Stereotyping of the elderly. *British Journal of Social Psychology*, 33, 63–82.

Snyder, M., Tanke, E.D. and Berscheid, E. (1977). Social perception and interpersonal behaviour: on the self-fulfilling nature of social stereotypes. *Journal of Personality and Social Psychology*, 35, 656–66.

Sproles, G.B. (1985). Behavioral science theories. In M.R. Solomon (ed.), *The Psychology of Fashion*. Lexington, MA: Lexington Books.

Stannard, U. (1971). The mask of beauty. In V. Gornick and B.K. Moran (eds), *Women in Sexist Society: Studies in Power and Powerlessness*. New York: Basic Books.

Steele, V. (1985). *Fashion and Eroticism: Ideals of Feminine Beauty from the Victorian era to the Jazz Age*. Oxford: Oxford University Press.

Steele, V. (1988). *Paris Fashion: A Cultural History*. New York: Oxford University Press.

Stokes, S.J. and Bickman, L. (1974). The effect of the physical attractiveness and role of the helper on help seeking. *Journal of Applied Social Psychology*, 4, 286–94.

Stone, G.P. (1962). Appearance and the self. In A. Rose (ed.), *Human Behavior and Social Processes*. Boston: Houghton-Mifflin.

Sypher, W. (1962). *Loss of the Self in Modern Literature and Art*. Westport, CT: Greenwood Press.

Tedeschi, J.T. (ed.) (1981). *Impression Management Theory and Social Psychological Research*. New York: Academic Press.

Tedeschi, J.T. and Norman, N. (1985). Social power, self presentation and the self. In B.R. Schlenker (ed.), *The Self and Social Life*. New York: McGraw-Hill.

Tedeschi, J.T. and Rosenfeld, P. (1981). Impression management theory and the forced compliance situation. In J.T. Tedeschi (ed.), *Impression Management Theory and Social Psychological Research*. New York: Academic Press.

The writings of Tertullianus (1869). *On Female Dress*. Ante-Nicene Christian Library. Translations of the writings of the fathers down to AD 325, ed. A. Roberts and D. James, Vol. 11. London: Hamilton.

The writings of Tertullianus (1870). *On the Veiling of Virgins*. Ante-Nicene Christian Library. Translations of the writings of the fathers down to AD 325, ed. A. Roberts and D. James, Vol. 18. London: Hamilton.

Thompson, J.K. and Thompson, C.M. (1986). Body size distortion and self esteem in asymptomatic, normal weight males and females. *International Journal of Eating Disorders*, 5, 1061–8.

Thompson, J.K., Dolce, J.J., Spana, R.E. and Register, A. (1987). Emotionally versus intellectually based estimates of body size. *International Journal of Eating Disorders*, 6, 507–13.

Tseëlon, E. (1989). *Communicating via Clothes*. PhD Thesis. Department of Experimental Psychology, University of Oxford.

Tseëlon, E. (1991a). Women and the private domain: a symbolic interactionist perspective. *Journal for the Theory of Social Behaviour*, 21, 111–24.

Tseëlon, E. (1991b). The method is the message: on the meaning of methods as ideologies. *Theory and Psychology*, 1, 299–316.

Tseëlon, E. (1992a). Is the presented self sincere? Goffman, impression management, and the postmodern self. *Theory, Culture and Society*, 9, 115–28.

Tseëlon, E. (1992b). What is beautiful is bad: physical attractiveness as stigma. *Journal for the Theory of Social Behaviour*, 22, 295–309.

Tseëlon, E. (1992c). Fashion and the signification of social order. *Semiotica*, 91, 1–14.

Tseëlon, E. (1992d). Self presentation through appearance: a manipulative vs. a dramaturgical approach. *Symbolic Interaction*, 15, 501–14.

Tseëlon, E. and Kaiser, S.B. (1992). A dialogue with feminist film theory: multiple readings of the gaze. *Studies in Symbolic Interaction*, 13, 119–37.

Tseëlon, E. (1994). Fashion and signification in Baudrillard. In D. Kellner (ed.), *Baudrillard: A Critical Reader*. Oxford: Blackwell.

Tual, A. (1986). Speech and silence: women in Iran. In L. Dube, E. Leacock and S. Ardener (eds), *Visibility and Power*. Delhi: Oxford University Press.

Turner, R.H. and Schutte, J. (1981). The true self method for studying the self conception. *Symbolic Interaction*, 4, 1–20.

Unger, R. (1985). Personal appearance and social control. In M. Safir, M. Mednick, D. Izraeli and J. Bernard (eds), *Women's Worlds: The New Scholarship*. New York: Praeger.

Van der Toorn, K. (1989). Female prostitution in payment of vows in ancient Israel. *Journal of Biblical Literature*, 108, 193–205.

Veblen, T. (1899/1912). *The Theory of the Leisure Class*. New York: Macmillan.

Wardle, J. and Foley, E. (1989). Body image: stability and sensitivity of body satisfaction and body size estimation. *International Journal of Eating Disorders*, 8, 55–62.

Wax, M. (1957). Themes in cosmetics and grooming. *American Journal of Sociology*, 62, 588–93.

Weeks, J. (1981/1989). The public and the private: moral regulation in the Victorian period. In *Sex, Politics & Society: The Regulation of Sexuality Since 1800*. London: Longman.

Weinberg, M.S. (1968). Sexual modesty, social meaning and the nudist camp. In M. Truzzi (ed.), *Sociology and Everyday Life*. Englewood Cliffs, NJ: Prentice Hall.

West, C. and Zimmerman, D.H. (1987). Doing gender. *Gender and Society*, 1, 125–51.

Wicklund, R.A. and Gollwitzer, P.M. (1982). *Symbolic Self Completion*. Hillsdale, NJ: Erlbaum.

Willett, C. and Cunnington, P. (1951/1981). *The History of Underclothes*. London: Faber and Faber. Revised by A.D. and V. Mansfield.

Wilson, E. (1985). *Adorned in Dreams: Fashion and Modernity*. London: Virago.

Wilson, E. (1992). Fashion and the postmodern body. In J. Ash and E. Wilson (eds), *Chic Thrills*. London: Pandora.

Winnicott, D.W. (1953/1986). Transitional objects and transitional phenomena. In P. Buckley (ed.), *Essential Papers on Object Relations*. New York: New York University Press.

Wolf, N. (1991). *The Beauty Myth*. London: Chatto & Windus.

Woodhouse, A. (1989). *Fantastic Women*. London: Macmillan.

Yeatman, A. (1984). Gender and the differentiation of social life into public and domestic domains. *Social Analysis*, 15, 32–49.

Zarchi, N. (1993). *Flyer*. Tel Aviv: Hakibbutz Hameuchad.

The Zohar (1931), trans. H. Sperling and M. Simon. London: The Soncino Press.

INDEX